PERSONAL EXPERIENCES OF PSYCHOLOGICAL THERAPY FOR PSYCHOSIS AND RELATED EXPERIENCES

For those struggling with experiences of psychosis, therapy can be beneficial and even life changing. However, there is no single type of therapy, and a great range and diversity of therapeutic approaches have been developed to help different individual needs, which means deciding which approach is most helpful for an individual not a straightforward choice. *Personal Experiences of Psychological Therapy for Psychosis and Related Experiences* uniquely presents personal accounts of those who have received therapy for psychosis alongside professional clinical commentary on these therapies, giving multiple perspectives on what they involve and how they work.

Presented in a clear and accessible way, each chapter includes accounts of a variety of different therapies, including Cognitive Behavioural Therapy, Trauma-Focused Therapy, Open Dialogue, and Systemic Family Therapy. The reader is encouraged to explore not only the clinical basis for these therapies but also understand what the treatments mean for the person experiencing them, as well as their challenges and limitations. The book also explores the importance of the individual's relationship with the therapist. As a whole, the perspectives presented here provide unique insight into a range of widely used psychological therapies for psychosis.

With its special combination of personal experiences and concise introductions to different therapies, this book offers a valuable resource for academics and students of psychiatry, clinical psychology, psychotherapy, mental health care, and mental health nursing. It will also be essential reading for those considering treatment, their friends and families, as well as mental health professionals, including psychiatrists, clinical psychologists, psychotherapists, and nurses.

Peter Taylor is a clinical psychologist and lecturer in clinical psychology at the University of Manchester, UK. His research includes a focus on interventions and therapy for those with experiences of psychosis as well as better understanding the causes of self-harm and suicide.

Olympia Gianfrancesco is an 'expert by experience' in psychosis, and has given talks about her experiences at conferences and on university courses. During her PhD, she researched the interaction between genes and environment in the context of psychosis. Olympia now works as a researcher in genetics at the University of Edinburgh, UK.

Naomi Fisher is a lecturer of mental health at the University of Lancaster, UK. Her research focuses on better understanding and reducing mental distress, and involves working closely alongside those affected by mental health difficulties in order to co-develop ways to promote mental health and well-being.

THE INTERNATIONAL SOCIETY FOR PSYCHOLOGICAL AND SOCIAL APPROACHES TO PSYCHOSIS BOOK SERIES

Series editors: Alison Summers and Anna Lavis
Series advisor for the monograph strand: Andrew Moskowitz

ISPS (The International Society for Psychological and Social Approaches to Psychosis) has a history stretching back more than five decades, during which it has witnessed the relentless pursuit of biological explanations for psychosis. This tide has been turning in recent years and there is growing international interest in a range of psychological, social and cultural factors that have considerable explanatory traction and distinct therapeutic possibilities. Governments, professional groups, people with personal experience of psychosis and family members are increasingly exploring interventions that involve more talking and listening. Many now regard practitioners skilled in psychological therapies as an essential component of the care of people with psychosis.

A global society active in at least twenty countries, ISPS is composed of a diverse range of individuals, networks and institutional members. Key to its ethos is that individuals with personal experience of psychosis, and their families and friends, are fully involved alongside practitioners and researchers, and that all benefit from this collaboration.

ISPS's core aim is to promote psychological and social approaches to understanding and treating psychosis. Recognising the humanitarian and therapeutic potential of these perspectives, ISPS embraces a wide spectrum of therapeutic approaches from psychodynamic, systemic, cognitive, and arts therapies, to need-adapted and dialogical approaches, family and group therapies and residential therapeutic communities. A further ambition is to draw together diverse viewpoints on psychosis and to foster discussion and debate across the biomedical and social sciences, including establishing meaningful dialogue with practitioners and researchers who are more familiar with biological-based approaches. Such discussion is now increasingly supported by empirical evidence of the interaction of genes and biology with the emotional and social environment especially in the fields of trauma, attachment, social relationships and therapy.

Ways in which ISPS pursues its aims include international and national conferences, real and virtual networks, and publication of the journal *Psychosis*. The book series is intended to complement these activities by providing a resource for those wanting to consider aspects of psychosis in detail. It now also includes a monograph strand primarily targeted at academics. Central to both strands is the combination of rigorous, in-depth intellectual content and accessibility to a wide range of readers. We aim for the series to be a resource for mental health professionals of all disciplines, for those developing and implementing policy, for academics in the social and clinical sciences, and for people whose interest in psychosis stems from personal or family experience. We hope that the book series will help challenge excessively biological ways of conceptualising and treating psychosis through the dissemination of existing knowledge and ideas and by fostering new interdisciplinary dialogues and perspectives.

For more information about ISPS, email isps@isps.org or visit our website, www.isps.org.

For more information about the journal *Psychosis* visit www.isps.org/index.php/publications/journal

MODELS OF MADNESS: PSYCHOLOGICAL, SOCIAL AND BIOLOGICAL APPROACHES TO SCHIZOPHRENIA 1ST EDITION
Edited by John Read, Loren R. Mosher & Richard P. Bentall

PSYCHOSES: AN INTEGRATIVE PERSPECTIVE
Edited by Johan Cullberg

EVOLVING PSYCHOSIS: DIFFERENT STAGES, DIFFERENT TREATMENTS
Edited by Jan Olav Johanessen, Brian V. Martindale & Johan Cullberg

FAMILY AND MULTI-FAMILY WORK WITH PSYCHOSIS
Gerd-Ragna Block Thorsen, Trond Gronnestad & Anne Lise Oxenvad

EXPERIENCES OF MENTAL HEALTH IN-PATIENT CARE: NARRATIVES FROM SERVICE USERS, CARERS AND PROFESSIONALS
Edited by Mark Hardcastle, David Kennard, Sheila Grandison & Leonard Fagin

PSYCHOTHERAPIES FOR THE PSYCHOSES: THEORETICAL, CULTURAL, AND CLINICAL INTEGRATION
Edited by John Gleeson, Eión Killackey & Helen Krstev

THERAPEUTIC COMMUNITIES FOR PSYCHOSIS: PHILOSOPHY, HISTORY AND CLINICAL PRACTICE
Edited by John Gale, Alba Realpe & Enrico Pedriali

MAKING SENSE OF MADNESS: CONTESTING THE MEANING OF SCHIZOPHRENIA
Jim Geekie and John Read

PSYCHOTHERAPEUTIC APPROACHES TO SCHIZOPHRENIA PSYCHOSIS
Edited by Yrjö O. Alanen, Manuel González de Chávez, Ann-Louise S. Silver & Brian Martindale

BEYOND MEDICATION: THERAPEUTIC ENGAGEMENT AND THE RECOVERY FROM PSYCHOSIS
Edited by David Garfield and Daniel Mackler

CBT FOR PSYCHOSIS: A SYMPTOM-BASED APPROACH
Edited by Roger Hagen, Douglas Turkington, Torkil Berge and Rolf W. Gråwe

EXPERIENCING PSYCHOSIS: PERSONAL AND PROFESSIONAL PERSPECTIVES
Edited by Jim Geekie, Patte Randal, Debra Lampshire and John Read

PSYCHOSIS AS A PERSONAL CRISIS: AN EXPERIENCE-BASED APPROACH
Edited by Marius Romme and Sandra Escher

MODELS OF MADNESS: PSYCHOLOGICAL, SOCIAL AND BIOLOGICAL APPROACHES TO PSYCHOSIS 2ND EDITION
Edited by John Read and Jacqui Dillon

SURVIVING, EXISTING, OR LIVING:
PHASE-SPECIFIC THERAPY FOR
SEVERE PSYCHOSIS
Pamela Fuller

PSYCHOSIS AND EMOTION:
THE ROLE OF EMOTIONS IN
UNDERSTANDING PSYCHOSIS,
THERAPY AND RECOVERY
Edited by Andrew Gumley,
Alf Gillham, Kathy Taylor and Matthias
Schwannauer

INSANITY AND DIVINITY:
STUDIES IN PSYCHOSIS AND
SPIRITUALITY
Edited by John Gale, Michael Robson and
Georgia Rapsomatioti

PSYCHOTHERAPY FOR
PEOPLE DIAGNOSED WITH
SCHIZOPHRENIA: SPECIFIC
TECHNIQUES
Andrew Lotterman

CREATIVITY AND PSYCHOTIC
STATES IN EXCEPTIONAL
PEOPLE: THE WORK OF
MURRAY JACKSON
Murray Jackson and Jeanne Magagna

ART THERAPY FOR PSYCHOSIS:
THEORY AND PRACTICE
Katherine Killick

CBT FOR PSYCHOSIS: PROCESS-
ORIENTATED THERAPIES AND
THE THIRD WAVE
Caroline Cupitt

PERSONAL EXPERIENCES OF
PSYCHOLOGICAL THERAPY
FOR PSYCHOSIS AND RELATED
EXPERIENCES
Peter Taylor, Olympia Gianfrancesco
and Naomi Fisher

MONOGRAPHS:

PSYCHOSIS, PSYCHOANALYSIS
AND PSYCHIATRY IN POSTWAR
USA: ON THE BORDERLAND
OF MADNESS
Orna Ophir

MEANING, MADNESS AND
POLITICAL SUBJECTIVITY:
A STUDY OF SCHIZOPHRENIA
AND CULTURE IN TURKEY
Sadeq Rahimi

PERSONAL EXPERIENCES OF PSYCHOLOGICAL THERAPY FOR PSYCHOSIS AND RELATED EXPERIENCES

Edited by Peter Taylor, Olympia Gianfrancesco and Naomi Fisher

LONDON AND NEW YORK

First published 2019
by Routledge
2 Park Square, Milton Park, Abingdon, Oxon OX14 4RN

and by Routledge
52 Vanderbilt Avenue, New York, NY 10017

Routledge is an imprint of the Taylor & Francis Group, an informa business

© 2019 selection and editorial matter, Peter Taylor, Olympia Gianfrancesco and Naomi Fisher; individual chapters, the contributors

The right of Peter Taylor, Olympia Gianfrancesco and Naomi Fisher to be identified as the authors of the editorial material, and of the authors for their individual chapters, has been asserted in accordance with sections 77 and 78 of the Copyright, Designs and Patents Act 1988.

All rights reserved. No part of this book may be reprinted or reproduced or utilised in any form or by any electronic, mechanical, or other means, now known or hereafter invented, including photocopying and recording, or in any information storage or retrieval system, without permission in writing from the publishers.

Trademark notice: Product or corporate names may be trademarks or registered trademarks, and are used only for identification and explanation without intent to infringe.

British Library Cataloguing-in-Publication Data
A catalogue record for this book is available from the British Library

Library of Congress Cataloging-in-Publication Data
A catalog record has been requested for this book

ISBN: 978-1-138-09049-1 (hbk)
ISBN: 978-1-138-09050-7 (pbk)
ISBN: 978-1-315-10860-5 (ebk)

Typeset in Times New Roman
by Apex CoVantage, LLC

Printed and bound in Great Britain by
TJ International Ltd, Padstow, Cornwall

EDITORS

Peter Taylor
Division of Psychology and Mental Health, University of Manchester
2nd Floor, Zochonis building, Brunswick Street, University of Manchester,
Manchester, M13 9PL;
peter.taylor-2@manchester.ac.uk; 01613060425

Olympia Gianfrancesco
Research Fellow, Institute of Genetics and Molecular Medicine,
University of Edinburgh
C3.14, MRC Human Genetics Unit, Institute of Genetics and Molecular
Medicine, University of Edinburgh, Crewe Road South,
Edinburgh, EH4 2XU; olympia.gianfrancesco@igmm.ed.ac.uk

Naomi Fisher
Lecturer in mental health, Division of Health Research, University of Lancaster
Furness Building, University of Lancaster, Bailrigg, Lancaster LA1 4YW;
n.r.fisher@lancaster.ac.uk

CONTENTS

Acknowledgements   xi
Brief biographies for all contributors   xii

1 **Introduction to the book**   1
PETER TAYLOR AND OLYMPIA GIANFRANCESCO

2 **Cognitive Behavioural Therapy (CBT)**   9
YARBURGH, PETER TAYLOR, AND JANE HUTTON

3 **Systemic Family Therapy (SFT)**   27
ZARA ZAKS AND PEKKA BORCHERS

4 **Care Co-Ordination**   44
JUNAID SARWAR, SIOBHAIN KOCH, AND JAMES KELLY

5 **Cognitive Analytic Therapy (CAT)**   61
ALEX AND CLAIRE SEDDON

6 **Trauma-focused therapy using cognitive-behavioural and EMDR approaches**   77
REBECCA, JOANNA WARD-BROWN AND DAVID KEANE

7 **Psychodynamic therapy**   96
PAUL-NEWELL REAVES AND ALISON SUMMERS

8 **Compassion Focused Therapy (CFT)**   115
MYSTIC LEAF AND JON CROSSLEY

CONTENTS

9 Open Dialogue (OD)   **133**
NICK HAYES AND NIKLAS GRANÖ

10 Person-Centred Therapy   **148**
JULES HALEY AND PETER CHATALOS

11 The relationship with the therapist   **166**
ANNIE BLAKE, AMANDA LARKIN, AND PETER TAYLOR

12 Conclusion   **185**
PETER TAYLOR AND NAOMI FISHER

Index   193

ACKNOWLEDGEMENTS

First of all we would like to thank the many contributors whose time, insight, and perseverance, have allowed this book to become a reality. Thanks go to our series editors at ISPS (The International Society for Psychological and Social approaches to Psychosis), Alison Summers and Anna Lavis, for their ongoing support, guidance, and feedback, and to ISPS for including this book as one of its series. Thanks to Anthony Greenwood for supporting the artwork editing. Additional thanks go to Susannah Frearson at Routledge for her advice and quick responses to the various queries we have had. Rory Byrne deserves thanks for this initial encouragement that this was an idea worth pursuing, in a pub overlooking Oxford Road in Manchester. John Read should also be thanked for initially linking us up with ISPS and supporting the idea.

BRIEF BIOGRAPHIES FOR ALL CONTRIBUTORS

Alex is 38 years old and from the North of England. From the age of 17 years she has experienced periods of depression that she put down to a genetic predisposition and received counselling and Cognitive Behavioural Therapy. At 35 years old Alex had an episode described as psychosis, spent time in a Psychiatric Intensive Care Unit and then was offered Cognitive Analytic Therapy (CAT). Alex found CAT particularly helpful in understanding her responses to distress and beliefs around her given diagnosis. The understanding of distress, self-compassion, and reclaimed future engendered through Alex's experience of CAT is hoped to be of interest to all involved in the therapeutic process and those living life following experiences of psychosis. Alex enjoys running, drawing, and life.

Pekka Borchers is a psychiatrist and family therapist based in Finland. He completed his Doctor of Medicine degree in 1982 before specialising in psychiatry. He completed further specialised training in family therapy at the University of Helsinki in 1990. Pekka has a longstanding interest in the use of family therapy with individuals with experiences of psychosis, and has undertaken research into how the experiences and inner-dialogues of clinicians can affect the treatments they provide.

Annie Blake is 30 years old and from London. At 27 she had her first manic psychotic episode after a traumatic revelation within her family. She was diagnosed with bipolar disorder and spent time in a psychiatric hospital. She received cognitive behavioural therapy for psychosis which helped her greatly. Annie spends her spare time playing the ukulele and watching live world music.

Peter Andrew Chatalos is a person-centred therapist in private practice, accredited with the British Association of Counselling and Psychotherapy. He has a background in mindfulness, facilitation, philosophy and human ecology, with interests that include trauma, addiction, and resilience. He has recently been counselling at the UK National Health Service's 'Club Drug Clinic' and with 'Antidote', London Friend's addictions focused agency for the Lesbian, Gay, Bisexual, and Transgender (LGBT) community. Peter has served as

BRIEF BIOGRAPHIES FOR ALL CONTRIBUTORS

trustee on the governing board of the Commonwealth Human Ecology Council, and is passionate about how holistic ecology can inform psychotherapy. His publications include contributions to the emerging field of eco-psychology, such as a chapter in "Vital Signs: Ecological responses to psychological crises". He continues to be inspired by the unique resourcefulness of each person he works with.

Jon Crossley is the Lead Clinical Psychologist for the Early Intervention for Psychosis Service in Leicestershire and Rutland. He is further trained as a Family Therapist and his clinical interests include using systemic and compassion focused approaches with service users and their families. He works part-time at the University of Leicester, where he organises and jointly delivers a Foundation Level Course in Systemic Family Therapy. He is Research Lead for the family, young people and children's service in Leicestershire Partnership NHS (National Health Service) Trust. He has supervised numerous doctoral research projects and has published several peer-reviewed papers. His current research interests include service users' experience of hearing voices and the formulation of psychosis by staff.

Naomi Fisher works as a lecturer of mental health at the University of Lancaster having completed her PhD looking into the benefits and mechanisms of mindfulness meditation. Her research focuses on better understanding and reducing mental distress. Her research involves working closely alongside those affected by mental health difficulties in order to better understand these problems and co-develop ways to promote mental health and well-being.

Olympia Gianfrancesco experience of psychosis began at the age of 16, after being faced with a difficult family situation. She was under the care of the Early Intervention for Psychosis Service for 4 years, during which time she moved to Sheffield to study at university. Whilst in Sheffield, Olympia was introduced to the ideas of the Hearing Voices Movement, and received Cognitive Analytic Therapy. These approaches allowed her to understand her experiences with self-compassion and make a full recovery. Olympia later completed her PhD at the University of Liverpool, researching how our genes and environment can interact to influence risk of mental health conditions. She currently resides in Scotland, where she works as a researcher in genetics at the University of Edinburgh.

Niklas Granö, PhD, is Doctor in clinical psychology at Helsinki University and is working as a clinical psychologist and researcher in Helsinki University Hospital, Finland. He has been working with young people in acute crisis since 2001 as a clinical psychologist and researcher at Jorvi Hospital inpatient unit, in an early psychosis outpatient centre, and in an early intervention and detection team, JERI (Jorvi Early psychosis Recognition and Intervention). He currently teaches courses at Helsinki University on early psychosis detection and intervention, he supervises PhD students, and he has published 20 peer-reviewed papers related to help seeking adolescents and psychotic-like experiences.

Jules Haley lives in London and is a volunteer counsellor. She worked through her mental distress with a person-centred therapist and now is beginning to build a life that she enjoys. Proving that 'psychosis' and recovery is possible for anyone, Jules hopes that this account of how therapy helped her will inspire others to take that next step in their journey towards healing and recovery.

Nick Hayes is a 45 year old teacher who has worked in schools for the last 20 years. His first experience of mental illness was when he was 25 and led to a diagnosis of bipolar disorder. Open Dialogue sessions have been instrumental in helping him back to work and back to good health. Nick spends most of his time away from work with his family, including two young children. When he finds the time, he enjoys writing poetry and prose, going to the cinema and to occasional football matches.

Jane Hutton before qualifying as a clinical psychologist in 2013, Jane worked with people identified as being 'at-risk' of experiencing psychosis as part of EDIE-2 (Earl Detection and Intervention Evaluation) and completed a specialist placement in Lancashire Early Intervention Service. For the last two years Jane has been working for a multi-site randomised controlled trial of Cognitive Behavioural Therapy for Psychosis. She has contributed to teaching CBT as part of the Edinburgh University Doctoral Training Programme and supervises on applied practitioner CBT courses. Her current interest is in improving access to psychological therapies for people experiencing psychosis across Scotland.

David Keane is a Senior Cognitive Therapist and accredited Eye-Movement Desensitisation and Re-processing (EMDR) practitioner. During the last 20 years he has worked in a range of mental health services across Lancashire. This has included community mental health teams, Early Intervention for Psychosis Services, crisis resolution and home treatment, inpatient services, and specialist trauma services. Currently David divides his time between the Lancashire Traumatic Stress Service and Central Lancashire Crisis Resolution and Home Treatment Services. Initially qualifying as a mental health nurse, David has gone on to attain a breadth of knowledge and experience through opportunities to study and enhance his skills in Psychosomatic Integration, Family Interventions, and Cognitive Behavioural Therapy for Psychosis and EMDR. In the last few years, David's work has increasingly focused on collaborating to provide evidence based trauma treatments with service users who have received a diagnosis of psychosis.

James Kelly is a Senior Clinical Psychologist working at Lancashire Care NHS (National Health Service) Foundation Trust. He works within the Early Intervention for Psychosis Service and is the project manager for the Improving

Access to Psychological Therapies Severe Mental Illness (IAPT-SMI) demonstrator site. He is an honorary lecturer in Clinical Psychology at the University of Manchester. He is a co-author of Cognitive Behavioural Suicide Prevention in Psychosis by Routledge and has published numerous peer-reviewed papers. Last year, James developed a mobile application, in collaboration with the University of Chester and the Hearing Voices Network, to improve understanding and empathy about voice hearing. His current clinical and research interests include cognitive therapy for psychosis, with a special interest in developing care pathways for negative symptoms, suicide prevention, and using mobile technology to deliver cognitive behavioural strategies in the course of everyday life.

Siobhain Koch is a team leader and clinical co-ordinator in an Early Intervention for Psychosis Service in the North West of England. Siobhain completed her degree in nursing studies in 1997 and has since undertaken further training in counselling and Cognitive Behavioural Therapy. She has previously worked as a Community Psychiatric Nurse in mental health settings including within a Community Mental Health Team. Siobhain's professional interests include psychosis, social functioning and recovery, maternal mental health, and carer's experiences. Outside of work, Siobhain enjoys yoga, music, travel, and time with family and friends.

Amanda Larkin is a clinical psychologist who works delivering psychological therapy across the research trials that are being conducted at the Psychosis Research Unit in Manchester. Amanda completed her Clinical Psychology doctorate training at the University of Edinburgh, from 2013 to 2016. She worked on placement for NHS Dumfries and Galloway in the southwest of Scotland. During this time, she began to develop her interest in working with people who experience psychosis, and undertook her final year specialist placement working on an inpatient mental health ward, and delivering CBT for psychosis on an outpatient basis. Amanda has a strong interest in working with families, and has received training to deliver Behavioural Family Therapy (BFT). Amanda has also worked with the charity Support in Mind in Scotland to complete a report on the experience of living with a diagnosis of schizophrenia or psychosis in Scotland.

Mystic Leaf is a 31 year old British Asian female. From the age of 24 years she began to develop psychotic symptoms whilst in a stressful job as a junior doctor. These symptoms increased in severity as she struggled with interpersonal issues such as trying to find a romantic life partner and the loss of her career and earning potential all within the context of a traditional Indian community with traditional values. She experienced both Cognitive Behavioural Therapy and Compassion Focused Therapy from two clinical trainee psychologists, as well as Family Therapy. In particular, she connected with the compassion focused approach best. Mystic Leaf is keen to talk openly about her experiences and has done so at a Psychosis conference and is also involved in teaching clinical psychologist trainees by speaking about her experience. Mystic Leaf is currently progressing in the field of charity retail and enjoys watercolour art and listening to music in her spare time.

Paul-Newell Reaves is a poet and educator from Washington, DC. He is owner and co-editor of defenestrationism.net where he reads for twice annual fiction contests. As a member of the Mad Pride community, he is honoured to be a part of this book. He hopes his story will enable other people who have experienced psychoses to consider psychodynamic therapy. He wishes you peace and contentment.

Rebecca Becky is 24 years old and lives in Preston. She has had a lot of bad life experiences, such as being bullied her whole school life, and being sexually abused by her uncle when she was 16. She found before treatment that she needed help, and the Early Intervention for Psychosis Service did just that. It took a lot of hard work and commitment for her to go to therapy every week, but she did go. Becky received a modular Trauma Focused Therapy, including elements of Eye-Movement Desensitisation and Re-processing therapy and Cognitive Behavioural Therapy. Therapy meant that she had to relive very difficult past experiences of abuse. With the patience and support of the therapist, Becky was able to do this. Since she has been discharged from the Early Intervention for Psychosis Service, she has started a new job role as an activities co-ordinator in a dementia care home. Becky has also started her National Vocational Qualification (NVQ) level 3 in health and social care, and her NVQ level 3 in activities. Things are looking better for the future, as she want to become a paramedic. Becky feels she is getting her life back to some kind of normality, but to get fully back it will take some time.

Junaid Sarwar is 29 years old. He was 18 when he started having headaches, low moods, and feelings of fatigue. After 6 years of problems, at the age of 24, he became so ill that he was referred to the Early Intervention for Psychosis Service. The staff who came to assess Junaid told his parents that he needed medical help and diagnosed him with psychosis. Junaid received various types of help from his clinical team including Cognitive Behavioural Therapy. Junaid has also participated in a football group organised by his service which included other people who had psychosis. Junaid has since successfully completed a National Vocational Qualification, Level 2 Apprenticeship in Business Administration. He has gone on to work as a secretary for mental health services within the National Health Service. Junaid feels his progress has been amazing and believes his family played a crucial part in his recovery, as well as the support and hope he received from the clinical team, which was life changing.

Claire Seddon is a Consultant Clinical Psychologist within an Early Intervention for Psychosis Service at Mersey Care NHS Trust, UK. Claire has over 15 years' experience working with individuals experiencing psychosis. Claire's clinical experience involves working with clients and families to help make meaning of distressing experiences, drawing on a range of psychological approaches. Claire is an accredited Cognitive Analytic Therapy (CAT) practitioner and is involved in research to develop the evidence base for CAT with psychosis. Claire is an honorary teacher and holds a research honorary appointment at The University of Liverpool.

Alison Summers is a psychodynamic psychotherapist and general psychiatrist, currently working in part-time psychotherapy posts in the UK National Health Service with Lancashire Care Foundation Trust and in the voluntary sector with the charity Freedom from Torture. She is co-editor for the International Society for Psychological and Social approaches to Psychosis (ISPS) book series and past current chair of the UK ISPS network. Alison has previously worked for over 10 years as a consultant psychiatrist in an Early Intervention for Psychosis Service in Lancashire. She has a particular interest in the use of psychodynamic approaches with people experiencing psychotic and related difficulties, and has published a number of papers in this area.

Peter Taylor is a Clinical Psychologist and lecturer in clinical psychology at the University of Manchester. His research focuses on understanding the causes of self-harm and suicide, including what contributes to these problems in those who experience psychosis. Peter is also interested in interventions and therapy for those with experiences of psychosis, and has undertaken research looking at Cognitive Behavioural and Cognitive Analytic Therapy for psychosis. He is an advocate of greater involvement of Experts by Experience in teaching, research and clinical practice.

Joanna Ward-Brown is a clinical psychologist and has recently started a new role as an inpatient and community mental health team psychologist in Bolton, England. Before that she worked at the Lancashire Early Intervention for Psychosis Service from 2012 to 2015. Jo has particular interests in attachment, trauma, and psychosis and has recently completed a specialist secondment at Lancashire Care traumatic stress service which focused on trauma-focused Cognitive Behavioural Therapy and Eye-Movement Desensitisation and Reprocessing within a phasic treatment approach. She is currently working with service users who have received these approaches to support them to become involved in training and research. Jo teaches on the Manchester clinical psychology doctorate and is involved in research on trauma and psychosis.

Yarburgh lives in the UK and struggled with experiences of psychosis for much of his early life, and received Cognitive Behavioural Therapy (CBT) as part of a trial looking at the benefits of CBT for psychosis. He now works with clinicians and researchers to help improve the way we support and help people with psychosis.

Zara Zaks is in her mid-20s and has struggled with repeat experiences of psychosis since she was in her late teens. Over this time she has had various interventions including counselling, Cognitive Behavioural Therapy, Cognitive Analytic Therapy, and Family Therapy. She is now stable on medication and is holding down a full time job. Zara is passionate about reducing mental health stigma and keeps a mental health blog. In her spare time she enjoys illustration, live music, and collecting vintage photographs.

1

INTRODUCTION TO THE BOOK

Peter Taylor and Olympia Gianfrancesco

Overview

The main goal of this book is to give an overview and introduction to a variety of different psychological or 'talking therapies' that are aimed at helping people who are struggling with experiences of psychosis. We do this in two ways: 1) by sharing the first-hand experiences of individuals who have received these therapies; and 2) by sharing therapists' accounts of the therapies they provide. In this first chapter, we aim to give a general introduction to the book. In particular, we explain some of the terms used in the book, including 'psychosis' and 'psychological therapy'. We also give a rationale for the book and discuss who may benefit from reading it. Lastly, we consider the benefits of looking to first-hand accounts in order to learn more about a therapy, and also some of the challenges in doing this.

What do we mean by psychosis?

The word 'psychosis' does not refer to one thing, but in fact covers a broad range of very different experiences. A number of these involve some sense of being out of touch with the world around us. For example, some experiences associated with psychosis include hearing voices that others cannot hear, and having strongly held, unusual beliefs or ideas that appear to be unsupported or excessive (British Psychological Society [BPS], 2014; Freudenreich, 2007). These experiences may be distressing for some people, but not necessarily for everyone. Unfounded or excessive fears that others will hurt you or wish you harm, usually called paranoia, are another common experience of psychosis. Psychosis can also include a loss of motivation (avolition), and social or emotional withdrawal.

Traditionally, these experiences have been linked to particular psychiatric diagnoses, most commonly, schizophrenia. However, in recent years there has been much debate about how valid or helpful these diagnoses are (Bentall, 2017; BPS, 2014). There is now evidence that many experiences of psychosis exist on a continuum (e.g. Shevlin, McElroy, Bentall, Reininghaus, & Murphy, 2016), and that experiences of psychosis are common, to a greater or lesser extent, across the population, including people whom we would normally say are mentally well and people who might traditionally be seen as mentally unwell. In this chapter we refer to psychosis, rather than to a specific diagnosis, for the same reasons. One implication of seeing psychosis in this way is that it suggests that, for many people, psychosis is not a problem. Some people may hear benign or even supportive voices for example, which do not negatively affect their lives or how they feel. However, for other people, psychosis can be very difficult and disruptive. For some, the psychosis itself may not be their main problem, but the way it affects their lives. For example, it may prevent them going outside, meeting people, doing the things they would like to. It is not uncommon for people struggling with their psychosis to feel anxious or depressed at times. As a result, therapies that are designed to help people with psychosis may focus on the experiences of psychosis itself, but may also focus more on related problems, such as low self-esteem or low mood.

It is important to note that there is still much debate around the idea of psychosis, and some people would question the definition we give above. Some would argue against the use of the word 'psychosis' at all, due to the psychiatric connotations and the stigma that can become linked to such words. We feel the term 'psychosis' is helpful in outlining a set of particular experiences (e.g. hearing voices, paranoia), but would agree that it has its limitations. Here we have given a relatively brief definition of psychosis, and we would suggest that those interested in knowing more about it do further reading on this subject or talk with a health professional about this (for example see BPS, 2014).

What is psychological therapy?

As with psychosis, there is no single thing called 'psychological therapy'. Instead, a wide range of different types of therapy exist. What many have in common is that they rely on conversation between the therapist and the client as a means of bringing about improvements in the client's problems (although some approaches such as art therapy are a little different, in that they do not rely on conversation). Some individuals may be sceptical about the idea that simply talking about their problem could bring about any meaningful improvements in the problems they are facing. However, it is common for people to discuss their difficulties with supportive others (e.g. friends, family), and such conversations have the potential to be helpful, changing how a person feels, or how they see their problems. Thus, the idea that conversation alone can be helpful does not seem so far-fetched. Also, for many therapies, the conversations that take place in therapy serve the purpose of trying to bring about a change in a person's day-to-day life, such as in the way they cope, interact with others, or think about themselves and the world around them. Through such day-to-day changes, improvements in a person's problems can emerge. Different therapies make use of a variety of different techniques and tools to help achieve improvements for the client.

Psychological therapy in psychosis

Over recent decades we have seen a growing recognition of the value of psychological therapies for people who are struggling with mental health difficulties. Research has steadily grown into understanding how these therapies can and do help many individuals with a wide range of different problems, from depression to anxiety, to problems with using substances or alcohol (e.g. Hofmann, Asnaani, Vonk, Sawyer, & Fang, 2012; Linde et al., 2015). The growing recognition of the value of psychological therapy has also extended to psychosis. This has been aided by increasing evidence that psychological mechanisms such as differences in the way individuals perceive others and the world around them, reach conclusions, cope with difficult feelings, or think about their problems, may be important to understanding their experience of psychosis and the associated distress they feel (e.g. Bentall et al., 2014; Dudley, Taylor, Wickham, & Hutton, 2015; Freeman, Garety, Kuipers, Fowler, & Bebbington, 2002). We have started to see evidence that talking therapies do have a role to play in helping people who are struggling with psychosis (BPS, 2014), including specific psychosis-related experiences like hearing voices (e.g. Thomas et al., 2014). One good example of this is that psychological therapies are now recommended as a front-line treatment for people with experiences of psychosis in some national guidelines (e.g. National Institute for Health and Care Excellence, 2014).

This is not to suggest, of course, that there is no longer any controversy around the use of psychological therapy for psychosis. Many people still dispute the value of such therapies, and debate continues (Kinderman, McKenna, & Laws, 2015). Nonetheless, our own perspective is that evidence coming forward from trials and research studies suggests that psychological therapies can help people who are facing problems associated with psychosis. However, debate remains about which therapies are most effective for experiences of psychosis, or which aspects of a particular therapy are most important in helping clients. Different therapies may look similar to the individual receiving them. Alternatively, the same therapy may be practised differently depending on the therapist, and the same therapist may alter their way of working for different clients even whilst using the same therapy model. Moreover, there is evidence that the relationship between client and therapist is particularly important in determining the outcome, irrespective of the type of therapy being used (e.g. Goldsmith, Lewis, Dunn, & Bentall, 2015; Horvath, Del Re, Flückiger, & Symonds, 2011).

The challenge of choice

The growing recognition of the value of talking therapies for mental health problems has led to an explosion in the range of different talking therapies that are available. This has been the case for therapies for psychosis, as with other types of problems. Whilst for some, the possibility of having a choice between different therapies can be empowering, it also has the potential to be bewildering and confusing, especially if we know little about what these therapies involve or how they differ from each other. What is the difference between Cognitive Behavioural Therapy (CBT) and Cognitive Analytic Therapy (CAT)? Which would I prefer? Which of these focuses more on my early experiences? How will they make sense of my problems? It does not help that many therapies have similar sounding names and abbreviations: CAT, CBT, CFT (Compassion Focused Therapy). The decisions we can make about which therapy to go with are of course limited by various factors, not least the services available to us. Mental health services for people with psychosis are usually limited to a small number of different therapeutic approaches. In the UK, for example, available therapies are usually those that currently have the most developed evidence (e.g. CBT, Behavioural Family Therapy) and which are recommended by national bodies (e.g. National Institute for Health and Care Excellence [NICE]). However, even in such contexts, there is still a choice to be made about whether to take up the offer of a particular therapy.

In order to make an informed choice about whether or not to pursue or become involved in a particular therapy for psychosis, we need to know something of what that therapy involves and what it is like. This brings us back to the main aim of this book: to provide an introduction to, and an overview of, a variety of different therapies for psychosis. The accounts of therapists explaining what their work involves are clearly helpful here, but only provide half the story. First-hand accounts from people who have received a particular therapy are also very important. In the current book, we therefore offer a combination of first-hand accounts of different therapies and accounts written by the therapists who deliver these approaches.

Although it has not been possible to cover every therapy in this book, we do cover a number of the dominant and recommended therapies for people with experiences of psychosis within the UK, including CBT and family therapy, as well as more recently developed approaches such as CFT. This book also focuses on therapies aimed at adults, which can differ to recommended therapies for children, and on therapies for individuals or families, rather than groups (although group therapies for psychosis also exist).

The power of the first-hand account

Learning about others' experiences of a particularly therapy is a helpful way of gathering information about that approach and deciding whether that is the therapy for us. In other, perhaps more mundane aspects of life, it is common to check others' experiences before we make decisions, such as booking a holiday or picking a restaurant. The choice of whether to take part in therapy, or of which therapy to undertake, is clearly a bigger decision, and so knowing what others went through when they received these therapies can be helpful. First-hand accounts are informative because they can go beyond just giving us an idea of what tasks and discussions a particular therapy may involve, and can describe how it may feel to experience that therapy. Such accounts are valuable not just in identifying some potential strengths and benefits of a particular therapy, but also in noting some possible challenges and difficulties.

Despite the value of considering others' experiences when making up our minds about therapy, there also needs to be some caution here. Everybody's experience of therapy will be different, even if they receive the same type of therapy. A huge array of factors will play a role in an individual's experience of therapy, some relating to themselves (e.g. their expectations and goals for therapy, their own understanding of their difficulties), and some relating to external factors (e.g. the qualities and preferences of the therapist, the nature of the service). A particular therapeutic approach, like CBT, does prescribe a certain set of methods and techniques. However, the way one therapist applies this approach may differ from that of another therapist. As a result, first-hand accounts of therapy provide a useful guide or outline of what a therapy might be like, but we can never assume that our own therapy journey will feel quite the same. This caution can also be extended to the accounts written by the therapists themselves, of course, because as noted above, one therapist's way of working may differ to another's.

It is also important to note that one person's account of their therapy does not necessarily constitute evidence that a particular therapy does or does not work. There is ongoing research with the goal of determining which therapies are helpful, in what way and to whom. One of the challenges facing the researcher is that if any single individual gets better after receiving therapy, it is hard to know why. Perhaps the therapy helped them, but perhaps they would have got better anyway, or perhaps it was just the act of talking to someone about it, and so nothing special about that particular therapy that helped. It could even be that something small, like the act of regularly travelling to see the therapist, was enough to bring about some improvement. Researchers draw upon various methods and approaches, and look at the experiences of large numbers of people, to establish whether it is the therapy that helps, as opposed to some other unknown factor. Considering this, we can see that an individual first-hand account where someone found a therapy helpful does not necessarily provide good evidence that therapy will work for most people. For this reason, we would suggest that, in considering therapy, it is important to also consider the evidence that currently exists for that therapy. Within this book, the chapters written by therapists provide a brief overview of the research behind each approach.

About this book

We hope this book will be helpful for a number of different people. We particularly hope it will assist those who have been offered therapy, or are seeking a referral for therapy to help with difficulties related to psychosis, and the friends and family of people in these situations. We also hope this book will be of value to therapists and other clinicians (and those training in these professions), either as a resource to provide to clients, or to support their own learning and development as practitioners.

Indeed, our own opinion is that there is much to be learned from first-hand accounts for the therapists themselves in terms of how they introduce and conduct therapy. Many of the therapies covered in this book, whilst used in the UK, are also used internationally (e.g. CAT, CBT, family therapy, open dialogue), and so we believe this book will be relevant to many readers from around the globe.

The book has been structured so that each chapter concerns a different therapeutic approach. Within each chapter there is a section giving a first-hand account of the therapy, and a section giving an introduction to that therapy from the perspective of the therapist. In putting this volume together, we are particularly indebted to those who have shared their experiences, progress, and achievements, as well as their difficulties. The chapters have demonstrated to us both the potential for therapy to change the lives of those who are faced with the challenges that psychosis can bring.

References

Bentall, R. P. (2017). Six myths about schizophrenia: A paradigm well beyond its use-by date? In J. Poland & S. Tekin (Eds.), *Extraordinary science and psychiatry: Responses to the crisis in mental health research* (pp. 221–248). Cambridge, MA: MIT Press.

Bentall, R. P., de Sousa, P., Varese, F., Wickham, S., Sitko, K., Haarmans, M., & Read, J. (2014). From adversity to psychosis: Pathways and mechanisms from specific adversities to specific symptoms. *Social Psychiatry and Psychiatric Epidemiology, 49*, 1011–1022. doi:10.1007/s00127-014-0914-0

British Psychological Society. (2014). *Understanding psychosis and schizophrenia*. Leicester: British Psychological Society. Retrieved from www.bps.org.uk/system/files/Public%20files/aa%20Standard%20Docs/understanding_psychosis.pdf

Dudley, R., Taylor, P. J., Wickham, S., & Hutton, P. (2015). Psychosis, delusions and the "Jumping to conclusions" reasoning bias: A systematic review and meta-analysis. *Schizophrenia Bulletin, 42*, 652–665. doi:10.1093/schbul/sbv150

Freeman, D., Garety, P. A., Kuipers, E., Fowler, D., & Bebbington, P. E. (2002). A cognitive model of persecutory delusions. *British Journal of Clinical Psychology, 41*, 331–347. doi:10.1348/014466502760387461

Freudenreich, O. (2007). *Psychotic disorders: A practical guide* (pp. 2–13). Philadelphia, PA: Lippincott Williams & Wilkins.

Goldsmith, L. P., Lewis, S. W., Dunn, G., & Bentall, R. P. (2015). Psychological treatments for early psychosis can be beneficial or harmful, depending on the therapeutic alliance: An instrumental variable analysis. *Psychological Medicine, 45*, 2365–2373. doi:https://doi.org/10.1017/S003329171500032X

Hofmann, S. G., Asnaani, A., Vonk, I. J. J., Sawyer, A. T., & Fang, A. (2012). The efficacy of cognitive behavioural therapy: A review of meta-analyses. *Cognitive Therapy and Research, 36*, 427–440. doi:10.1007/s10608-012-9476-1

Horvath, A. O., Del Re, A. C., Flükiger, C., & Symonds, D. (2011). Alliance in individual psychotherapy. *Psychotherapy, 48*, 9–16. doi:10.1037/a0022186

Kinderman, P., McKenna, P., & Laws, K. (2015). Are psychological therapies effective in treating psychosis? *Progress in Neurology and Psychiatry, 19*, 17–20. doi:10.1002/pnp.365

Linde, K., Sigterman, K., Kriston, L., Rücker, G., Jamil, S., Meissner, K., & Schneider, A. (2015). Effectiveness of psychological treatments for depressive disorders in primary care: Systematic review and meta-analysis. *Annals of Family Medicine, 13*, 56–68. doi:10.1370/afm.1719

National Institute for Health and Care Excellence. (2014). *Psychosis and schizophrenia in adults: Prevention and management.* London: National Institute for Health and Care Excellence.

Shevlin, M., McElroy, E., Bentall, R. P., Reininghaus, U., & Murphy, J. (2016). The psychosis continuum: Testing a bifactor model of psychosis in a general population sample. *Schizophrenia Bulletin, 43*, 133–141. doi:10.1093/schbul/sbw067

Thomas, N., Hayward, M., Peters, E., van der Gaag, M., Bentall, R. P., Jenner, J., . . . McCarthy-Jones, S. (2014). Psychological therapies for auditory hallucinations (voices): Current status and key directions for future research. *Schizophrenia Bulletin, 40*(suppl 3), S202–S212. doi:10.1093/schbul/sbu037

'In search of help', a short comic on experiences of therapy by Annie Blake

2

COGNITIVE BEHAVIOURAL THERAPY (CBT)

Client's perspective

Yarburgh[1] and Peter Taylor

> Although cognitive behavioural therapy is perhaps the most well-known therapy offered in the UK for people experiencing psychosis reading this chapter gave me a much better understanding of what is involved. It gives a real insight into how different ways of seeing thoughts and beliefs can lead to positive change and how this is process that can take time.
>
> – Naomi Fisher

Background

This section focuses on my experiences of Cognitive Behavioural Therapy (CBT), which I undertook as part of a research trial of CBT for people with experiences of psychosis. I had many misconceptions about CBT, and therapy in general, before starting including what it would be like and what it would involve. In this section, I hope to provide a picture of what this therapy is actually like. I will start with an outline of what led to me receiving CBT, before going on to describe the CBT itself. I will emphasise the things that helped but also the challenging parts of this therapy.

What led me to therapy

When I now look back, I think I have suffered from mental health problems from a young age. Experiences like suspicious thoughts were common for me but I did not see this as being any different to what other people went through. Then there was one big psychotic incident that happened when I was 18 years old. I was facing a lot of stress at the time, I had been burgled, lost my home, my mum went into hospital, and my dad had killed himself after years of being confined to a hospital bed. When I moved into my new house after this, I had an experience where I thought my friends were planning to steal my music. It may sound silly but the experience itself was really overwhelming. I could hear voices outside of my head and was experiencing full-on hallucinations where I could see people that were not there.

Following this episode, I was shaken up at first, but relaxed in some ways over time. I continued to have mini-experiences, like suspicious thoughts, trust issues, getting obsessed with ideas and overthinking things, and problems falling asleep at night.

Soon afterwards I moved away to go to university. I think I was suffering from Post-Traumatic Stress Disorder (PTSD) in some ways and blocking out events, particularly in relation to my dad. I did struggle in certain life situations, but unknowingly had set up natural coping mechanisms to deal with them. I had always thought talking to yourself and hearing voices in your head was normal and that some people just did it more than others. I felt like a lot of these experiences were normal and not a sign of any bigger problems at this time, I just thought I was depressed.

Years later I got into a toxic relationship in which I started taking drugs a lot. I think this began to undo my natural coping mechanisms and over time I gradually started having more and more psychotic episodes closer together. At this point I began to feel like I was mad, people were evil, and the world was not real. All this made me want to escape even more through even more drug taking. It was hard to distinguish what was real and what was not at times, both on and off drugs. There was a night when my girlfriend was talking about family names and found my family coat of arms; this gave me a massive overwhelming blast of information, flashbacks of the past, mainly in relation to my dad, but also the other incidents and emotions that surrounded it. The difficult decision to leave my partner, which also meant me losing my home, my daughter's home, and my business, led to more stress. At this point I tried to get help from the National Health Service (NHS).

I tried to get help from friends and services, but moving around a lot and with others not understanding psychosis it was hard for them to help. I was struggling with delusional thoughts (the world was full of bad people) and was having suicidal feelings. Because I moved into temporary accommodation, I was not seen by a professional in time before I had to move area again. This happened a couple of times until I was back in Manchester in a good friend's house who allowed me enough time to stay for me to get help. I was seen by a new doctor at first who referred me to the early intervention for psychosis service. After my assessment with them, I was seen by a psychiatrist who diagnosed me with psychosis and gave me a prescription for medication to try and help with the psychosis. The drugs did not work for me. If anything they seemed to be making me worse. I tried a few variations of medication before being made aware that there was a research trial that was running, in which candidates were assigned a course of CBT or meds, the outcome of the trial being how effective CBT is in comparison to prescribed medication for psychosis. I was lucky to be assigned the CBT group.

Overview of the therapy

The therapy I experienced went on longer than was initially planned, and I think I received over 20 sessions. The sessions took place every week in my home and lasted about an hour. This was one aspect of therapy I initially found hard. Our sessions would often run over and my therapist started to try and keep us to time, using a clock or a 15-minute warning. I did not like the clock, it felt very much like way therapy is presented in movies where the therapist says 'your time is up' and ushers the client out of their office. However, this was something we were able to address head on and discuss in the therapy, and this helped a lot in easing these tensions.

It is important to note that the therapy I received was part of a research trial. This means it might be different to the therapy that you would normally receive through health services, for example in terms of the number of sessions given (I was offered more sessions than might be available through the NHS) or where the therapy took place, but I know this can vary a lot anyway depending on the service you are with. Being part of a trial also meant I was required to complete other questionnaires and assessments in addition to the therapy I was doing.

Initial impressions

The first meeting with the therapist was very difficult. I think this is the case for everyone, even if you know what to expect. I was meeting with a total stranger and would be asked to share very personal information about the problems I had faced! However, it really helped that the therapist I had seemed very good. She quickly gave me the impressions that she was listening to everything I was saying, but instead of judging me, she seemed to understand. She showed a genuine interest in hearing about myself and my experiences, and this really helped me to open in these early sessions. Very quickly it got easier to talk about these things, and I was able to feel comfortable in the sessions. I have a tendency to overthink things, and ruminate over ideas and possibilities, and I suspect this is one of the factors that contributed to my experiences of psychosis. However, in sessions together I found that this tendency also had a positive side, as it meant that I could talk about the difficulties I faced and things I had been through. Our sessions together felt very like active ongoing discussions between myself and the therapist.

I had a big misconception when I started therapy about what it would involve. Though I had been told I was going to receive CBT, I thought it would be more like how I imagine counselling is, where I would talk about whatever was on my mind and therapist would sit back and listen. In reality, I wanted to tell the therapist everything that was going on in my life and she would stop me to say that she had the information she needed and might move us onto a different topic. I thought the therapy would be more like me talking about past experiences and what they meant to me personally. Instead, the focus was very much in the 'here and now'. My therapist explained this to me and how the focus of CBT might be different in this way to other types of therapy. I was struggling, trying to make sense of the therapy and how it worked, as this is how my mind works, I can overthink things trying to make sense of what is going on around me. It was therefore helpful having this direct discussion with my therapist about what the therapy involved, and it all made a little more sense from this point onwards.

Making sense

The early sessions of therapy were very much about gathering information, finding out about me and my experiences. As we talked about this, my therapist started to draw out what is called a 'formulation'. Formulations in CBT are drawn diagrams that help to show how different experiences link to certain ways of thinking, feeling, or behaving, and so begin to make sense of the difficulties you have been facing. When the idea of formulation was first introduced to me, I was not really clear on what to expect, the language felt quite foreign and clinical. However, as my therapist started to develop and draw out these formulations with me, it started to make sense. I could see these cycles of events and behaviour that kept my problems going, for example how the voices I heard affected my feelings about going out of the house, or how drinking coffee before bed affected my sleep and the consequences of not getting enough sleep.

The formulations were helpful, because it can often be hard to take advice around bad or unhelpful habits. Like when your mum asks you not to do something as a child, you might know it's a good idea but still ignore this advice. But seeing these cycles and the links between what you are doing one minute, and what happens next, was a much more powerful tool for me in helping my understanding. It helped to reinforce the changes I was trying to make in how I dealt with difficult situations. In a way I feel having a formulation of what was going on behind my psychosis gave me a new set of ways to make sense of a situation. Another way of thinking about this is that it gave me a different path to go down, when faced with a situation that would trigger anxiety or paranoia (e.g. a stranger knocking on the door), and so started to break with the automatic response to these situations that I had always had.

My therapist would give me copies of these diagrams to take home, alongside other handouts, with the goal of helping me to understand what caused my current difficulties and kept them going. However, I did not like taking these handouts home. I did not keep hold of any of the diagrams and handouts, as I was concerned about the stigma associated with my experiences and what others might think of me if they saw them. Personally, I much preferred it when the therapist talked with me and explained things in the sessions, rather than it being put down on paper to read.

As I mentioned, the focus of the therapy was often on the here and now. One way my therapist would try to understand what was going on for me was by looking at recent experiences, over the last week or so, where things had been difficult. An example of this would be going to a supermarket and finding this provoked my anxiety and paranoid feelings. My concerns were both around the way I appeared (was I making a face or standing in an odd way?) and how others reacted (were they looking at me?). My therapist wanted to understand this better. She would encourage me to talk through exactly what happened, moment-by-moment, sometimes asking me to stop or go back, to get a really clear picture of what happened. This process was hard at first, having to revisit these experiences again and again. However, through doing this she was able to give me a step-by-step explanation of what had happened to me that day. Doing this helped me to step back from the raw emotion of these experiences and start to make sense of why I felt I particular way.

Challenging beliefs and ideas

One of the important things we hit upon in therapy was that the thoughts and ideas that I had about myself and other people were not necessarily true, and so could be tested out and challenged. As the therapy progressed, a lot of what we did together was therefore about finding ways to test out the truth of some of the paranoid or upsetting thoughts I was experiencing.

My therapist asked to actually go with me to a local supermarket, to see firsthand how I found this. This was something we started to do regularly. My therapist used this as an opportunity to challenge and question the beliefs and ideas I had in this setting. We did not always agree, sometimes I felt someone had looked at me a certain way and my therapist missed this, but I think ultimately this exercise was helpful in changing the way I felt about and responded to these situations. My therapist also suggested filming me at the supermarket, as another way to check out whether some of the thoughts I was having were true or not, with video evidence. However, I did not like the idea of having to watch myself on the screen and so this was something we did not do. My therapist listened to these concerns and was okay about not doing this.

Intrusive thoughts and voices

Another area of the therapy was around intrusive thoughts and voices. These would pop into my mind and I would then find it hard to let go of them. The result was that I would often end up stuck, ruminating, with the same thoughts or voices running around and around in my mind. Three techniques that my therapist introduced to me to help here were *attentional training, mindfulness,* and *worry postponement.*

Attentional training involved practicing trying to shift my attention from one thing (thought, sound, image) to another, for example from one sound to another. The idea was to help me feel in control of my attention, rather than it being distracted and grabbed by unhelpful or distressing thoughts or ideas. I had an audio recording, which I was asked to listen to, to practice between sessions. Being honest, the attentional training practice was one part of the therapy I found less helpful. The recording had a man's voice talking to me and asking me to ignore him and listen to the noises of water in the background. I have a background in sound recording, and so insight into how people hear sounds. To me, the idea of following the man's instruction to not listen to him, whilst he was telling me what to do, made no sense at all. As a result I found it hard to get on board with this exercise and did less practice than I was asked to.

In contrast, *mindfulness* was something I found very helpful. This is essentially a kind of meditation practice, to help keep your focus in the present moment, rather than being distracted by thoughts about the past or the future. I already had some experience of mindfulness, which may have helped me engage with this. I remember a moment when I had a stark realisation that the mindfulness was helping. I had always been, and still am at times, anxious about leaving the house. I was living in Manchester and took a walk from my friend's house to the shop. During this walk I suddenly noticed that I was not focused on the route ahead of me, but instead was looking over at the canal, and the ducks that were on it, and that I was feeling good. Rather than being focused on the destination or what I had to do next, or what might happen, I was noticing the journey, and what was going on around me in that moment. At this point, what it meant to be mindful and living in the moment really clicked.

Another technique I was introduced to in therapy was *worry postponement*. Whilst attentional training and mindfulness were more about keeping my attention and focus on the present, worry postponement was more around communicating with voices and thoughts, and reaching an agreement. So I would strike a deal with a voice, that I would not talk with it or give it my attention now, but would do so another time (maybe tomorrow morning, for example). This was an odd one because it was something I had already been doing. I think we all develop our own, almost automatic ways of coping with stress and problems. When I was growing up and struggling with intrusive thoughts, ideas and voices, I had started to do this sort of postponement. This had been helping me to get along day-to-day, but then something big happened, I had a major psychotic episode, and I seemed to lose touch with these helpful techniques. They were blown out of the water. So I started again to use this technique and this did help me for a little while. This was until, having put off giving a particular voice my attention for a while, it exploded and gave me a real bollocking (a telling off). The voice said, and quite accurately, that I had been lying to it, and had no intention of giving it my attention at some later point. This was an important event and something we discussed in the therapy. I think, personally in some ways, voices are like children. They require a certain amount of attention and can start to cause more trouble when you do not give them this time. Whilst worry postponement was only partially helpful, having it as part of therapy did help me to gain a new recognition of the value of these old coping mechanisms.

Homework

Homework is a big part of CBT, and I would often have pieces of work to do between sessions, including mindfulness practice, reading handouts or watching videos, or completing small tasks like going outside or noticing my surroundings more. My therapist would often share bits and pieces of information with me about psychosis to look at, at home. One particularly helpful thing she shared was a video of a TED presentation by Eleanor Longden (a psychologist and researcher with her own experiences of psychosis), about her experiences of psychosis (www.youtube.com/watch?v=syjEN3peCJw). This talk gave me hope, seeing someone with experiences of psychosis in such a prominent role. The talk also helped to show that it was not just me with these experiences, and so defeated some of the self-reflected stigma I felt at times. Another really helpful video is about mindfulness and intrusive thoughts by Andy Puddicombe (www.youtube.com/watch?v=qzR62JJCMBQ). Andy uses his juggling skills to help explain these ideas in a way that made a lot of sense to me.

One piece of homework that was particularly helpful, however, was homework that I set for my therapist, rather than the other way around. When you experience psychosis, you are faced with events and things that you had never known could happen before, and I found this can shatter the way you look at and understand the world. For me, faced with these experiences, I had a need to try and make sense of what had happened, and discover the truth of some of these experiences. As a result I would do research and look into strange phenomena, the paranormal or supernatural, as well as philosophy and other ideas. In doing this, I found it hard to differentiate what was good information from misleading information. I think this tendency to research even reinforced some of my less helpful beliefs and ideas at times. It was not possible to talk to family about this, they did not understand the place I was coming from and simply warned me to stay away from everything. So I spoke to my therapist and set her homework to look into this, to watch a documentary or read a presentation, and tell me what she thought. She did not say that it was all nonsense, and importantly we were able to discuss these ideas and what value they had.

For me, the weekly gaps between therapy sessions were as important as the sessions themselves, including the homework and the thinking space it gave me. I am a DJ and create music, and sometimes find that you need time away from what you are doing to master it. I think it is the same in therapy as the gaps are essential. I do not think that 16 back-to-back days of therapy would therefore be as good as 16 sessions occurring once a week.

Change

The way I understand CBT is that it gave me different templates that I could carry with me, for how to look at situations, and new tools for helping myself at these times. However, these new templates and tools do not work at first. I found that even with a new understanding of why, for example, I found going into a busy supermarket difficult, this did not make it easier to cope with. Instead, I found it was something that takes time, you learn to apply these new tools and templates more automatically, and it is like you are learning to re-programme the way you think and react in difficult situations. But this process takes a long time, as you are essentially trying to re-wire the way you think and act.

I still do not feel the 20 or so sessions I had were enough and I think I might have benefited from longer therapy. I am now 35 years old, and so have had 35 years for problems and difficult experiences to build up, and so I am not sure if 16 or 20 sessions will be enough to resolve this completely. I still have ups and downs and times when it is hard to break away from my automatic ways of responding and reacting to situations (those habits I had learned). The skills and knowledge I have gained is still no magic pill. Sometimes I know there is a different way to think or act, but I'm so overstimulated by what is going on, the voices or the situation I am in, that it is impossible to use these techniques.

Despite these ongoing challenges, I feel I have gained a great deal from the CBT, and have been able to do many things that I struggled with before. I am now actively involved in voluntary psychiatric services and do work with the Psychosis Research Unit, helping them to better support and understand people with psychosis.

Whilst the techniques and approaches used in CBT were helpful, I think a big part of what helped me were the qualities of my therapist. I have often had different mental health staff come in and out of my life, but I felt there was something different about my therapist. She seemed to show a real empathy for me, and was able to move beyond being another psychiatric team staff member to being a human being, someone in my life who I felt, beyond her professional role, cared about how I was doing. This feeling was a massive thing for me. The flip side of having this relationship is that it can be very hard when therapy comes to an end, and I personally found the ending of therapy very difficult.

Conclusion

Hopefully this chapter has given you a good feeling for what CBT for psychosis involves, the challenges and the benefits of this therapy. I wanted to end this section by noting that, for me, it was the understanding of my problems and what kept them going that helped me to engage with the practical parts of therapy. Understanding why, for example, I might feel paranoid or anxious in a particular situation really gave power to those actions that might break these cycles. It is also important to note that this all takes effort. A therapist will not push you through therapy – this is a path you have to walk yourself with the therapist's help.

Practitioner's perspective

Jane Hutton

In this section I aim to offer a sense of what Cognitive Behavioural Therapy (CBT) for psychosis may look like in practice. I draw heavily on the ideas of Antony Morrison and colleagues who are leading researchers in this area and with whom much of my own training and experience lies (for further details of this approach see Morrison, Renton, Dunn, Williams, & Bentall, 2004; www.psychosisresearch.com).

The cognitive model

Meet Anne, Bob, and Claire. By a remarkable coincidence, they all decide to text their mutual friend Dave, to invite him out for a drink. Unbeknownst to them, Dave is off on a two day hike without his phone and will not pick up their messages until he returns. So what do our trio make of Dave's lack of reply?

Anne has a history of being let down by other people. She generally believes that others are mean and untrustworthy. Anne decides that Dave is being incredibly rude and in fact might be ignoring her on purpose. She feels hurt and angry and quickly sends further text messages to Dave telling him just how unreasonable he is being.

Bob was brought up with highly critical parents and experienced bullying throughout school. He does not have a very good opinion of himself and believes that you should always try to please others. Bob thinks that Dave must be upset with him and so he sits at home and thinks through all the possible things that he could have done to offend Dave, feeling more and more anxious and upset as he does so.

Claire on the other hand does not particularly worry about what others think of her and believes that people are generally ok. She reasons that Dave must be busy; she feels relaxed and carries on with her day. She will text Dave again in a few days if she has not heard from him.

These examples illustrate the key components of the cognitive model. Originally developed by Aaron T. Beck in the 1960s (Beck, 1964), the cognitive model suggests that it is our interpretation of events, rather than the events themselves, that leads to negative (or indeed positive) emotional responses. These interpretations

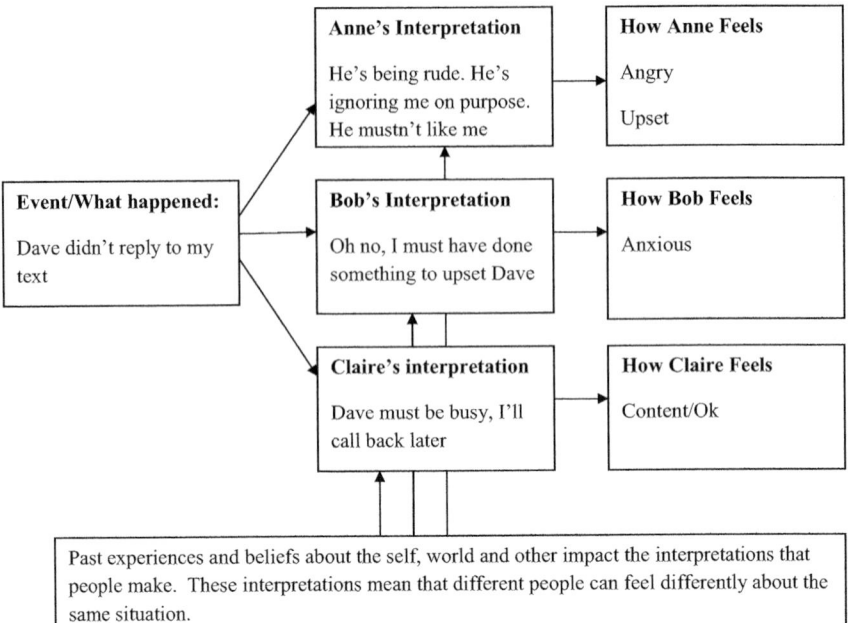

Figure 2.1 How thoughts influence feelings; the cognitive model

are thought to be largely influenced by sets of beliefs and assumptions that we hold about ourselves, others, and the world around us, which develop as a result of our past experiences. The way we interpret, and subsequently feel about, a situation will influence how we respond to it (Figure 2.1). Using the cognitive model to understand the interplay between our thoughts, feelings, and behaviour is the foundation on which CBT is based.

The cognitive model and psychosis

The cognitive model can help us understand a whole range of experiences including those associated with psychosis. Suspicious thinking, for example, worrying that others are trying to hurt you, is one experience often associated with psychosis. Let us consider this example first.

Andrew is 50 years old and has experienced a number of difficult events in his life. He witnessed repeated violence between his parents, he was bullied severely at school, and suffered a physical assault in his early twenties. Andrew may, quite understandably, have come to believe that other people are dangerous and mean him harm, that the world is unsafe, and that he himself is vulnerable. He may also hold positive beliefs about the importance of being suspicious (e.g. "being on

COGNITIVE BEHAVIOURAL THERAPY (CBT)

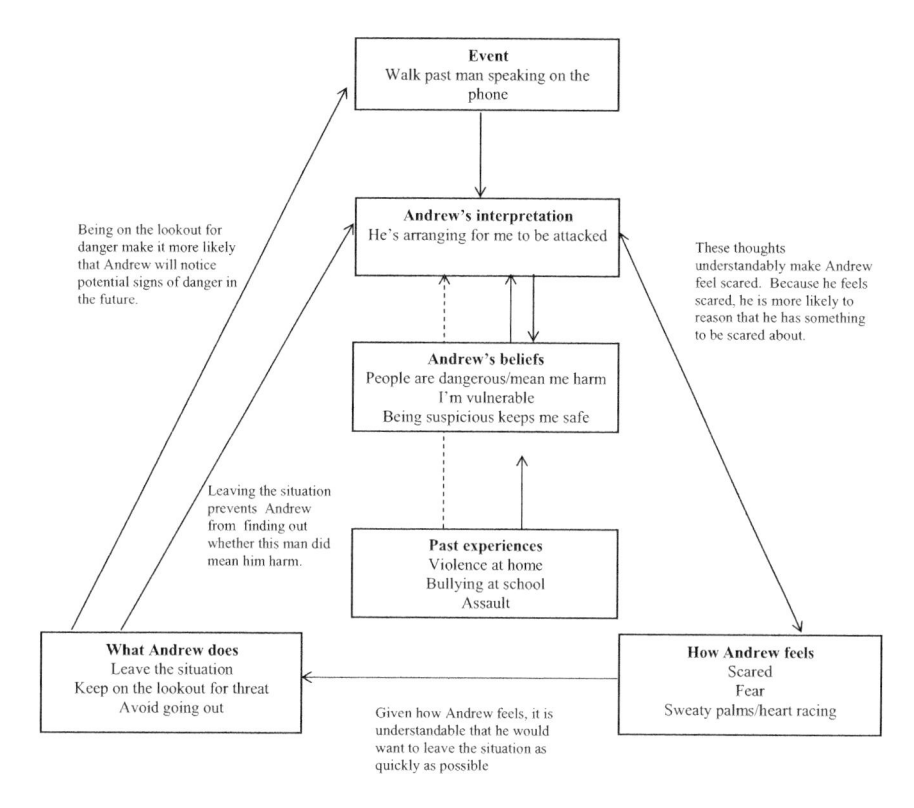

Figure 2.2 A diagram representing the development and maintenance of Andrew's distressing experiences. Based on Morrison's model (Morrison, 2001).

guard keeps me safe"). As such, Andrew may be prone to jumping to suspicious conclusions when faced with ambiguous situations, especially if other people are involved.

So, if Andrew walks past a rather stocky, grumpy looking fellow, who is talking on the phone, he may well interpret this in a threatening way (e.g. "he's arranging for me to be attacked"). This interpretation may lead Andrew to feel scared; quickly leaving the situation as a result. He is prevented from finding out whether the gentleman in question did in fact mean him harm, later reasoning "phew, I had a lucky escape there". He continues to be on the lookout for signs of threat and avoids leaving his home whenever possible. His beliefs that the world is unsafe and that people mean him harm are maintained, and he continues to experience distressing suspicious thoughts.

As with the earlier examples, we see how past experiences can influence the way in which we make sense of the things that happen to us. Figure 2.2 shows how the cognitive model can be applied to Andrew's experiences.

From model to practice: CBT in action

Having introduced the cognitive model and considered how it can apply to psychosis, the remainder of this section will focus on how this model is used in CBT. CBT is a time limited therapy. While the duration of CBT can vary, UK national guidelines recommend that all people experiencing psychosis are offered "at least 16 planned sessions" of CBT (NICE, 2014). Sessions typically occur on a weekly basis, usually lasting for about an hour at a time. Given its foundations in the cognitive model, CBT aims to reduce psychological distress and improve quality of life by helping people to:

a   Understand the links between events, thoughts (or interpretations of events), feelings, and behaviour.
b   Identify and re-evaluate the validity and usefulness of interpretations that are repeatedly linked to distress or that interfere with quality of life.
c   Identify unhelpful behavioural responses (e.g. avoiding people, spending time worrying) and experiment with alternative ways of responding.

Other core features of CBT for psychosis are considered below.

Problem list and goals: CBT is orientated around specific problems and goals. A key task of early sessions is to develop a clear understanding of what an individual hopes to gain from therapy. Developing a prioritised problem list and setting realistic and shared goals in relation to these problems will direct subsequent work. While therapy goals may be linked directly to experiences associated with psychosis, such as hearing voices or unusual beliefs, this may not be the case. Research indicates that goals associated with developing a sense hope and purpose as well as increasing control over or coping with distressing experiences are often prioritised by service users undertaking CBT for psychosis (Greenwood et al., 2010).

Work between sessions: A key feature of CBT is completing work between sessions, in order to maximise the gains that can be made from therapy. These tasks may involve collecting information, testing out ideas, or practising new skills. Research involving over 2000 people indicated that better therapy outcomes are related to the level of work completed between sessions (Mausbach, Moore, Roesch, Cardenas, & Patterson, 2010). That is to say, those that complete more home tasks tend to achieve better results. Nevertheless, the thought of 'homework' can strike fear in the heart of many an adult. The collaborative nature of CBT helps ensure that home tasks are agreed in line with what people feel is both important and achievable.

Agenda setting: Agenda setting typically occurs at the start of CBT sessions. The therapist and client decide together what they hope to cover in a particular appointment. This ensures that sessions are collaborative and proceed in accordance with an individual's goals. In addition to one or two mutually agreed items to be covered, a typical agenda includes a review of the preceding week and home tasks attempted.

Normalisation: Conceptualising 'psychotic experiences' as being understandable reactions to difficult life events is a fundamental principle of CBT for psychosis. This stance is supported by research demonstrating a strong relationship between traumatic events and the development of psychosis (Varese et al., 2012). Furthermore, experiences associated with psychosis such as suspicious thinking and perceptual differences (e.g. hearing, seeing, or feeling things that others do not) are commonly observed, to varying degrees, by people both with and without psychiatric diagnoses (Johns et al., 2004). Providing information such as this during therapy, referred to as *normalisation,* can help people to feel less stigmatised and alienated by their experiences, as well as promoting hope for recovery (Kingdon & Turkington, 1991).

Collaborative empiricism: Collaborative empiricism is the cornerstone of CBT and arguably one of its most important features (Hutton & Morrison, 2013). Collaborative empiricism refers to the practice of working together to develop and test ideas, with the goal of broadening understanding and knowledge. In CBT, therapist and client work together in a collaborative effort to explore alternative ways of understanding and making sense of the client's experiences. A CBT therapist does not make assumptions about the validity of people's experiences, but will, in agreement with individual clients, help to evaluate thoughts and experiences that are linked to distress.

CBT in practice: an illustrative example

To help illustrate what CBT for psychosis may look like in practice, I would like to introduce you to Sue (this is a made up case based on work with lots of different clients). Sue is a 32 year old lady who lives on her own. She has some family members close by but has little social contact beyond this. Sue began hearing distressing voices (sometimes referred to as auditory hallucinations) around seven years ago. This continues to be problematic for Sue, particularly when she is in public places. At these times, the voices become more intense and call Sue horrible names. As a result, Sue avoids going out wherever possible.

Initial stages of therapy: problem list, goals, and informed consent

After meeting with Sue to discuss CBT and establishing that this was an approach that she would like to try, Sue and the therapist started to develop a shared sense of what they would target together. Sue and the therapist developed an initial therapy goal of helping Sue to feel less distressed by voices when out in her local community. Sue rated her current level of anxiety when out as eight out of 10 (10 being the worst it could be). She hoped that reducing this to five or six out of 10 would be more manageable and would allow her to complete daily tasks more easily. Measuring her distress in this way would help Sue and her therapist to monitor progress towards her goal.

Many experiences associated with psychosis can have both positive and negative consequences. For example, while hearing voices may be highly distressing and intrusive, this experience can also provide people with a sense of companionship and support (Mawson, Cohen, & Berry, 2010). It was therefore important to help Sue weigh up the possible advantages and disadvantages of change before proceeding. Sue had become very isolated over recent years and reflected that whilst the voices were often distressing and stopped her from doing the things that she wanted to do, they could also make her feel less alone. Although Sue came to the decision to proceed with CBT, this was done with an understanding that voices may reduce or even stop completely. It also highlighted a concurrent therapy goal of reducing social isolation; an associated goal of joining a local art class was set.

Developing an understanding of the prioritised problem

Using the cognitive model, Sue and the therapist looked at recent times in which she had felt anxious when out (Figure 2.3). Sue noticed that the voices tended to become more intense and derogatory as she approached other people. Sue believed that people could hear the voices and, as a result, thought that everybody

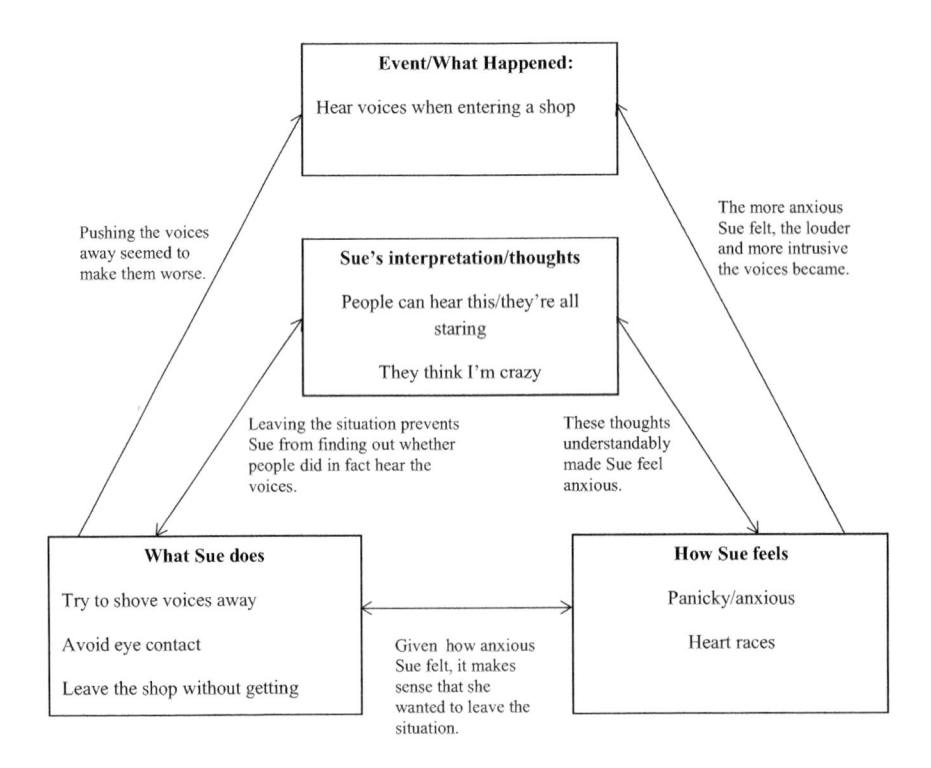

```
                    Event/What Happened:
                 Hear voices when entering a shop

                                                        The more anxious
 Pushing the voices                                     Sue felt, the louder
 away seemed to      Sue's interpretation/thoughts      and more intrusive
 make them worse.                                       the voices became.
                     People can hear this/they're all
                              staring

                         They think I'm crazy

              Leaving the situation prevents    These thoughts
              Sue from finding out whether      understandably
              people did in fact hear the       made Sue feel
              voices.                           anxious.

    What Sue does                                How Sue feels
 Try to shove voices away                      Panicky/anxious
 Avoid eye contact        Given how anxious    Heart races
                          Sue felt, it makes
 Leave the shop without getting   sense that she
                          wanted to leave the
                          situation.
```

Figure 2.3 Mapping out Sue's worries using the cognitive model

was looking at her and judging her ('they'll think I'm crazy'). Making sense of the situation in this way understandably made Sue feel anxious and panicky. Sue and the therapist realised that the more anxious Sue felt, the louder the voices became, and the more difficult it became for Sue to stay in the situation. Sue would try to push the voices away, avoid looking at people, and exit the situation as quickly as possible.

Testing out Sue's worries

Sue and the therapist designed an experiment to test out her worry that others could hear the voices. They agreed that they would go out to a busy shop together. Sue would hold a phone to her ear and press record whenever she heard the voices. Sue predicted that the voices would show up on the recording; if they did not, this would provide evidence against the possibility that other people could hear the voices. Sue was shocked and relieved when listening back to the recording and discovering that the voices could not be heard. Additional work focused on testing Sue's worry that 'everybody was looking at her' by encouraging Sue to look around when she was out instead of looking at the ground. While she noted a few glances, this was nowhere near the level that she had expected and in fact was at a comparable number of glances noted by the therapist when he carried out the same task.

After completing the above and similar experiments together, Sue's belief that others could hear her voices dropped from eight out of 10 to two out of 10, as did her belief that everybody was looking at her. Her level of distress related to this experience also dropped from eight out of 10 to five out of 10. Although she was still anxious in public places, this felt a lot more manageable.

Sue's beliefs about voices

Sue believed that she had no control over the voices and often worried that they might have the power to cause her physical harm (as they often threatened to do). Each of these beliefs led Sue to feel more distressed by voices (which in turn seemed to make them worse). Sue and the therapist agreed that it might therefore be helpful to investigate these beliefs together.

They wondered whether some of the strategies that Sue currently used in response to voices may be making them worse. Sue would often argue back with the voices for long periods, which would leave her feeling tired, exhausted, and defeated. At other times, she would try to ignore the voices and push them away, but this did not seem to work either. It is therefore not surprising that Sue believed that her voices were uncontrollable.

Sue and the therapist set out to test of different ways of responding to voices. In one session, when Sue noticed hearing voices, they found that playing a game of noughts and crosses reduced the intensity of this experience. Sue tried similar distraction techniques at home and recorded the impact that these had on voices.

These experiments not only helped Sue to test out alternative ways of responding to voices, they also helped her to re-evaluate her beliefs about how controllable and powerful the voices were. She came to the conclusion that:

1   I have more control over the voices than I thought.
2   If playing noughts and crosses can weaken voices, they can't be that powerful after all.

In relation to the latter belief, Sue and the therapist looked at the evidence for and against the voices having power to do her harm. While there was little evidence supporting this being true (other than their constant barrage of threats), there was a lot of evidence against this being true. This lead to Sue feeling confident enough to test out what would happen if she disobeyed the voices by leaving the house even when the voices told her not to. Sue found that while the voices continued to make their threats, these did not come true. This further bolstered Sue's belief that the voices were not as powerful as she had once thought.

It is important to note that this is just a snapshot of what CBT may look like in practice. These particular strategies may not be helpful for everybody. Together client and therapist can generate ideas regarding what might be helpful, and test these out in a safe, controlled, and measurable way.

Cognitive behavioural therapy and psychosis: what is the evidence?

CBT is often cited as being the most widely and rigorously tested psychological intervention. Its effectiveness has been demonstrated for a range of psychological problems including psychosis (Hofmann, Asnaani, Vonk, Sawyer, & Fang, 2012). Given this, we are able to have more certainty when considering whether or not CBT can be a useful approach for people experiencing psychosis. We can now say with relative confidence that CBT, for some people at least, can be effective at reducing distressing experiences and improving outcomes associated with quality of life. As a result of the cumulative evidence supporting CBT for psychosis, UK national guidelines currently recommend that CBT should be offered to all people experiencing psychosis, and to those who may be at risk of experiencing psychosis (NICE, 2014). While most of this evidence has been accumulated for people also taking medication for psychosis, research is now emerging which suggests that CBT may also benefit people who choose not to take such medication (Morrison et al., 2014).

With all of that being said, we also know that CBT is not helpful for everybody, and the benefits that individuals derive from therapy can vary widely. While there is some evidence to suggest that CBT is more effective than other therapies for experiences such as hallucinations and delusional thinking (Turner, van der Gaag, Karyotaki, & Cuijpers, 2014), this has not been consistently reported (Jones, Hacker, Cormac, Meaden, & Irving, 2012). More research is needed to directly contrast models of therapy and to better establish what form intervention may be most helpful to which individuals. While CBT is currently one of the most widely used talking therapies for psychosis, having a range of psychological interventions that we have tested, and can say with confidence can help the individuals with whom we are working, is of upmost importance. This will allow service users to make a truly informed decision about which taking therapy, if any, they might like to try.

Concluding remarks

In this section we have looked at the theory underlying this CBT for psychosis, specifically how the cognitive model applies to experiences associated with psychosis. As well as looking at the structure and content of CBT sessions, we have discussed the guiding principles of normalisation and collaboration. Individual experiences of CBT for psychosis will vary depending on a number of factors including particular goals being targeted, the experiences of different services users and the approach and style of the individual therapist involved. Nevertheless, I hope that this chapter has provided a sense of what CBT for psychosis may look like in practice, and what you might expect if you are considering trying this form of therapy.

Note

1 The author has preferred to remain anonymous and to use a pseudonym. (Peter has worked alongside Yarburgh to record his account of his experience of having therapy.)

References

Beck, A. T. (1964). Thinking and depression: Ii. theory and therapy. *Archives of General Psychiatry, 10*(6), 561–571.

Greenwood, K. E., Sweeney, A., Williams, S., Garety, P., Kuipers, E., Scott, J., & Peters, E. (2010). CHoice of Outcome In Cbt for psychosEs (CHOICE): The development of a new service user-led outcome measure of CBT for psychosis. *Schizophrenia Bulletin, 36*(1), 126–135.

Hofmann, S. G., Asnaani, A., Vonk, I. J. J., Sawyer, A. T., & Fang, A. (2012). The efficacy of cognitive behavioral therapy: A review of meta-analyses. *Cognitive Therapy and Research, 36*(5), 427–440.

Hutton, P., & Morrison, A. P. (2013). Collaborative empiricism in cognitive therapy for psychosis: A practice guide. *Cognitive and Behavioral Practice, 20*(4), 429–444.

Johns, L. C., Cannon, M., Singleton, N., Murray, R. M., Farrell, M., Brugha, T., . . . Meltzer, H. (2004). Prevalence and correlates of self-reported psychotic symptoms in the British population. *The British Journal of Psychiatry, 185*, 298–305.

Jones, C., Hacker, D., Cormac, I., Meaden, A., & Irving, C. B. (2012). Cognitive behaviour therapy versus other psychosocial treatments for schizophrenia. *Cochrane Database of Systematic Reviews, 4*, CD008712.

Kingdon, D. G., & Turkington, D. (1991). The use of cognitive behavior therapy with a normalizing rationale in schizophrenia. Preliminary report. *The Journal of Nervous and Mental Disease, 179*(4), 207–211.

Mausbach, B. T., Moore, R., Roesch, S., Cardenas, V., & Patterson, T. L. (2010). The relationship between homework compliance and therapy outcomes: An updated meta-analysis. [journal article]. *Cognitive Therapy and Research, 34*(5), 429–438.

Mawson, A., Cohen, K., & Berry, K. (2010). Reviewing evidence for the cognitive model of auditory hallucinations: The relationship between cognitive voice appraisals and distress during psychosis. *Clinical Psychology Review, 30*(2), 248–258.

Morrison, A., Renton, J., Dunn, H., Williams, S., & Bentall, R. (2004). *Cognitive therapy for psychosis: A formulation-based approach.* Hove: Routledge.

Morrison, A. P., Turkington, D., Pyle, M., Spencer, H., Brabban, A., Dunn, G., . . . Hutton, P. (2014). Cognitive therapy for people with schizophrenia spectrum disorders not taking antipsychotic drugs: A single-blind randomised controlled trial. *The Lancet, 383*(9926), 1395–1403.

NICE. (2014). *Psychosis and schizophrenia in adults: Prevention and management (update)* [CG178]. London: National Institute for Health and Care Excellence.

Turner, D. T., van der Gaag, M., Karyotaki, E., & Cuijpers, P. (2014). Psychological interventions for psychosis: A meta-analysis of comparative outcome studies. *The American Journal of Psychiatry, 171*(5), 523–538.

Varese, F., Smeets, F., Drukker, M., Lieverse, R., Lataster, T., Viechtbauer, W., . . . Bentall, R. P. (2012). Childhood adversities increase the risk of psychosis: A meta-analysis of patient-control, prospective- and cross-sectional cohort studies. *Schizophrenia Bulletin, 38*, 661–671. doi: 10.1093/schbul/sbs050

3

SYSTEMIC FAMILY THERAPY (SFT)
Client's perspective

Zara Zaks[1]

> Family relationships have been shown to be an important factor in our mental health. While many of the therapies in this book recognise and discuss the importance of our relationships with others, this chapter on Systemic Family Therapy is one of the few that directly involves both the client and their family members. In this chapter, Zara and Pekka describe how the experience of psychosis can affect relationships with those close to us, and how communication and a shared understanding of the client's experience among family members can help in supporting the individual and maintaining a positive family atmosphere.
>
> – Olympia Gianfrancesco

Background

Out of all the different interventions I have had for psychosis, family therapy has been one of the most unusual. I am not sure what I was expecting when my community psychiatric nurse suggested this type of talking therapy for my family, but I was willing to give it a try. My experience of psychosis had had a great impact on my relationships with my family. Psychosis had affected the way my family related to me due to my symptoms and in turn how they related to each other. They were struggling with the grief of seeing someone close to them descend into a place that is both frightening and wholly difficult to understand. This grief was often unexpressed, and whilst my family wanted to help me and stay positive, they were also concealing their own panic and fear within themselves and from one another, including me.

The reasons for our referral to family therapy were related to my experiences with repeated episodes of psychosis. Psychosis is difficult to describe (see Chapter 1 for an overview), but involves a number of different psychological difficulties that are often about losing touch with reality, for example, hallucinations or paranoid thoughts. My experiences of psychosis followed many years of struggling with anxiety. I began to experience my first set of psychotic symptoms, paranoid delusions and a set of auditory hallucinations or 'voices', at the age of

18 years. Delusions are unfounded beliefs, thoughts that are not based in reality yet held with a strong conviction, even when others try to persuade you otherwise. These thoughts are extremely convincing, real to you, and practically impossible to shake. Auditory hallucinations are sounds that you can hear or sense, but no-one else can. In my case they manifested as people talking to me in my head with voices that were not my own, with derogatory phrases towards myself and often strong commands. The whole experience is one of fear and confusion. These experiences feel wholly uncontrollable when left alone. I often had the feeling that the experiences themselves were multiplying by the day with no ability to halt them.

Knowing absolutely nothing about psychosis prior to this made the experiences even more frightening for me, as I was unsure about what was happening to my mind. I had been seeing a therapist practicing Cognitive Behavioural Therapy (CBT) at the child and adolescent mental health service to help with my anxiety. However, during this time, my persecutory beliefs grew stronger and multiplied into a complex web of unreality until I was referred to the early intervention for psychosis service by my then CBT therapist. A diagnosis of a psychotic disorder followed, and my first prescription for medication for psychosis. I managed to hide my experiences of psychosis from my family for a while, although they were aware that I was seeing a therapist for anxiety. Of course, something like this is hard to hide and it was only a matter of time before my parents found out about my experiences of psychosis. What followed were months of total despair for my parents, who had no knowledge of mental illness. There was also confusion for my then 13 year old sister who had to watch the person she had looked up to descend further and further into madness.

Expectation and reality

It was these experiences that led me and my family to receive family therapy. We had six sessions of family therapy in total, interrupted in the middle by a further relapse and my fifth and final hospital admission to date. In all, I had a few sessions well, a few unwell, and then a further few well again. This is interesting to remember, because my experience in each of these states was very different.

I have experienced numerous types of talking therapy: counselling (see Chapter 10), cognitive behavioural therapy (see Chapter 2), and cognitive analytic therapy (see Chapter 5). All of these were one-to-one interventions, where it was just the therapist and myself in the room and the focus was on me. Suddenly, with family therapy, I was not the focus. This therapy involved my whole family and we all played an equal part in the progression of the therapy. This meant having equal opportunities to express our feelings and opinions, and our therapist certainly made sure that none of us sat in silence. This was a real change from the one-to-one therapy I was used to.

Many people's perception of family therapy, or indeed any therapy, is that you sit around in a room and doctors or professionals scrutinise your every word and every movement and make notes about you. This was not the case with any of the therapies I have experienced, including family therapy. However, there was a difference between one-to-one therapy and family therapy, as in the latter there were three professionals in the room: the lead family therapist, and two psychologists. The lead therapist took the reins with asking the questions, while it was the responsibility of the psychologists to listen to the family talk, and then to talk to each other about what had just been discussed by the family. This is referred to as the 'reflecting teams' approach. The lead therapist would ask specific questions to each of us about how we felt, and then invite the rest of us to respond. She would direct the questions at each of us by using our names, and they seemed carefully chosen to promote discussion. For example, "how do you feel about what Dad just said? Do you agree with him about needing a crisis plan?" or "what would you prefer your sister to do when you are pacing around the kitchen?" or "Mum, how would you like Dad to behave when you are feeling stressed that Zara is not keeping her bedroom clean?" The psychologists would then discuss what we had said: "so it seems like Zara's sister feels she needs to give her a hug and ask her if she'd like to watch TV instead, which might help distract her".

The structure of therapy was in a way very rigid, but in another way quite liberal; we sat down to talk for a set time with set therapists, but not with specific objectives in that discussion was open but under the umbrella of therapeutic intervention. This somehow made it less clinical and more like a frank discussion, which I thought made it easier as there was no solid list of questions and the discussion could be very open ended. The lead therapist would direct the therapy so that everyone would get a chance to speak, and each for a similar amount of time. In that way, there were boundaries for each of us. The topics of discussion, however, were up to us as a family. The therapist did not have a rigid list of things that she wanted us to talk about, she asked questions based on what sort of themes were coming from our discussion. For example, she asked how the symptoms I was experiencing made everyone feel, or how my sister felt being bullied at school, or how my mum would have preferred my dad to behave during my hospitalisations.

Content of the therapy

The main topic of conversation in family therapy was, for us, about my journey with psychosis. When we first started the therapy, I had just been discharged from my fourth hospital admission after my fourth episode of psychosis. My community psychiatric nurse thought that perhaps through the therapy we could create better family dynamics: a greater understanding of how my family could help me should I become unwell again, and generally learning to become more open and honest with each other. It was a chance to analyse my past experience with psychosis together, and to explore if anything could be done differently should I get unwell again, as well as being a chance to reflect on what might have contributed towards my first episode. The goal of this was to determine if, next time, something might be done differently, to either prevent my psychosis snowballing or at least help me to cope during my episode.

The discussions we had in therapy focused in particular around when I started teenage life. Before this time, things had not been that bad. We had a very good upbringing, we were sent to good schools and my parents cared about our education, welfare, and health. My parents worked full time when my sister and I were children, but we had a childminder who treated us well. Family therapy is not just about the bad experiences and we were encouraged to recognise the good too.

When I was a teenager, my sister was also starting secondary school. She was unfortunately badly bullied at junior school and a little way into secondary school, and this had a substantial impact on me. My confidence was never very high, but in secondary school it decreased so much to the point of severe anxiety on my part. I think both these unfortunate aspects of life really played into the family dynamics. I remember my sister's bullying causing my mum extreme stress and anguish, and my sister extreme unhappiness, which then impacted the rest of the family. Since the stress was high, arguments happened often, mainly surrounding school work and school life. I have always found examinations extremely stressful, and these arguments were happening often since I was doing my GCSEs (General Certificate of Secondary Education, a qualification in the UK), and during my first episode of psychosis, my A Levels (Advanced Levels, another UK qualification). My sister struggled with her work and this was a focus of concern within the family until she was finally diagnosed with dyslexia and Attention Deficit Hyperactivity Disorder (ADHD). This was another area of discussions in therapy. Since both my parents' children had 'problems', I am sure this took a toll on them.

It was clear that both my sister's experience of bullying and learning difficulties, and my spiralling mental health, rocked the boat. A lot was unspoken in my family, and at the time my psychosis started, I believe it was not only me keeping quiet. My mother and father also kept quiet, not wanting to make me worse or upset me. So when we started family therapy, I knew it was these unspoken feelings that would be the most prominent.

The course of therapy and how it changed

In addition to the sessions where we all sat together, our therapist also offered us separate sessions: one session for my parents, one for my sister and me. This was talked about fairly early on in therapy as an option for us to think about. I thought this was a good option for my parents. They obviously talk together about their daughters anyway, but I felt that this might provide them with some gentle guidance about how to process my experiences. It was also a good idea for my sister and myself as we also often talked together about my parents and how they felt about my illness, but often kept this to ourselves. It seemed a therapist in the discussion might help us to talk more rationally or reflect on the way we looked at things. Attending a session with my family and then attending a session with my sister was quite different. I respect my parents, and sometimes in family therapy there were things I wanted to say but I had to make sure I worded them carefully.

There is no worse feeling than knowing you have said something offensive or upsetting to someone you care about. For instance, whilst my mother still loved me when I was first psychotic, she did not handle it very well. When I had to go back to this in the sessions, I could not be as blunt as I wanted to be. I think the point of family therapy is to be honest and open, but there is a subtle and unspoken boundary that exists, or certainly existed for us. My mother has always been very emotional regarding my illness and has always blamed herself. As a result, going into sessions, my father, my sister, and I had to be cautious over our wording regarding my mother's feelings, so as not to make her feel worse than she already did. However, when it was a session with just my sister and me, we could be a little more open regarding our feelings towards our mother, and also our father. I found this a positive aspect of therapy. My sister and I have always talked about my parents together, but the therapist was able to give us some gentle guidance and also encouraged us to feel that talking together is healthy and useful. Our relationship became closer and to this day we maintain good honesty with each other around how we think our parents are behaving towards my illness, and how my sister feels about it too. I often give her guidance on how I would like them to behave, and she relays this in a neutral and confidential way. In return, I think they value her honesty and find her a good sounding board. Often then she will relay to me how they feel. This way in which our relationship works does not feel sneaky or secretive, I find it highly useful and honest and it works for us.

Challenges

I found the discussions between the psychologists particularly odd (the 'reflecting teams'), and I know my sister did too. It is very strange to be discussed by professionals whilst they are in front of you. In the past, I often found that I was being discussed behind my back, in offices or handover meetings. But here we listened to the psychologists analysing parts of our session in front of us. An example being something like: "what I hear Zara saying to Dad is that she is getting frustrated because he doesn't communicate enough with her, but in return, Dad has explained that he finds it hard to articulate himself". The other psychologist would then agree, and follow with their mirrored opinion or anything else they thought was important to bring up. It was these parts, the discussion between the psychologists, which I found most uncomfortable. I wanted to hear what they thought of our discussion with one another, but I found myself holding my breath just in case any of what we had discussed was considered to be unusual or even uninteresting. It was an elephant in the room, but I think we all wanted as a family to just be seen as 'normal'.

It was the feeling of wanting to be normal that made the experience so uncomfortable for me. I found it hard to have professionals nodding at us in the sessions, as if they understood what we were going through when really I felt that no-one could understand what it is truly like to live with psychosis, be it yourself or your family. Of course, it was not simply the psychosis we talked about. We talked about our relationships with one another and how that felt, our family dynamics and our frustrations, but also our love for one another.

The therapy presented other challenges for me. We were not speaking every second of the therapy. As with other interventions there were many silences and some of these felt awkward. I have always found this in therapy, I hate the silences. There is some sort of unspoken tension that I feel. I feel like I should be talking and not wasting the therapist's time, although I am sure most therapists would say that this silence is healthy and to be expected. The difference between individual and family therapy, however, was that the silence was shared between all of us, so I did not feel as guilty for not saying anything and so creating a silent moment. I thought that as therapy went on I would grow more comfortable with talking in a family setting and in the family therapy setup. I never did. However, I have been much the same with individual therapy. I have always found it difficult to talk, not because I cannot express my feelings, but because I am afraid of being judged. Family therapy was no different in this regard, and I had similar fears.

In terms of having the family therapy when I was ill and when I was well, there were some differences. When I was well, I could be much more verbose and articulate and I had insight into my previous episodes. When I was unwell, I found myself retreating and anxious, confused about the world around me and unable to relate to the real world. Therefore, when I was unwell I found the family therapy sessions more difficult. I found myself daydreaming and zoning out. I also felt embarrassed that the focus was on me and how I felt and how people could help me. I am not one to turn down support, but when you are unwell with psychosis, you feel so alone that you think no-one can relate to you, and so it feels that there is no point in talking at all. In fact, in one session I was there for only a few minutes before, as the attention turned to me, I had to leave because I just could not take talking anymore. Instead, I waited for the session to finish in the waiting room, crying with my legs curled up into a ball. Talking to an audience was far too difficult for me and it was not something that I wanted. In contrast, when I was well, I was able to contribute to the discussions and speak with insight about my psychotic experiences.

The therapists seemed very optimistic when we first met them, and I felt like the sessions would be useful as they explained exactly how the therapy would work, how it would be structured and what their role would be. I was cautious to begin with as I did not want to feel patronised. Initially I did feel a little patronised, but I soon grew to understand this to be more like compassion and understanding for my situation, rather than a false demeanour. It took time for me to trust that this was the right intervention: I worried that we would not get anywhere because the relationships we had built around my psychosis were so longstanding and embedded. However, I did feel from the beginning that we were in safe hands and that the therapists were going to be thorough. This was a feeling I had after the first session and this feeling turned out to be accurate. I think my parents and sister had similar feelings, although I know that my sister continued to feel very slightly patronised since the tone of voice of the therapists throughout was one of slightly exaggerated compassion. I think this came from a good place however, so I decided to overlook this aspect of the sessions.

What I got from therapy

The outcome of the discussions we had in therapy was mainly a chance to be open and honest with each other, but not just during therapy. In fact, the resounding and remaining impact is that we talk more together, not just about psychosis, but about everything. We often do family things together, such as going for meals out or for long walks. I am in turn more open and honest with my family about my feelings, including any early symptoms I might be experiencing, or any general worries or anxieties. I have managed to move away from home, but I still talk to my family every night. It is so important that I try to stop any psychotic experiences as soon as they happen, and talking to my family about these is my biggest safeguard against relapse. Family therapy really helped us to realise that talking to each other and communicating how we feel is absolutely vital, not just about my psychosis but about general aspects of life within the family and outside of it.

Talking about my psychosis with my family has produced greater insight for all of us. My family can now recognise when I am having paranoid thoughts because they now know my history of delusional ideas. My new openness since family therapy has been so refreshing. If something matches the way I thought before, they can express this, and it is useful for me to have someone point this out and gently challenge my ideas, questioning the reality of these thoughts. Because of this gentle challenging, I then generally do not think any further about the ideas. Of course, sometimes this is not as easy as other times. There was a period where my paranoid ideas lasted more than a few months. But there was always a doubt in my head saying that my family think it is unfounded, so therefore I should not think about it anymore. It is hard to completely stop my symptoms in their tracks, but my family manage keep me on the rails.

My advice for anyone offered family therapy is to try it, with an awareness that the first few sessions might be a little awkward and uncomfortable. It takes a few sessions to get used to the structure and used to talking to each other openly in a safe space. But despite this initial adjustment, my experience is that it can help those supporting someone with psychosis to understand their point of view and adjust according to their wishes, whilst also allowing the family to raise any concerns or frustrations. It can leave a lasting impact: the ability to be honest and therefore catch any initial symptoms of psychosis before they multiply.

Practitioner's perspective

Pekka Borchers

What is Systemic Family Therapy?

Research shows consistently that family relationships have a major impact on mental health (Stratton, 2011). When our loved ones experience a crisis, anxiety and other difficult emotions are transmitted. Because of these emotions, we risk losing our ability to act as a resource for our family members, and instead can respond in unhelpful ways. Problems in our close relationships will also present major challenges for our own well-being. In this way, we can see that human problems have relational dimensions, which are best treated within those relationships.

The concept of Systemic Family Therapy (SFT) has different meanings and different clinical manifestations for different practitioners. SFT has often been used to refer to the Milan model of family therapy (Hoffman, 1981). The Milan team (e.g. Boscolo, Cecchin, Hoffman, & Penn, 1987) succeeded in summarising important aspects of the therapeutic conversation of SFT. However, there are several modifications of SFT, and in real life clinicians use different approaches according to the needs of the clients. Thus, in this chapter, a broader conceptualisation of SFT is chosen.

Families can be seen as human systems: a unit of individuals who share a common history, culture, patterns of communication, emotional atmosphere, social norms, and goals. Families are more than the individuals that make up this system. Although no single family member has a direct power over the whole system, the individuals in the family can influence each other. Naturally, other systems in society also have an impact on families. Families can also be seen as consisting of smaller, interacting units or systems, such as parents or siblings.

According to Stratton (2011), SFT aims to help people to utilise the strengths of their relationships in order to reduce distress. It is often more useful to understand what is preventing the problem from being resolved than what caused the problem to begin with. My understanding of SFT is based on my family therapy training, and my history of being a psychiatrist treating psychosis according to the Finnish need adapted approach (Alanen, 2009). In the need adapted approach, the individual, integrative, and flexible therapeutic plan, which is focused on the real and changing needs of the clients and their family members, is created and followed up in therapy meetings together with the clients and their personal and professional network. These are also forums for trying to find a psychotherapeutic understanding of the psychotic crisis. In this chapter, the term 'clients' can refer not just to the individual with experiences of psychosis, but also their family members.

The evolution of Systemic Family Therapy

Psychosis has had an important impact on SFT. Initially, it was mainly psychoanalysts who started to meet the families of their clients who were experiencing psychosis, trying to find more effective therapies for psychosis (e.g. Wynne, Ryckoff, Day, & Hirsch, 1958). In the early years of SFT, the researchers and therapists assumed that they would see the real communication patterns of the families. They did not take into account their own impact on the discussion (Hoffman, 1981; Bateson, Jackson, Haley, & Weakland, 1956; Boscolo et al., 1987). The tradition of having co-therapists working with a family has remained a part of different modifications of SFT.

Strategic Therapy was developed in late 1950s and in the 1960s. According to this approach, humans are vulnerable to developing vicious patterns or cycles, whereby an initial challenge or life crisis becomes a worsening problem because of our unsuccessful ways of dealing with or solving the original difficulty (e.g. Weakland, 1974). When an adolescent or a young adult has a psychotic crisis, the understandable tendency of the parents to try to protect them can become irritating or stressful for the client, whose natural effort is to try to be more independent. These conflicting forces might make the atmosphere in the family difficult, and cause further challenges for the client, which may then evoke further irritation and criticism from the parents. A strategic family therapist would try to build a picture of these patterns and find a way to stop the unsuccessful communication patterns and replace them with more fruitful ones.

Solution Focused Therapy has its roots in the strategic therapy model. However, where the strategic therapist interviews the client to get a picture of the problematic communication patterns, the solution focused practitioner prefers to jump directly to finding the solutions and exceptions where things have gone well with relation to the problem (e.g. De Shazer, 1991). The solution focused therapist might encourage clients to speak more about situations where there are no psychotic symptoms, or where the clients are able to deal with auditory hallucinations, and then try to find ways of interacting that will increase the frequency and meaning or significance of these occasions.

Structural Family Therapy (e.g. Minuchin, 1981) assumes that it is important that families have some kind of sufficient but flexible norms, which separate the subsystems (e.g. parents and offspring) inside the family, as well as the whole family from the other systems of the community they are a part of. This might mean that it is important that adolescents have some clear duties in the family and common rules exist, but that parents have autonomy in how they interpret and implement these rules in a given situation. A family therapist working from a structural point of view might propose having a separate meeting with the parents or with the siblings. A structural family therapist would probably be very sensitive to the needs of the children of a parent with psychosis, and to the strengths of the spouse.

The innovators of **Milan Systemic Family Therapy** (e.g. Boscolo et al., 1987) developed concepts and ways of working which were designed to help clients gain new and more helpful perspectives on their difficulties. They use particular kinds of open questions called *circular questions*, which are designed to help family members become aware of new perspectives on a problem, for example, asking how a sibling of the client sees their parents' relation to the client. The therapists are making *hypotheses* about what has happened in the life and relations of the family to cause the current difficulties. They emphasise the attitude of *neutrality* towards all clients, meaning that the views of everyone are seen as equally important. The Milan model has been influential in the development of Systemic Family Therapy. However, this approach sees the family system as a factor which contributes to the problem, in a way that can increase family members' feelings of guilt. This can be a major problem for families of people with psychosis.

The so called **post-Milan approaches** in Systemic Family Therapy base their thinking largely in **social constructivism**, which claims that there is no single correct version of reality, but instead we humans develop and change our own understanding of the world around us through our social interactions with others. According to social constructivism, dysfunctional family systems do not cause problems. Instead, difficulties in human life cause problems in family systems. From this perspective, therapists should assist the clients in resolving their problem systems, either by finding solutions to the problems or by developing new and more favourable meanings for them (Anderson & Goolishian, 1988). The tendency for a person to hear voices can then be seen as a personal characteristic, rather than a sign of dysfunction that needs fixing.

An important turning point in the evolution of Systemic Family Therapy was the development of the ***reflecting team***. Tom Andersen (1991) discovered that instead of the team having discussions together without the clients, it is better to try to find novel understandings by having an open discussion between the professionals in front of the clients, who are then able to listen and respond. This facilitates a more respectful way of speaking and thinking about the clients. The members of the reflecting team turn to each other when they are speaking, while the clients and the therapist are listening. Rather than offering any ready-made conclusions or interpretations, the reflecting team base their conversation on words that the clients have actually said. Those words which, for example, have aroused emotions in the reflecting team or in the clients, are the starting point of the reflective talk, the purpose of which is to learn and understand more about the family members' views. Similar reflective practices have become one of the key elements of **Open Dialogue** (see Chapter 9; Olson, Seikkula, & Ziedonis, 2014).

The basis of ***narrative therapies*** is an understanding that we humans need to build narratives: we seem to need explanations and descriptions of the experiences in our lives in order to maintain our agency, the capacity to make choices and to act upon them. In crisis situations such as psychosis, either our story of ourselves, or the story which significant others have about us, is challenged or even lost. This shakes our sense of agency. The purpose in narrative family therapy is to construct a new and more favourable narrative of ourselves and our social relationships, a story which takes account of what has happened in the crisis. According to narrative thinking, this assists us to leave the often unpleasant happenings in the crisis situation behind and continue our lives (Holma, 1999; White & Epston, 1990).

A family therapist using a narrative therapy model (e.g. White & Epston, 1990) might try to 'externalise' the diagnosis of schizophrenia, treating it as a kind of alien family member rather than an intrinsic part of an individual. This can help the discussion of 'schizophrenia' to feel less blaming or judgemental. The therapist would inquire how schizophrenia impacts on clients and their relationships. After finding situations in which the client has managed to have desirable impact on it, the therapist focuses on using these experiences to increase the client's power in these situation, as well as to help them to construct a favourable narrative of themselves in their new life situation.

Dialogical and reflective practices (Andersen, 1991; Seikkula & Arnkill, 2014) can be considered as different kinds of narrative approaches in family therapy. Here the focus of therapists is on listening to what the clients actually say in the present moment, and accepting them as they are. After listening (to both the outer dialogue and the therapist's own inner dialogue including bodily responses), the therapist replies often using reflective discussion with her or his co-therapists. This procedure of separating the turns of speaking and listening in emotionally difficult occasions often gives the clients and the practitioners more room to listen and have an inner dialogue at the same time. Instead of attempting to understand the client using diagnostic stories or labels, in which personal meanings are not shared, if the family members take part in therapy meetings from the beginning of a psychotic crisis, it is possible to find a self-narrative which will make psychotic experiences meaningful for the clients and professionals (Holma, 1999). When family members and professionals take part in the dialogue, the client can find their own words for their frightening psychotic experiences (Seikkula, 2002), which can be an extremely important starting point for constructing a rationale normalising narrative for these experiences.

Zara Zaks wrote in her section describing her experiences of family therapy, that she had found the reflecting discussion between professionals as well as the silences in the middle of therapy sessions challenging. Her comments are very important, not least because reflecting talks and silences are seen as important elements of family therapy. According to my experience, in open reflections therapists are able to say a bit more about what they have heard and felt whilst trying to learn more about their clients' lives, and the clients have a better opportunity to hear them. The silences are often important for everyone to have time and space for their inner conversations. However, as families and individual clients have different needs, in my own practice I try to modify my way of working from session to session according the feedback from all family members (see below).

What does research say about Systemic Family Therapy and psychosis?

Carr (2014) undertook a review of the literature, using a very broad definition of systemic practices, which suggested that evidence from around the world supports the effectiveness of systemic therapy for families of people who have a diagnosis of schizophrenia. There has been convincing evidence of the effectiveness of psycho-educational family interventions for psychosis since the start of the 1980s (e.g. Berry, 2008). These interventions mainly consist of giving information about psychosis, and learning communication and problem solving skills to lower stress within families. The research evidence suggests that case-specific approaches which acknowledge and normalise clients' experiences and circumstances, and which give a voice to their inevitable confusion, ambivalence, and feelings of guilt, are beneficial (Aderhold & Gottwalz, 2013; Read & Seymour, 2013). A psychotherapeutic attitude and the open discussion of the changing needs of all family members are fundamental elements of the Finnish Need Adapted Approach to psychosis (Alanen, 2009). In particular, research indicates that the Open Dialogue approach (see Chapter 9), which is a modification of the Need Adapted Approach, shows exceptional promise in treating psychosis (e.g. Seikkula & Arnkill, 2014).

Psychotherapy research (Wampold & Imel, 2015) suggests that the therapeutic method has only a small impact on the results of different therapies. The collaboration between therapist and client seems to be the most important factor in determining the outcome. There is also research indicating that a positive therapeutic relationship predicts better outcomes for those with psychosis (e.g. Priebe, Richardson, Cooney, Adedeji, & McCabe, 2011; Goldsmith, Lewis, Dunn, & Bentall, 2015; see also Chapter 11). Psychotherapy research has demonstrated that measuring the therapeutic relationship and the outcome can improve the success rate and predict failures in therapy (Lambert et al., 2002), and there are some examples of such findings concerning therapy for psychosis (e.g. Priebe et al., 2007, 2011). Qualitative research concerning recovery from difficult psychiatric disorders (e.g. Topor, 2004) indicates that the therapist's ability to evoke confidence and hope in the client can be even more important when working with individuals who are experiencing psychosis compared to individuals with less challenging problems. Most studies assessing the effectiveness of therapy deal with individual therapy between a therapist and a single client, however, the current research concerning family therapy suggests that different therapeutic models are equally effective, and the factors which impact the therapeutic relationship are the most important concerning outcomes (Sprenkle, Davis, & Lebow, 2009). Nonetheless, the expansion of the direct treatment system (inclusion of family members) and the therapeutic relationship are particular benefits of SFT compared to individual approaches. As a result, family members can learn to speak together about difficult issues without a therapist.

The development of the Finnish need adapted approach has involved a considerable amount of qualitative research, which supports the results of the psychotherapy research described above. It indicates that, instead of focusing on trying to 'get rid of psychosis', the therapist should create a shared dialogue with the family, be mindful of the client's use of language (e.g. Seikkula, 1991), ensure the continuity of therapeutic relationships (Lehtinen, 1993), and use reflective conversations in therapy meetings (Haarakangas, 1997). The Finnish need adapted approach seems to give opportunities for clients to create trusting relationships, to experience feelings of safety, and to focus on maintaining hope (Piippo, 2008). The study by Holma (1999) indicates the importance of forming of a narrative with the family.

What does the therapy I offer look like?

As a private practitioner, I work alone. The work starts most often with a contact from one of the clients. The clients choose which family members will come to the first meeting. However, if there is major violence in the family, it is important to take this account when deciding who will participate in the family meeting. I start the sessions by asking the clients to fill the Outcome Rating Scale (ORS), and at the end of each discussion I ask them to fill the Session Rating Scale (SRS; Miller, Duncan, Sorrell, & Brown, 2005). These are tools for a therapist to evaluate session-by-session changes in clients' well-being and perceptions of the therapy.

The clients have a dominance in the discussion. However, according to their feedback, I can be more active. I am interested in hearing every client's perspective, but I can also respect if somebody wants to be silent and concentrate on listening. Occasionally I might ensure that we are talking about the right issues and in an appropriate manner. I base my own questions and reflections on the actual words clients have used. In particular, I concentrate on words that seem to arouse emotions or bodily sensations in the clients or in myself. I am interested in the psychotic experiences, but also in the skills, strenghts, resources, and successes of the clients. I respect if they would rather not discuss distressing issues or experiences. Throughout the session, I will ask participants of the session who have been listening to respond to what has been said. I prefer to wait with my own questions and comments until the clients have finished having their say and if they interrupt each other I might also ask them to wait until the family member has finished. I prefer to have silent moments in the conversation. I myself use these as a space to listen to my own thoughts, emotions, and bodily sensations, which might be the basis of my next response. Especially in the context of couples therapy, I sometimes talk with one client first, while the spouse is listening, and then the clients change positions. When the clients want to hear my thoughts, I tend to share the inner conversation I am having in my head out loud and speak in a speculative manner. If the clients ask me to give some information about psychosis, I mainly refer to studies which increase hope – often connected to the recovery tradition (e.g. Topor, 2004). In the end of every session, after the clients have filled the SRS (Miller et al., 2005), we have a short discussion of their experiences of the meeting. I also encourage them to say aloud their disappointments and critical views and try to modify my way of working according the feedback (see the challenges experienced by Zara Zaks).

I am willing to be flexible, collaborate with other professionals, and meet clients in different combinations, also alone. I encourage all relevant family members to get involved in the therapy, as well as significant others in their social network. I usually propose that clients have at least five family sessions lasting 1.5 hours each. However, usually the therapies last much longer. In the beginning of the process, we usually meet at least once a week or fortnightly, but later on we tend to have sessions less frequently.

In summary, the Systemic Family Therapy tradition as a whole gives a good background for a therapist to try to strengthen hope and construct a positive therapeutic relationship with an individual who is experiencing psychosis, and their family members. On the other hand, one should bear in mind that all approaches of SFT can be of limited value if there is a poor therapeutic relationship, and in such situations this approach can even be harmful for the clients (Goldsmith et al., 2015).

Note

1 The author has preferred to remain anonymous and use a pseudonym.

References

Aderhold, V., & Gottwalz, E. (2013). Family therapy and psychosis: Replacing ideology with openness. In J. Read & J. Dillon (Eds.), *Models of madness: Psychological, social and biological approaches to psychosis* (2nd ed., pp. 378–391). London: Routledge.

Alanen, Y. O. (2009). Towards a more humanistic psychiatry: Development of need-adapted treatment of schizophrenia group psychoses. *Psychosis, 1,* 156–166. doi:10.1080/17522430902795667

Andersen, T. (1991). *The reflecting team: Dialogues and dialogues about the dialogues.* New York: Norton.

Anderson, H., & Goolishian, H. A. (1988). Human systems as linguistic systems: Preliminary and evolving ideas about the implications for clinical theory. *Family Process, 27,* 371–393.

Bateson, G., Jackson, D., Haley, J., & Weakland, J. (1956). Toward a theory of schizophrenia. *Behavioral Science, 1,* 251–264. doi:10.1002/bs.3830010402

Berry, K. (2008). The implementation of the NICE guidelines for schizophrenia: Barriers to the implementation of psychological interventions and recommendations for the future. *Psychology and Psychotherapy, 81,* 419–436. doi:10.1348/147608308X329540

Boscolo, L., Cecchin, G., Hoffman, L., & Penn, P. (1987). *Milan systemic family therapy: Conversations in theory and practice.* New York: Basic Books.

Carr, A. (2014). The evidence base for couple therapy, family therapy and systemic interventions for adult-focused problems. *Journal of Family Therapy, 36,* 158. doi:10.1111/1467-6427.12033

De Shazer, S. (1991). *Putting difference to work.* New York: Norton.

Goldsmith, L. P., Lewis, S. W., Dunn, G., & Bentall, R. P. (2015). Psychological treatments for early psychosis can be beneficial or harmful, depending on the therapeutic alliance: An instrumental variable analysis. *Psychological Medicine, 45,* 2365–2373. doi:10.1017/S003329171500032X

Haarakangas, K. (1997). *Hoitokokouksen äänet: Dialoginen analyysi perhekeskeisen psykiatrisen hoitoprosessin hoitokokouskeskusteluista työryhmän toiminnan näkökulmasta [English summary: The voices in treatment meeting: A dialogical analysis of the treatment meeting conversations on family-centered psychiatric treatment process in regard to the team activity].* Jyväskylä: University of Jyväskylä.

Hoffman, L. (1981). *Foundations of family therapy a conceptual framework for systems change.* New York: Basic Books.

Holma, J. M. (1999). *The search for a narrative: Investigating acute psychosis and the need- adapted treatment model from the narrative viewpoint.* Jyväskylä: University of Jyväskylä.

Lambert, M. J., Whipple, J. L., Vermeersch, D. A., Smart, D. W., Hawkins, E. J., Nielsen, S. L., & Goates, M. (2002). Enhancing psychotherapy outcomes via providing feedback on client progress: A replication. *Clinical Psychology & Psychotherapy, 9,* 91–103. doi:10.1002/cpp.324

Lehtinen, K. (1993). *Family therapy and schizophrenia in public mental health care.* Turku: University of Turku.

Miller, S. D., Duncan, B. L., Sorrell, R., & Brown, G. S. (2005). The partners for change outcome management system. *Journal of Clinical Psychology, 61,* 199–208. doi:10.1037/a0027762

Minuchin, S. (1981). *Family therapy techniques.* Cambridge, MA: Harvard University Press.

Olson, M. E., Seikkula, J., & Ziedonis, D. (2014). *The key elements of dialogic practice in open dialogue: Fidelity criteria* (Version 1.1). September 2. Retrieved from http://umassmed.edu/globalassets/psychiatry/open-dialogue/keyelementsv1.109022014.pdf

Piippo, J. (2008). *Trust, autonomy and safety at integrated network- and family-oriented model for co-operation: A qualitative study.* Jyväskylä: University of Jyväskylä.

Priebe, S., McCabe, R., Bullenkamp, J., Hansson, L., Lauber, C., Martinez-Leal, R., et al. (2007). Structured patient-clinician communication and 1-year outcome in community mental healthcare: Cluster randomized controlled trial. *The British Journal of Psychiatry, 191,* 420–426. doi:10.1192/bjp.bp.107.036939

Priebe, S., Richardson, M., Cooney, M., Adedeji, O., & McCabe, R. (2011). Does the therapeutic relationship predict outcomes of psychiatric treatment in patients with psychosis? A systematic review. *Psychotherapy and Psychosomatics, 80,* 70–77. doi:10.1159/000320976. Epub 2010

Read, J., & Seymour, F. (2013). Psychosis and families: Intergenerational parenting problems. In J. Read & J. Dillon (Eds.), *Models of madness: Psychological, social and biological approaches to psychosis* (2nd ed., pp. 276–291). London: Routledge.

Seikkula, J. (1991). *Perheen ja sairaalan rajasysteemi potilaan sosiaalisessa verkostossa [English summary: The family-hospital boundary system in the social network].* Jyväskylä: University of Jyväskylä.

Seikkula, J. (2002). Open dialogues with good and poor outcomes for psychotic crises: Examples from families with violence. *Journal of Marital & Family Therapy, 28*, 263–274. doi:10.1111/j.1752-0606.2002.tb01183.x

Seikkula, J., & Arnkil, T. E. (2014). *Open dialogues and anticipations: Respecting otherness in the present moment.* Helsinki: National Institute for Health and Welfare.

Sprenkle, D. H., Davis, S. D., & Lebow, J. L. (2009). *Common factors in couple and family therapy: The overlooked foundation for effective practice.* New York: Guilford Press.

Stratton, P. (2011). *The evidence base of systemic family and couples therapies.* Warrington: Association for Family Therapy.

Topor, A. (2004). *Vad hjälper? vägar till återhämtning från svåra psykiska problem [English summary: What helps? Roads to recovery from severe mental illness.].* Stockholm: Natur och kultur.

Wampold, B. E., & Imel, Z. E. (2015). *The great psychotherapy debate the evidence for what makes psychotherapy work.* New York: Routledge.

Weakland, J. (1974). Brief therapy: Focused problem resolution. *Family Process, 1*, 141–168. doi:10.1111/j.1545-5300.1974.00141.x

White, M., & Epston, D. (1990). *Narrative means to therapeutic ends.* New York: Norton.

Wynne, L. C., Ryckoff, I. M., Day, J., & Hirsch, S. I. (1958). Pseudo-mutuality in the family relations of schizophrenics. *Psychiatry, 21*, 205–220. doi:10.1080/00332747.1958.11023128

'Finding a connection', a short comic on experiences of therapy by Annie Blake

4

CARE CO-ORDINATION

Client's perspective

Junaid Sarwar

Care Co-Ordination is a key part of the standard, front-line treatment for psychosis in the UK. It is not conventionally seen as a therapy. However, at the heart of care co-ordination there is a therapeutic relationship between the client and their care co-ordinator. Within this relationship there exists a great potential for therapeutic gains. The care co-ordinator may also offer psychosocial interventions and family interventions. Care Co-Ordination continues alongside other therapies, so they need to be understood in this context. For these reasons, it felt important that we include a chapter on this form of intervention in the book.

– Peter Taylor

Introduction

This section will provide detailed information on the care and support I received from my care co-ordinator as part of the Early Intervention for Psychosis Service (EIPS) that aided my ongoing recovery from psychosis. I will also provide some brief background information on the difficulties that led to my contact with the EIPS, and on my life following this support.

Beginning of my journey

I encountered various problems in my childhood and teenage years including anxiety and low confidence. These difficulties continued into college, where I experienced stress and low mood. Nonetheless, I followed college with my Islamic education at the local mosque, studying to memorise the Holy Quran. Due to my difficulty in socialising with people I found myself alone. I isolated myself a lot from people and those feelings of loneliness hurt me a lot. I also lost much weight, self-esteem and confidence. One day in 2010 I woke up and started screaming as I felt the pressure of failing in life. The thought of me going alone into the big wide world had scared me. This was one of the most difficult experiences I have ever had to face in life. These problems escalated. There was a time when I was unable to feed myself. During the nights I struggled with many fearful feelings. In the mornings I often awoke feeling very low in mood or scared.

As things were not getting better I was given an appointment to see a psychiatrist at a local Mental Health Service. In the waiting room I just kept pacing around the room. I was prescribed medication but there was no way I was going to take this; I felt there was nothing wrong with me and I was afraid of feeling like a zombie. However, that night a family member put the medication in my drink.

My problems continued and I was referred to see the psychiatrist again. I remember that I was moving my hands around constantly due to negative thoughts. The psychiatrist told us that he was going to refer me to a team called the Early Intervention for Psychosis Service (EIPS) who specialise in helping people with psychosis. The psychiatrist also told us that I was in the early stages of psychosis. I did not believe I had psychosis at the time. This is something I have since come to terms with. The term psychosis now means to me someone who has an illness and not someone who is a 'psycho'. People who have psychosis should have other people's empathy.

The journey of recovery

Within a week two people from the EIPS team came to visit me at home to see if I needed help from the service. On seeing my agitated state they said they would be accepting me into their service. The EIPS help people who are struggling with experiences of psychosis. The service helps you up to a total of three years. A care plan is completed that guides the care you receive during your time with EIPS and afterwards. The care plan is there to help you notice and respond to the warning signs of psychosis that may result in a relapse. That day I felt a pressure was off my shoulders. I had been worried about what people were saying about me. Within my culture problems related to psychosis sometimes are attributed to other spiritual causes such as *Jinn*, and so I was concerned about how others were making sense of my difficulties. Knowing that EIPS would be accepting me into their service removed the worry of what people might be thinking about me. This is because it gave me a clear explanation and label for my difficulties, 'psychosis', and legitimised this as a recognised health problem.

The team that was helping me was made up of a care co-ordinator, consultant psychiatrist, psychologist and a support worker. This section focuses on my experiences of working with my care co-ordinator. Initially this was a woman called S, and later on she was replaced by a new care co-ordinator called D. A care co-ordinator acts as your main point of contact with mental health services, and helps to organise the care and support you receive. Whilst being with an EIPS entailed seeing many different professionals (psychiatrists, support workers, psychological therapists), my care co-ordinators, S, and then D, remained in touch through this process and helped me to navigate the different roles and interventions that I experienced.

My first care co-ordinator

I do not recall what I expected S to be like. I did not feel anxious about the visit. I had already had visitors from the EIPS, taking my blood pressure and other assessments related to my medication, a few weeks before. I think because of this meeting another new person from the service did not feel so daunting.

S was a big part of the therapy and support I received through the service. I would say that S was the best you could get, she had such a personality that she would liven up the house when she came to see me. Her character, her way of talking, and the advice she gave helped me a lot.

The first time I met S she told me that when she read my notes she had wanted to work with, and help me. It made me feel special hearing this. She also told me that she would be my care co-ordinator. I saw S on a regular basis for about three months. She would visit me at least once a week at my home. After that she started to see me once every two weeks and then finally started to reduce her visits to once every two months.

For the first few sessions I did not feel comfortable sitting alone with S, and so my father would sit with us. This was a time when I still found talking and communicating with others, especially strangers, a real challenge. In these early sessions with S I would either say 'no comment' and 'no problem' to her questions, or respond to these questions through my dad. The flexibility S allowed in having my dad present was therefore really important and helped me to not feel too overwhelmed with these early sessions.

S one day asked my dad and me if it was OK that from the next session it could be one-to-one meetings only. Both I and my father agreed to this. In the beginning I was unable to talk directly with S but here I was in my first one-to-one session, sitting alone with her and communicating directly with her. This was evidence that things were starting to change. Up to this point I had been very isolated, and this gradual and sensitive approach to building my confidence and our relationship was an important aspect of how S helped me.

These early meetings were very difficult because of the anxiety, distress and isolation I had been experiencing. Change happened slowly but S persevered. As our meetings progressed I gradually became more able to talk with S, to move beyond 'no comment' to short sentences.

As my confidence in talking with her gradually increased we talked about many things. The conversation often focused on how I had been feeling that week, and the difficulties I had been struggling with. In one of the sessions with S she asked me about my pacing, gasping, and spitting. I told her that I was gasping and spitting because I did not want to breathe the smoke in. In reality there was no smoke but I perceived that there was. During one session S reinforced my view that previously I was concentrating only on my religion. She taught me that a person has to have a holistic approach. By this she meant that a person has spiritual or religious needs, physical needs and emotional needs. If any of these needs are not being fulfilled then the body will get ill. As I had decided to concentrate on my religious needs only I started to experience problems. Looking back I can see a gradual breakdown stemming from my social anxiety, negative thinking, and decisions in life. This resulted in a decline from a confident, happy person to becoming a shadow of my former self. Everything did not happen at once. My confidence, self-esteem, wanting to mix with people slowly left me.

Another way that S supported me was by introducing me to a football group that was set up by the EIPS. This helped me with mixing with people, getting physically fit, improving my mood. The group was held every Thursday evening at a local college. S had introduced me to a support worker to get me back into doing social activities as a way of improving my physical health. The support worker is a different role to the care co-ordinator. I was introduced to my support worker after several weeks of working with S and received help from them for about a year and a half. My support worker would come to my house at least once a week, sometimes twice a week and would help me access other groups and services. This included taking me to the football club and bringing me back home. I played football with this group for over four years. Playing football helped give me some type of exercise in a week. I also gradually got to know other members of the group. Doing some type of activity to keep fit is very important. Personally, I would recommend playing any sport that one enjoys, but walking, jogging, running, and going to the gym are also very good. My support worker also took me to the local college to gain information about a course, to the gym, library, park, and to visit the local imam.

The way that S involved my family in meetings was another important part of the support she offered. It helped that she got on with all my family. When she would come to my house my parents' tensions would be gone. After our sessions together S would then come and sit with the family in the living room, and this felt really helpful in allowing my family to get to know S. She mixed in like she was family and my parents would always talk highly of her when she left. I would therefore say she not only provided me directly with therapy but also helped me indirectly, through the advice and support she gave to my family. This was exactly what I and my family needed. For example, she advised my father to let me do things at my own pace. My father acted on this advice, which helped me as it removed the stress of trying to do many things at once and just to accept that I should do things steadily. S was also able to answer questions and quell some of the concerns and anxieties my family understandably had. I recall my mother asking S whether I would ever recover from psychosis. S was able to answer positively that I could certainly recover, and gave examples of other people, including doctors, who had faced psychosis and recovered enough to carry on working afterwards. I remember S told my mum that even when she was jogging in the evenings she was thinking about how she could help me. Even after work S was thinking about how she could support me. To me this felt like proof of genuine care.

A new care co-ordinator

One day S told me and my father that she would be transferring my care to another care co-ordinator as she had completed the work she needed to do with me. By this I think she meant that she had got me out of a critical state and that I was now more stable. This change reflects the way this particular EIPS team worked, but for others you may have the same care co-ordinator throughout your time with a service. S believed I was ready to change to a new care co-ordinator where our focus would be on more in-depth work around the difficult thoughts and feelings I had. Ending my time with S was really difficult. We had built up a strong attachment over our meetings, and I recall the separation and feeling of loss being a challenge. I was also anxious about having a new care co-ordinator and what they would be like.

On her last visit S introduced me to my new care co-ordinator called D. He also had a good personality and had such good humour that he would make me and my family laugh. He built a really good relationship with me and my family, and I enjoyed spending my time with him.

With D I did work around negative thoughts and making realistic goals. I talked to D about the bad thoughts that I experienced, but when he asked me what these thoughts were I would go quiet. Talking about the thoughts was just too difficult. Because of this, these initial sessions with D left me feeling like we were not getting anywhere or making any progress. Week by week we would have the same discussions, and I would face the same barriers to sharing these difficult thoughts I had. Then one day I finally felt able to open up and started to tell him about the thoughts. The barrier was broken. It is hard to say what changed to eventually allow me to talk about these difficult thoughts. I think it was the gradual build-up of confidence, through the sessions with D, that I would be able to share these things and that this would be okay. To be talking to D about these negative, distorted thoughts was another sign that I was recovering. I would never have thought before that I would be able to talk about these horrible thoughts with anyone, so this was a big step forward. When talking about my thoughts I felt the tension go from my heart. D helped me rationalise these intrusive thoughts by telling me that these thoughts happen to everyone. It made me feel that these thoughts were normal, not something unusual or to be feared.

The work I did with D about making realistic goals for my life involved me using the SMART goals technique. A SMART goal should be Specific, Measurable (i.e. you can tell when you have achieved it), Achievable (i.e. it can be done), Relevant (i.e. they mattered to me), and Time-limited (i.e. there is a time-frame for completing these goals). An example of a SMART goal for me was when I was trying to lose weight. I used this technique to help lose weight slowly.

I also used this technique to do certain activities. This technique helped me to think about the things I wanted to do in a structured way and to set achievable targets. I also did work around how my beliefs and thoughts affected my feelings and behaviours. I had to write down these on paper and then we would talk about them. These techniques helped give me more of an insight into how my feelings were affected by what was going on around me and how I was thinking. These sorts of techniques are taken from Cognitive Behavioural Therapy (CBT; see Chapter 2) but were used as part of the Care Co-Ordination I received from D. When S first started to see me I do not think I would have benefited from CBT.

After two years going to football with my support worker, D recommended I make my own way to football as it would give me some independence. I then started to go by train. It made me feel good about myself and gave me back some of my autonomy.

S and D were each able to act as a linchpin, linking me in with other aspects of the care I received from the EIPS, such as my support worker.

I was initially placed on two medications. They were Quietiapine and Sertraline. The Quietiapine was for the psychosis, and Sertraline was for depression and anxiety. D had a role in checking in with me about the medication, monitoring this and how I was finding it. This is another important part of the care co-ordinator role. Quietiapine is known to increase weight (Hutton, Taylor, Mulligan, Tully, & Moncrieff, 2015) as it makes one very hungry. My weight increased; however, I am not sure if medication was the only factor, as my activity levels were low as well. I also used to eat a lot due to boredom and eating would give me some sort of pleasure. I am aware that medication is not for everybody, but with hindsight I feel that my medication has helped me a lot. In the beginning I was against it but now I feel that medication was the best thing for me.

How my care co-ordinators helped

The support that I received from S and D was first class. In times of hardship this team allowed me to see light at the end of the tunnel. Something in particular that stood out for me was that S and D seemed genuinely interested in me as a person, and wanted to help me. This sense of being genuinely cared about was key to the positive relationship I formed with both S and D. There were many challenging parts to the care I received from the EIPS, and especially from S and D. Being open about the troubling experiences and negative thoughts that had plagued me was something I found extremely difficult. I was at times pushed to do things outside of my comfort zone, such as taking part in the football group sessions. However, these steps were vital parts of my recovery.

A parent of someone who is struggling with psychosis may at times get upset, especially if the psychosis impacts on things like their child's personal hygiene, or contributes to a lack of routine or daily activities. I know that my own parents found my experience of psychosis and the way it affected me very difficult. Parents have to remember as time goes by things will get better. One of the real benefits of the support I received from S and D was the way they worked not just with myself, but also my parents and family, providing advice and support and answering their questions.

During my time with EIPS I worked with many different professionals, including psychiatrists, psychologists, and support workers. S and D were a consistent presence throughout this time, and I saw more of them than I did any of these other professionals. Early on S took the time to explain these different professional roles, and guided me through the different ways they might be able to help me. Whilst I received support and input from these various roles I think the involvement of my care co-ordinators was key to my recovery.

Improvements and achievements after therapy with EIS

During my three years with the EIS there was a lot of improvement in my health. The darkness within me that I had felt when I first experienced psychosis improved and my low moods started to get better. Following my discharge from the service I applied for and gained a business administration apprenticeship post where I would be working within the EIPS department. I later successfully applied for a job with the Attention Deficit and Hyperactivity Disorder (ADHD) service. I also worked for the improving access to psychological therapy service and did some reception work. I have gained a great deal of confidence and have built many good friendships with my co-workers. I do not believe this would have been possible without the input of S and D, helping me to recover from psychosis.

Practitioner's perspective

Siobhain Koch and James Kelly

Introduction

This section aims to give a general introduction to Care Co-Ordination. We will outline the underpinning principles of Care Co-Ordination for psychosis, and the nature of this role as providing a therapeutic relationship, comprehensive assessment, formulation and care planning and the provision of psychosocial interventions. The care co-ordinator (CCO) also provides the client with access to a multi-disciplinary team who offer evidence based interventions across a broad spectrum, such as psychological (e.g. cognitive behavioural therapy), social (e.g. help with accommodation, access to voluntary sector organisations) and biological interventions (e.g. assessment and treatment with anti-psychotics, anti-depressants). We use the example of how this role works in an Early Interventions for Psychosis Service (EIPS), but we also recognise that CCOs work within a variety of different mental health services.

The CCO is a client's key contact person within mental health services. When we read of the specific therapies in this book, for example of Cognitive Behavioural Therapy (CBT) or Cognitive Analytic Therapy (CAT), we should bear in mind that this is often in addition to what is termed 'treatment as usual'. People have often already been engaged by a CCO, had their needs assessed and a care plan formulated. The following section outlines the development of this important role in the UK. This chapter describes Care Co-Ordination in a mental health system that is particular to the UK, but similar approaches to providing support to individuals experiencing psychosis in the community across many domains of their lives, exist elsewhere. Open dialogue, which originated in Finland, builds and expands on some of the principles and ideas behind good Care Co-Ordination (see Chapter 9), for example.

History of Care Co-Ordination

The role of the CCO first came into the mental health dictionary back in 1991. It saw the change from having a nurse or social worker visiting an individual every few weeks or months, to embedding in the UK National Health Service (NHS) delivery a process in which a named mental health professional would oversee a co-ordinated approach to managing an individual's mental health care and well-being, in the community where they live. This was called the Care Programme Approach (CPA). It followed the closure of mental health institutions or asylums across the UK in the mid 1980's, and the shift from hospital-based care to care in the community for individuals experiencing mental health problems.

The CPA involves regular meetings with the client, multi-disciplinary team members (e.g. nurse, social worker, support worker, probation, therapist, family worker, etc.) and where appropriate, significant others in the person's life, such as family and friends. In these meetings, the individual's mental well-being is central to reviewing, planning, and identifying interventions to promote improved stability and well-being. The CPA also places a sense of accountability on the mental health team to deliver a service which has defined expectations and measurable outcomes. The Care CPA has three main elements which enable it to provide a framework for effective mental health care. These are:

- Plans for systematically assessing the health and social needs of people accepted into specialist mental health services.
- The formation of a care plan which identifies the health and social care required from a variety of providers to support the client.
- The appointment of a CCO to keep in close touch with the client and to monitor and co-ordinate care (and where necessary revise the care plan as things change).

It can be seen therefore that the CCO was at the heart of the CPA and has come to be the front-line of intervention and support for those struggling with complex mental health problems in the UK, including psychosis.

The role of a care co-ordinator

A CCO working in a community-based mental health service typically has a professional qualification as a mental health nurse, a social worker or an occupational therapist. This means that there is a mix of professionals and skills in the team. The CCO role has always been central to the way mental health services within the community work, individualising the service to the specific needs of the individual.

In the UK, the national guidance (National Collaborating Centre for Mental Health, 2014) specifies that people with psychosis should be offered eight evidence based interventions, guided by the care plan, which are listed as follows:

1   Referral to early intervention in psychosis services (EIPS).
2   CBT.
3   Family intervention.
4   Medications that aim to help with psychosis.

5   Supported employment programmes.
6   Assessment of physical health.
7   Promotion of healthy eating.
8   Carer focused education and support.

The CCO provides access to these interventions whilst also empowering the person and carers or family members to access health and social care and navigate the broader 'system' of benefits, education, and housing. The emphasis in EIPS is on recovery focused work, helping the client to live a life consistent with their own values and work towards personally meaningful goals, such as education and employment, as well as helping the person to prevent relapse. Finally, the CCO prepares the person to leave the EIPS, putting together a discharge plan and referring back to primary care and their doctor, or onto specialist services. For example if the person is in an EIPS, they may be referred to a community mental health team (this would mean referring on to a new CCO).

The day-to-day practice of Care Co-Ordination

Initially, the primary role of the CCO is to meet with the client and, with their consent, family members. The remit of these meetings is to begin to identify a shared understanding of the client's experiences and the impact these have had on them and their family. This identifies the strengths and values of the client and their family. It is hoped that these early conversations will set the foundations for a therapeutic and collaborative relationship which will instil a sense of hope and confidence for a positive future for the client.

Experiences of psychosis and the disruption that can accompany these can leave many individuals scared, worried, and concerned about their future or the meaning of their experiences (Byrne & Morrison, 2010; Taylor, Pyle, Schwannauer, Hutton, & Morrison, 2015). We believe that a CCO can help by containing these fears and concerns, and providing a stable figure of support during what is often a challenging time for individuals.

This initial phase of contact with the client may identify a need for the CCO to have a more extensive understanding of the cultural and religious beliefs within the family unit. This may involve making contact with community and cultural leaders for their expertise and guidance. It is, however, an important part of these meetings to create realistic and shared expectations which will reduce the perceived potential burden of expectation on the client and those involved in their care.

The development of trust and of a therapeutic alliance is key (see Chapter 11); personal qualities such as the ability to engage, as well as offering hope and conveying a sense of expertise are likely to be important components of this. The CCO should always be mindful of the potentially distressing events and experiences, which have brought about seeking help and their engagement in the assessment process for the client and their family, which for most families in the UK is not an everyday experience. Within this work we believe it is important to help the client to feel understood and valued as an individual, and not just seen as a diagnosis or a set of symptoms. The help offered may be in talking through concerns about returning to work or study or any activities that are important to recovery. Acknowledging concerns beyond symptoms feels key to developing a positive and productive relationship with the client, which in turn may help to foster their recovery.

As soon as the client meets their CCO the proactive and individual planning of their care begins. The care plan will describe the needs of the client and outline the interventions offered to them. It will also provide information on other services involved with an individual such as public or voluntary organisations that may help with housing, finances or benefits, and social support. It will include what responsibilities the client agreed to take in working towards their goals and what expectations they can have of services. The care plan will begin to evolve into a picture of the journey towards recovery and reflect the actions that have taken place on that journey.

Experiencing psychosis and taking medication can be confusing for clients and those around them. Clients may have contact with a confusing array of different health professionals, including support workers, psychologists, psychiatrists, and occupational therapists. The particular role these health professionals have, or the type of work they do is not always clear, and professionals may come and go at different times during an individual's involvement with mental health services. The CCO is therefore intended to be an accessible figure, within this potentially confusing and changing environment. They help guide the client through the package of care they receive, and help explain to the client these different professional roles and how they might help. In this way a CCO can help clients to navigate an often complex health care system. Because of this aspect of CCOs role, the intention is for CCOs to be, as much as possible, a constant in clients' tie with a service. Often services aim to have a single CCO or to minimise changes between CCO, although sometimes these are unavoidable.

The work a CCO undertakes with a client can be highly varied depending on their individual needs. Below are outlined some of the key interventions and conversations that might take place. These interventions are not meant to be prescriptive or followed in any particular order. They are examples of good practice, and should be offered, when and if appropriate and at times which are sensitive to the client's circumstances and safety.

Developing a shared understanding of the client's experiences and an early formulation of their strengths and needs

Time is offered and spent getting to know and understand the thoughts and feelings of the client, and building a trusting relationship. This is a time to offer support, reassurance, and information at a pace which is sensitive to the individual's needs. During this work we have found it important that the CCO adopts an understanding and compassionate stance, and views the client as an individual rather than a set of symptoms. A formulation is developed that takes into account the person's current problems, (e.g. low mood, distressing beliefs) the triggering events to these problems (e.g. arguments or tension with others), factors that maintain them (e.g. social withdrawal), protective factors (e.g. good social relationships), and, if appropriate, predisposing factors (e.g. trauma).

Identify significant life events that may have contributed to psychosis

The CCO will work with the client to build a picture of significant life events. The client's memory of early and recent life experiences is explored and if possible added to with further information gained from others such as friends and family. This helps to gain a more complete picture of the client's journey to becoming unwell. In the future, it is highly likely to give insight into markers, which inform individually tailored interventions and a relapse prevention plan.

'Psychoeducation' and 'normalising' information

Psychoeducation refers to sharing information about mental health difficulties such as psychosis, their causes, consequences, and characteristics. Normalising refers to specifically sharing information about how common experiences like psychosis actually are, and how they can be a common reaction to extreme circumstances. An important stage for the client can be to realise that they are 'not alone' and others have had similar experiences. There is a wealth of literature available in the public arena on the internet. The document "Understanding Psychosis and Schizophrenia" is a good example of such literature (British Psychological Society [BPS], 2014). It is important to instil a sense of hope and learning about the experiences of others, this can often have a strong and reassuring impact.

Medication

The CCO will have shared the information gathered in the initial assessments with a psychiatrist who then conducts a medical assessment and considers the appropriateness of prescribing medication (National Collaborating Centre for Mental Health, 2014). Often, alternatives or choices will be given and information and literature will be shared to help the client to make an informed decision regarding their treatment.

Physical health

The physical health of people with psychosis has become an area of increasing concern with research consistently finding links with obesity, diabetes and cardiovascular disease (Shiers, Bradshaw, & Campion, 2015; Shiers & Curtis, 2014;

Shiers, Jones, & Field, 2009). The CCO therefore is often the person who initiates a comprehensive assessment of physical health status (e.g. blood tests, family history of physical health problems) in order to identify factors relevant to the experience of psychosis, or to the general health of the client. Discussions will also take place around health promotion and well-being based on current research, for example healthy eating, smoking, exercise, alcohol and drug use (Gates, Killackey, Phillip, & Álvarez-Jiménez, 2015).

Risk assessment and management

CCOs play a critical role in ensuring the safety of clients by assessing risky behaviours such as harm to self and others, and in carrying out safeguarding assessments to protect vulnerable children and adults. Although best practice is to always support clients to make their own decisions where possible, when needed a CCO may request a Mental Health Act (Department of Health, 1983) assessment or undertake an assessment of capacity. Identifying risks is important for protecting the individual and others from physical, financial and legal harm (Brobbey, 2011; Tarrier et al., 2014). Thorough assessments inform the development of formulations of risk, using the structure outlined above (e.g. triggers, maintaining factors, protective factors, and predisposing factors). This informs the care plan and decisions of how best to keep clients safe. It may be that intervention is needed immediately to ensure safety, and this may prompt a mental health act assessment, consideration of admission to inpatient wards, or involvement with other services such as crisis teams. The least restrictive option should always inform this work and risk prevention is key.

Use of specialist therapy skills

Many CCOs have undertaken further training in psychosocial interventions (i.e. specific talking therapies like those covered in this book). These interventions may focus on developing a problem and goal list, improving sleep, reducing worry or changing how worry is coped with, working on how emotions are managed, or working with specific difficulties like voice hearing, paranoia or low self-esteem. These interventions are prioritised in order to reduce risk and then promote recovery.

Family work and carer support

There is widespread acknowledgement that the social context within which a person lives, and the quality of their interpersonal relationships, has a major impact on their recovery from distressing experiences of psychosis. In particular, it has been found that families can assist recovery from psychosis by interacting with the individual in a supportive way that is not critical or emotionally over-involved

(Bebbington & Kuipers, 1994; Butzlaff & Hooley, 1998). It is therefore important to engage with a person's family and immediate social network, with the aim of supporting the person's family in their efforts to help them.

Focus on education and employment

Identifying meaningful and fulfilling roles is a vital part of a person's well-being. This will be a theme that will be regularly visited with the client and their CCO, as the service aims for a recovery focused approach which is sensitive to each individual's journey.

Challenges

CCO work can often be complex and involve many challenges. It is not uncommon for a client to disagree with their CCO over the way the difficulties are addressed. If such disagreements are not effectively managed they can cause a rupture in that therapeutic relationship, which affects how well a CCO can support a client. A particular challenge to the work undertaken between client and CCO comes later in their contact when the client may well feel that they have engaged in, 'the plan' that has been initially offered, but this is no longer required as they are feeling better. However, from the perspective of the CCO this is just the beginning of the journey. A key aspect of this role is therefore to tread the delicate path of normalising experiences and reducing catastrophic appraisals of these experiences, whilst also increasing the awareness of the client that some patterns of thoughts and behaviours may increase the risk of further distressing experiences of psychosis. This phase strikes a major note of concern for the CCO, as the client may begin to move away from them and the service, around the optimal time for starting work on relapse prevention for the individual and their family.

There is also a risk that following an initial experience of psychosis an individual may 'seal over' their experiences as a way of coping, whereby they avoid thinking about the experiences leading up to and surrounding their episode of psychosis (McGlashan, Docherty, & Siris, 1976; Tait, Birchwood, & Trower, 2004). This creates a barrier to 'relapse prevention', work that ideally involves thinking back over these earlier experiences. Carefully pacing the work with the client and ensuring this work is done in a collaborative way can help with navigating these challenges.

CCOs are often under a great deal of pressure, having large numbers of clients to work with. High stress and problems like burnout can be a result of this pressure if CCOs are not adequately supported (Edwards et al., 2006). It is, therefore, imperative that they are able to access appropriate professional supervision and have the protected time to reflect on and critically review their clinical involvement and the interventions offered to each client they care co-ordinate.

The evidence for the role of Care Co-Ordination

A large number of studies have been undertaken comparing approaches like Care Co-Ordination to other forms of health care for people struggling with mental difficulties like psychosis. Together these studies suggest that Care Co-Ordination is beneficial for a range of outcomes including less time in hospital, getting a job, and staying in touch with services (Dieterich et al., 2017; Rapp & Goscha, 2008; Ziguras & Stuart, 2000). Comparing these studies is difficult because they take place within different countries with different health care systems. However, this research does suggest that Care Co-Ordination can be helpful.

There is also a small but burgeoning evidence base for interventions offered by CCO for people with psychosis. A small trial showed that under the supervision of a trained psychological therapist, it was feasible for CCOs to deliver structured therapies based on CBT principles (see Chapter 2). These include techniques like behavioural activation (using a structured approach to planning activities to reduce low mood) or exposure therapy (reducing fearful reactions by facing the situation rather than avoiding it; Hazell, Hayward, Cavanagh, & Strauss, 2016; Waller et al., 2013). Techniques such as these are likely to be an area of continued interest and development, given the shortage of trained therapists.

In interviews on the experience of receiving support from an EIPS, individuals reflected positively on the relationship they had with their CCO, this relationship becoming a key source of support and information about psychosis. This research also illustrated how influential the relationship with the CCO was for how people saw the EIPS more widely, and how they understood their problems (Harris, Collinson, & Das Nair, 2012). Further research is needed to understand the role of the CCO and the impact they have on recovery for people with psychosis.

Final reflections

The CCO plays a vital role in empowering the individual to receive an individualised package of care that is consistent with their individual, cultural, and family values, and meets their needs to promote recovery. The therapeutic relationship developed as part of the role of CCO, in which the client feels understood and valued as an individual, forms the foundation of this work. This view, about the importance of the relationship with clients, is based on my (SK) experience of over 30 years working in mental health hospitals and in the community setting.

References

Bebbington, P., & Kuipers, L. (1994). The predictive utility of expressed emotion in schizophrenia: An aggregate analysis. *Psychological Medicine*, *24*(3), 707. https://doi.org/10.1017/S0033291700027860.

British Psychological Society. (2014). *Understanding psychosis and schizophrenia*. Leicester: British Psychological Society. Retrieved from www.bps.org.uk/system/files/Public%20files/aa%20Standard%20Docs/understanding_psychosis.pdf

Brobbey, H. (2011). Problematic and risk behaviours in psychosis: A shared formulation approach. *Journal of Mental Health*, *20*(4), 419. https://doi.org/10.3109/09638237.2011.586743

Butzlaff, R. L., & Hooley, J. M. (1998). Expressed emotion and psychiatric relapse: A meta-analysis. *Archives of General Psychiatry*, *55*(6), 547–552. https://doi.org/10.1001/archpsyc.55.6.547

Byrne, R., & Morrison, A. P. (2010). Young people at risk of psychosis: A user-led exploration of interpersonal relationships and communication of psychological difficulties. *Early Intervention in Psychiatry*, *4*, 162–168. doi:10.1111/j.1751–7893.2010.00171.x

Department of Health. (1983). *Mental Health Act 1983*. London: The Stationery Office.

Dieterich, M., Irving, C. B., Bergman, H., Khokhar, M. A., Park, B., & Marshall, M. (2017). Intensive case management for people with severe mental illness. *Cochrane Database of Systematic Reviews*. doi:10.1002/14651858.CD007906.pub3

Edwards, D., Burnard, P., Hannigan, B., Cooper, L., Adams, J., Juggessur, T., . . . Coyle, D. (2006). Clinical supervision and burnout: The influence of clinical supervision for community mental health nurses. *Journal of Clinical Nursing*, *15*(8), 1007–1015. https://doi.org/10.1111/j.1365-2702.2006.01370.x

Gates, J., Killackey, E., Phillips, L., & Álvarez-Jiménez, M. (2015). Mental health starts with physical health: Current status and future directions of non-pharmacological interventions to improve physical health in first-episode psychosis. *The Lancet Psychiatry*, *12*, 726–742. https://doi.org/10.1016/S2215-0366(15)00213-8

Harris, K., Collinson, C., & Das Nair, R. (2012). Service-users' experiences of an early intervention in psychosis service: An interpretative phenomenological analysis. *Psychology and Psychotherapy: Theory, Research and Practice*, *85*(4), 456–469. https://doi.org/10.1111/j.2044-8341.2011.02043.x

Hazell, C. M., Hayward, M., Cavanagh, K., & Strauss, C. (2016). A systematic review and meta-analysis of low intensity CBT for psychosis. *Clinical Psychology Review*, *45*, 183–192. https://doi.org/10.1016/j.cpr.2016.03.004

Hutton, P., Taylor, P. J., Mulligan, L., Tully, S., & Moncrieff, J. (2015). Quetiapine immediate release v. placebo for schizophrenia: Systematic review, meta-analysis and reappraisal. *British Journal of Psychiatry*, *206*, 360–370. doi:10.1192/bjp.bp.114.154377

Longden, E. (2012). Negative symptom: More, not less. In J. Geekie, P. Randal, D. Lampshire, & J. Read (Eds.), *Experiencing psychosis: Personal and professional perspectives* (pp. 179–186). East Sussex: Routledge.

McGlashan, T. H., Docherty, J. P., & Siris, S. (1976). Integrative and sealing-over recoveries from schizophrenia: Distinguishing case studies. *Psychiatry*, *39*(4), 325–338. https://doi.org/10.1521/00332747.1976.11023903

National Collaborating Centre for Mental Health. (2014). *Psychosis and schizophrenia in adults: Treatment and management* (NICE, (February), Feb 54 Clinical Guidelines no. 178). https://doi.org/10.1002/14651858.CD010823.pub2.Copyright

Rapp, C. A., & Goscha, R. J. (2008). The principles of effective case management of mental health services. *Psychiatric Rehabilitation Journals*, *27*, 319–333. doi:10.2975/27.2004.319.333

Shiers, D., Bradshaw, T., & Campion, J. (2015). Health inequalities and psychosis: Time for action. *British Journal of Psychiatry*, *207*, 471–473. https://doi.org/10.1192/bjp.bp.114.152595

Shiers, D., & Curtis, J. (2014). Cardiometabolic health in young people with psychosis. *The Lancet Psychiatry*, *1*, 492–494. https://doi.org/10.1016/S2215-0366(14)00072-8

Shiers, D., Jones, P. B., & Field, S. (2009). Early intervention in psychosis: Keeping the body in mind. *British Journal of General Practice, 59*(563), 395–396. https://doi.org/10.3399/bjgp09X420888

Tait, L., Birchwood, M., & Trower, P. (2004). Adapting to the challenge of psychosis: Personal resilience and the use of sealing-over (avoidant) coping strategies. *British Journal of Psychiatry, 185*(NOV.), 410–415. https://doi.org/10.1192/bjp.185.5.410

Tarrier, N., Kelly, J., Maqsood, S., Snelson, N., Maxwell, J., Law, H., . . . Gooding, P. (2014). The cognitive behavioural prevention of suicide in psychosis: A clinical trial. *Schizophrenia Research, 156*(2–3), 204–210. https://doi.org/10.1016/j.schres.2014.04.029

Taylor, P. J., Pyle, M., Schwannauer, M., Hutton, P., & Morrsion, A. (2015). Confirming the structure of negative beliefs about psychosis and bipolar disorder: A confirmatory factor analysis study of the personal beliefs about experience questionnaire and personal beliefs about illness questionnaire. *British Journal of Clinical Psychology, 54*, 361–377. doi:10.1111/bjc.12079

Waller, H., Garety, P. A., Jolley, S., Fornells-Ambrojo, M., Kuipers, E., Onwumere, J., . . . Craig, T. (2013). Low intensity cognitive behavioural therapy for psychosis: A pilot study. *Journal of Behavior Therapy and Experimental Psychiatry, 44*(1), 98–104. https://doi.org/10.1016/j.jbtep.2012.07.013

Ziguras, S. J., & Stuart, G. W. (2000). A Meta-analysis of the effectiveness of mental health case management over 20 years. *Psychiatric Services, 51*, 1410–1421. doi:10.1176/appi.ps.51.11.1410

5

COGNITIVE ANALYTIC THERAPY (CAT)

Client's perspective

Alex[1]

> It is known that our early experiences can shape the ways in which we think about and relate to ourselves and others. In this chapter, Alex and Claire describe the process of identifying and understanding such patterns of relating, and how this can allow the client to break out of negative patterns of thoughts or behaviour. I feel that Alex's story really captures the active and collaborative nature of Cognitive Analytic Therapy (CAT), and how the process of mapping out one's relationship patterns can help to bring about self-understanding and change. In particular, Alex describes both the challenges and successes that come with allowing oneself to be vulnerable in the presence of others, and how such experiences within the therapy relationship can be used to inform and support change.
> – Olympia Gianfrancesco

Starting at the beginning

I experienced Cognitive Analytic Therapy (CAT: Ryle & Kerr, 2002) following an experience of what can be described as psychosis. I had become so distressed, so out of touch with reality, that I had been hospitalised, something that I fought against with all my might. When I was offered the chance to see a clinical psychologist, I had been out of the acute psychiatric setting for just over six months. I was taking medication that aimed to help with the psychosis, and also anti-depressants to reduce the depressing effects of this medication. At that time, despite the smoke screen of recovery that I presented to the world, I stayed in bed for most of the day. I was occupied by thoughts of grief for the future that I had lost, and feelings of shame for having been publicly 'caught out' as someone with mental health issues. My punishing thoughts, feelings, and emotions meant that thinking about suicide had become a comforting release. The period of 'hypomania' (i.e., a state of heightened mood and energy levels; Mind, 2016) that had resulted in me receiving psychiatric care had been wonderful and protective in comparison to the unfeeling, disconnected, medicated state that seemed to be the price I had to pay to avoid another episode. I sought therapy for several reasons: I did not want to go on living this way; my Community Psychiatric Nurse (CPN) said she thought therapy might help; I felt that I had to be seen to be doing something; and it was the only thing in my diary.

Meeting with the clinical psychologist

I was invited to a meeting with my CPN and a clinical psychologist to talk about what therapy might be appropriate. With the exception of the 'staying well plan' that had been put together for me (a written plan about how I would avoid relapse and stay well), and my weekly meetings with my CPN, it was the first therapeutic event since my admission the previous year. Meeting my CPN in hospital had been the first time anyone had asked if I was OK and talked about what would happen when I left the ward. It is perhaps surprising and important to note that there had been no psychological therapy or support during my five month stay in various psychiatric units.

I arrived at the meeting all smiles, but I was very anxious. The meeting was held at a place I had stayed during my traumatic admission to hospital. My fear was that if I said what I was thinking, I would not be allowed to leave. When asked by the therapist if I was all right, I blurted out that the smell of the hospital had triggered frightening memories. To my relief, this was met with reassurance and understanding about how upsetting that must be. If I had not been open about my feelings at this meeting, however ridiculous they may have seemed, I might not have returned for the therapy sessions, or seen how compassionately my concerns would be received. By the end of the CAT sessions, I had even made 'nodding' friends with the same hospital receptionist who had not let me out when I had been sectioned the summer before.

Working out if CAT is for you

The first meetings were about what would work for me: would I benefit from a certain form of therapy? Would I want to receive therapy from Diane (the clinical psychologist)? How willing would I be to do the work involved in therapy? My biggest reservation was that I did not want to talk about my childhood experiences. Taking your history into consideration is one of the key elements in CAT. As an independent woman in her mid-thirties who had left home as soon as possible, I did not see the relevance of talking about my childhood. I just wanted to know how to get back to work, be allowed to stop taking medication, and avoid coming into contact with psychiatric services ever again. I was given a leaflet about CAT to take away and read. Diane had reservations about the appropriateness of CAT if I would not talk about my history. Diane carefully explained that, within CAT, the rationale for discussing early experiences is that it is through these experiences that we learn patterns of relating to others and ourselves. By 'relating' I mean the way we tend to be with others and ourselves, critical or compassionate, caring or concerned, worried or supportive. These patterns can be useful and even skilful, helping us to manage our relationships with others and navigate the world around us. Sometimes, though, these patterns can also become distorted, amplified, or muddled and lead to behaviour that can be unhelpful. Understanding how these patterns came about, and how the expression of the patterns plays out in our lives, can tell us about what we need as humans. For example, during my episode of psychosis my patterns had led to the certain belief that I was in touch with the universe in a meaningful and tangible way, and at times a member of the secret services. This meant that at the point at which I felt most disconnected and vulnerable, I comforted myself with the idea of being almost superhuman and able to look after myself. I decided to open up about my past with Diane and give CAT a try.

Even before the episode, the way I related to others in the past provided a template for my future. Specifically, having been parented by someone who would nowadays be described as having post-partum depression, I had decided by age six that I would not have children. This was based on a fear that having a child would make me ill and the determination not to inflict the associated suffering on another child. This unchecked belief and the self-limiting decision it had led me to make had decided the outcome of several relationships. Having then experienced an episode of psychosis, I had elaborated on these beliefs: "being ill meant I would not be able to get a job, partner, or be able to do the things that normal people could. I would have to avoid stressful situations and take medication for the rest of my life".

Setting out our expectations for the CAT sessions and the work involved

CAT can last for between 4 and 24 sessions. Although I had no way of knowing what would be enough, we decided to plan 16 weekly sessions with the idea that we would see how it felt after that. Like all talking therapies, there is a period where you get to know each other, in which one person takes the role of client, and the other, therapist. The first surprise I got was Diane's explanation of how we were equal and that the way we related to each other in therapy was part of the process. In CAT, the work is collaborative, rather than the client talking and the therapist coming up with explanations and ways to solve or avoid problems. At first this was unsettling, but in the end it felt right as any changes would have to work for me and my life. The second surprise was the amount of active work that would be involved in the form of maps (diagrams of patterns in your life), letters, and worksheets. However, faced with the chaos I was experiencing, the fact that I could capture these experiences in writing and diagrams was reassuring and offered a safe outlet for my emotions.

CAT in practice

The first few sessions are called the *'reformulation phase'*. In this phase, you have the opportunity to speak openly and in confidence about what is happening in your life, about your own personal history and life experiences. The focus here is not just on things that have gone wrong in your life, but also on identifying what has gone or is going right. This was a real challenge when my mind was focused on a diagnosis, illness, or grief around what might have been lost, but there will always be aspects of you that should be celebrated. You are not the sum total of the parts when things have all gone wrong. The therapist will encourage you to name what works well for you, what things have given you happiness, satisfaction, and a feeling of doing well in the world.

Diane described how talking through previous experiences would help us identify patterns that were happening now or in the past and work out how to reduce the negative influence that they were having on the present. It is not easy to look deeply into the ways that you have interacted with the world and how they might have led to mental distress. At times we both found ourselves really upset by some of the things that I described and how they had influenced my adult life. However, it was liberating to talk about my history in a way that showed how beliefs formed in a second or as a result of a child's upset and confusion, could continue to influence choices made years after the actual events.

Mapping part one

CAT is a very active therapy, and the process of understanding and self-discovery involves drawing the patterns of behaviours, thoughts, and emotional reactions in a visual map or diagram. Here, the patterns of how you relate to yourself and others are also mapped. Looking at our patterns and their consequences is a key part of CAT. Drawing a map at first felt incredibly minimising; I had lost everything and now I was asked to map how, and what, had led up to this point on an A4 piece of paper! Diane, however, was persistent. For me to actually be able to see what I had hidden so well from the world on a piece of paper made it less unspeakable. The map took shape and then reappeared as we talked about experiences I was having now. The map was tested against these experiences and then changed until it became a detailed and yet simple map of my beliefs and patterns up to this point, including what made me wonderful.

Further into the therapy, the map becomes something that allows you to identify places where alternative responses, actions, and thoughts could be suggested. Between weekly sessions, I would reflect on the map and offer changes, as would Diane. Not all of these changes would be made, but some of them reflected the new experiences and different understanding gained as therapy progressed.

The reformulation letter

At around session four or five, I was read a *'reformulation letter'* in which Diane had written an account of the understanding shared between us about the problems that had brought me into therapy, how I had tried to cope with them, and what we were trying to change through the therapy. This did feel a bit strange as we already discussed these things each week, but the letter format meant that it felt official and it was actually about summarising the 'me' that I had shared. When the letter was read, I was asked if it was accurate and helpful, which contrasts with the way I had been written about on a psychiatric ward. The letter evidenced that my story had been heard. This bearing witness was actually really emotional for me and gave me confidence that I was not wasting my time with therapy, as we had a shared understanding about the goals of this work.

Starting to make changes in life

Part of the active nature of CAT means that you are invited to take part in and shape how change happens. The mapping process builds your ability to recognise the patterns of relating, thinking, acting, and feelings that you want to change. The therapist might suggest ways of recording these patterns in between sessions, and together you will look out for these patterns happening within therapy itself. For example, when I, and my family, have to talk about something that is distressing, we make it into a sound bite or 'make a funny' about it to try to reduce how awkward talking about it might be for me or the listener. Minimising a distressing experience by using humour can be a way of reducing anxiety around recalling an event. For me, the use of humour was a way of shutting the listener out, controlling their responses. This pattern of interacting happened throughout my relationships with friends and family, who must have been confused that I was making jokes about things that should have invoked feeling of sadness.

When patterns like this are identified in CAT, they are acknowledged and discussed to see how they affect current ways of relating to yourself and others (Ryle & Kerr, 2002). This meant that although in the sessions I made jokes and 'got a laugh', we could both see there was a disconnect there, a non-verbal but loud 'don't go there'. For example, I would joke about my table-tennis skills, honed over years of playing unpredictable opponents when visiting my mum in psychiatric hospitals. If my use of humour as a defence had not been understood, it would have prevented me from checking out what would happen if I told the truth. Visiting my mum in psychiatric units had been scary and upsetting as a child, mainly because I did not want to leave her there. Together we identified this as an opportunity to do something different (sometimes referred to in CAT as an 'exit'; Ryle & Kerr, 2002). Telling the truth about events and feelings instead of joking allowed me to test the belief that others would not want to hear it or that these experiences were 'too bad' to be talked about. This may seem like a trivial example, but changing this pattern helped me to avoid missing future opportunities to talk about my emotions and experiences, and prevented me isolating myself from support when I needed it most. For the record, I am glad that I was able to visit my mum, to hold her hand, and I did get to play table-tennis at county level.

Using journals and worksheets

I cannot remember whose suggestion it was to keep a reflective journal, but I had begun a journal of secret outpourings since the episode. This had become a record of daily to-do lists that consisted of getting out of bed, eating something other than cereal, and answering my mobile when it rang. Adding in self-reflection about therapy shifted the emphasis from recording daily to-do list failures, and brought the therapy outside of the one-hour-a-week session and into my everyday life. Also, in some sessions, I became quite angry or upset by what came up and it was good for me to have an outlet for this. I also used the journal to record my feelings in relation to the medication, as these would change over the week. It was useful to notice changes in mood so that they were not a mystery or something to be feared as a warning sign of another episode. The journal was also where I recorded the strength and frequency of my suicidal thoughts as, for me, this was a key measure of whether therapy was helping.

At various points I was given worksheets to note down something that I was finding difficult, what I did when this thing happened, and how I felt afterwards. For example, when my mobile phone rang I would try to ignore it, then check who was calling whilst letting it ring out. At this time, I felt very isolated and could go for days without talking to anyone. I lied to everyone about what I had been doing in the day to reassure friends or family that I was doing well and looking after myself. Noting down my difficulty with answering the phone meant that we could talk about it in the session and try to understand it, and then come up with ideas to make changes that would reduce the difficulty. For me, the mobile felt like the outside world, in which I felt judged and too broken to be a part of. The mobile pierced my protective bubble of sleepiness and illness. The alternative ways of being with this was to challenge myself to answer the phone and see what happened. This allowed me to see that people could be different to how I feared they would be, and showed me how my beliefs and reactions to my diagnosis were wrong. It was my judgement, my supposed failings and unworthiness, that prevented me from talking to people. Of course, there have also been really awkward conversations where I have been asked if I have 'got over being mad now' or been told in hushed tones that "there is no need to talk about such things as it's all in the past".

Mapping part two: continuous revision and real life experiments

Throughout therapy, the map is worked on, revised, and questioned to see if it is still true or still relevant to the problems. Either of you might suggest ways of changing a pattern, but this is done with an understanding of the difficulties involved in change. One of the key difficulties can be the defensive barriers that come up when someone suggests changing something that has been going on for so long. In such situations it is hard to see where the patterns end and the personality starts. For example, my family had always described me as having an independent and self-sufficient personality. However, this was just how I had learnt to relate to them, as the ability to hide emotions and carry on was something they praised. Talking about distressing experiences is not something we did as a family.

Alternative behaviours or responses (sometimes referred to as 'experiments') are explored and even practised in sessions. Experiments can be small and controlled, but are still unsettling because anything could happen. My experiments included seeing what would happen if I told someone the truth about how I felt or that I had been in bed all day, or answering the phone. Some experiments were about seeing what would happen if I related to myself differently. How would it be to be happy that I had walked to the shop rather than comparing it negatively to doing ten kilometre runs like I used to? Exits and experiments are added to the map and it suddenly shows that you do not know what will happen if you do something different.

There were exits I could not take and experiments that I tried to avoid doing. This meant that I would either not turn up to therapy or have to pretend I had done the experiment and end up having to discuss something I had made up. Missing a session or not telling the truth is an example of a 'rupture' in a relationship. This is where honesty really helps. Like in all relationships, when it is tested you learn about each other, and working out how to get over a difficulty together often strengthens the relationship. We talked about what it meant when I had not turned up and why I had avoided doing the experiment.

Of all the experiments, the greatest was one that no-one could witness, but continues to influence how I relate to myself and others. I was a perfectionist, not just in work but also with the image I presented to the world. This meant that, at times, the weight of social events was so overwhelming that I would avoid them just so no-one would see my imperfection. So my experiment involved seeing if it was okay if I said I was finding something difficult, rather than presenting the perfect daughter, student, colleague, and friend. I had feared others' disappointment or that I would be rejected if I showed my self-doubt, but actually it helped me to feel real, relaxed, and connected to others. You might not know that many of the people you meet in life have also had experiences that have really shaken how they see themselves. When you are open, people and the support they offer can really surprise you.

The end of CAT sessions and the 'Goodbye Letter'

It is good to start a therapy knowing that it will end. This means that the work that happens has to be enough to let you continue afterwards without weekly sessions. There are often follow-up sessions after three or six months as CAT recognises that finishing the weekly therapy can be difficult, especially if endings in your life have been difficult in the past (Ryle & Kerr, 2002). The last three or four sessions are used to think back over the course of therapy, and to consider the ending of this therapeutic relationship. This allowed us to talk about the end with a structure and make a plan so that the work could continue. The therapist will write a '*goodbye letter*' and will invite you to do the same. This letter is a summary of the work you have done together and how that will continue. It was moving to share what we had both written. By this point, Diane knew more about my weaknesses, fears, and who I was after the episode than anyone in the world. But the letter itself was a reminder of all that had changed and a commitment to continuing to live well.

What happens after CAT and moving into unknown territory

It has been over two years since my last follow up, and even though I have not shown my partner my map, I have described certain patterns of relating that were unhelpful to allow him to better understand what happened. He can now spot when I am making light of something that is upsetting so that he can show me care rather than just laughing at the funny. Sharing some of the patterns enables us to experiment together with different exits in relating to each other. Talking about CAT has been a positive way to talk about the distress we both felt during and after the episode.

If I had not kept a journal during the CAT experience and the following months, I would not have been able to mark the fading and then disappearance of suicidal thoughts that had accompanied me for as long as I can remember. They stopped when I understood how unrealistic my expectations for myself had been and that being me was good enough. The greatest question I was asked in the CAT sessions is now one I ask myself when I feel the pull of unhelpful ways of coping: 'Are you OK? You look upset'. In that moment there is permission to have emotions, there is care and concern. The question, so disarmingly simple, allows space between the feeling of upset and the previously automatic need to prove myself strong or dash for the duvet. In the space created, I have the chance to do something different, to be compassionate, ask for help, or take a break.

When I left hospital or started CAT, if you had asked me why I had fallen apart, I would not have been able to say why. Now, without judgement, I could cite a destructive, isolating relationship, several weeks without sleep, and the effort of trying to disguise the fallout from a failed suicide attempt. I was so used to managing such events, so skilled at hiding the associated emotions, that even I could not recognise their full impact. The CAT approach allows a sustainable way of understanding experiences. The mapping process results in a personal understanding that does not devalue anyone else's. This has allowed me to talk with people who have had similar experiences or have supported, loved, or worked with others who have received diagnoses of bipolar or psychosis, in a way that respects all the ways we make sense of our lives.

Practitioner's perspective

Claire Seddon

Throughout life we form relationships with other people. If we look at these relationships we can often identify patterns in how we relate to others. We may be supportive or critical, passive or dominating. How we relate to others will in turn influence how they then relate back to us, which can set up relational patterns. We also have a relationship with ourselves. For example, we can be compassionate and supportive of ourselves, but also self-critical or judging. Cognitive Analytic Therapy (CAT) focuses on understanding patterns in how we relate to others and ourselves, and uses these as the basis for achieving change and resolving difficulties in our mental health.

CAT explores the development of the clients' relational patterns by understanding their early experience of relationships and how this has shaped their style of interacting with others and themselves. For example, as a result of emotional neglect a child may struggle to recognise their own distress and emotional needs or how to comfort themselves, and this difficulty may persist through their adult life. They may develop strategies to manage feelings such as pleasing others to reduce conflict or taking drugs to numb feelings. These patterns of relating may be understandable and functional but ultimately maintains the emotional neglect. CAT focuses on collaboratively identifying how to change and exit from understandable patterns of relating which the individual now experiences as problematic.

CAT draws on concepts from different theoretical perspectives focusing on the social and relational nature of humans. This section will introduce the theoretical underpinnings of CAT and, through the use of examples, will illustrate how suited this framework can be to developing an understanding of an individual's experience of psychosis. The section will focus on what CAT uniquely offers. An overview of the practical aspects of CAT will be provided as well as an overview of the limited but increasing evidence base to support the application of CAT with psychosis.

The theory and language of CAT

Anthony Ryle, who was a GP and psychotherapist, developed CAT through the 1970s and 80s as a brief, active, collaborative model of therapy suited to the

British National Health Service (NHS). Ryle drew on concepts and ideas from a variety of different theories and ideas in psychology (e.g. psychodynamic theory, including particularly object relations theory [see Chapter 7], personal construct theory (Kelly, 1955), and developments in cognitive psychology) to develop CAT as an integrative therapeutic approach (Ryle & Bennett, 1997; Ryle & Kerr, 2002). In particular, object relations theory influenced the development of CAT by offering an account of how early parental experiences can become internalised and influence the development of personality. Ryle was also heavily influenced by the work of Kelly (1955) and the use of the repertory grid technique, which he saw as an accessible tool for clients to conceptualise relational issues.

Fundamentally, CAT is based on the idea that our experiences when growing up provide us with a template of how to be with others, which we continue to draw on throughout our adult life, when relating to both ourselves and others. Within CAT, the term 'reciprocal roles' (RRs) has been coined to refer to the positions two people take when relating to each other, and can also refer to positions we can take when relating to ourselves. Examples include feeling bullied and humiliated in response to an attacking, bullying other, or feeling secure, safe, and loved in relation to a protecting, loving other. From a CAT perspective it would be expected that we each experience a number of key reciprocal roles that form a broad collection of ways of relating and being with others that we can draw on. Where a person has had a 'good enough' early experience of care (Winnicott, 1973) and a safe enough environment to grow up in, they are able to learn to adapt and move between these different roles as the environment around them changes, and they can do this whilst maintaining a fairly stable sense of who they are. The focus of CAT will be on problematic core RRs that are unhelpfully dominating an individual's pattern of relating with themselves or others. Figure 5.1 shows how RRs are represented diagrammatically within CAT.

As a result of the role we are in, we will then think, feel, and behave in ways that either anticipate or invite others to behave in a particular way towards us. These are known as 'reciprocal role procedures' (RRPs). For example, if you imagine an individual who experienced significant bullying as a child, they may come to expect bullying from others and relate to others as if they anticipate hostility, for example, by avoiding sharing their opinions and being overly placating. This can leave the individual in a difficult position as they may not feel able to say

Bullying Attacking	Loving Protecting	Neglecting Dismissing
Humiliated Bullied	Safe, loved secure	Ignored, missed unimportant

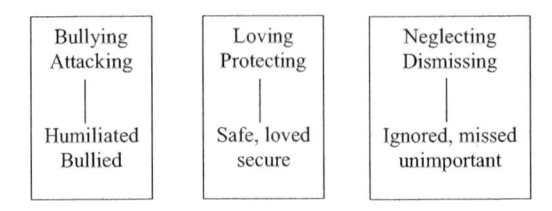

Figure 5.1 Examples of reciprocal roles (RRs)

how they really feel and what they really think. Some may see this as a weakness and go on to dominate and bully the person, which in turn maintains a relational pattern of feeling powerless and bullied in relation to a bullying other.

CAT theory evolved over time, later being influenced the work of Vygotsky (1962, 1978) and Bakhtin (1984). Both bodies of work emphasise how children draw upon their relationships and interactions with others in order to make sense of the world. Vygotsky showed that, before language skills develop, children learn to understand the world through signs, body language, and utterances. Bakhtin developed our understanding that the language children learn through communicating with others goes on to become the language and speech they use when relating to themselves, what we might call 'inner-voice' or 'inner-speech'. This concept is important in CAT as each RR is seen to have a related 'voice' of its own. This idea can be understood more simply by imagining yourself on your way to an interview and running late. Can you think what you would be saying to yourself? Would you be criticising yourself for not being organised and setting off earlier, or would you be reassuring yourself that it isn't your fault as the traffic is bad? This is an example of what is meant by our own 'inner-voice'. It is simply the way we talk to ourselves. It is not an activity we feel in control of and often we are not aware that this process is going on. However it can be very powerful. Building on the example used earlier, the bullied person will have developed a bullying inner-voice, which when active will leave the person feeling abused and attacked.

The CAT model understands that individuals who experience traumatic or depriving upbringings will develop negative inner-speech and adaptive ways of coping (RRPs). The adaptive RRPs develop to help the person survive, cope as best they are able and avoid unmanageable feelings associated with negative role positions (Ryle, 1990). However these once adaptive ways of coping can become problematic in subsequent different environments, as illustrated in the example above. The CAT model sees the self (who a person is) as fundamentally made up by interpersonal experience, and all mental activity is viewed as relational in nature.

CAT and psychosis

Whilst there is much debate around the causes of psychosis-type experiences, it is well-established in the literature that experiences of adversity, including trauma, in particular in childhood, link to the experience of psychosis (Varese et al., 2012; Longden & Read, 2016).

Ryle (1997) suggests that following experiences of neglect, abuse, trauma, and/or inconsistent and unresponsive parenting, a person's capacity to connect and move between their different roles becomes compromised, potentially leaving the person more disconnected and fragmented from parts of themselves. For the person, this can be very confusing. From a CAT perspective, psychosis-type experiences represent an individual's disconnection and dissociation from parts of themselves that become exaggerated and distorted (Kerr, Birkett, & Chanen, 2003; Kerr, Crowley, & Beard, 2006). For example, the experience of critical, abusive voices seen as coming from another may represent an exaggerated or extreme version of the inner-speech which all people experience, but which the individual has become disconnected from. Similarly, for an individual who believes themselves to be a prophet with the potential to save others, this belief could originate from an RRP of trying to help other people in order to not feel like a personal failure.

In CAT in general, and particularly with psychosis, the aim of the therapy is to support the individual to get back in contact with themselves. The aim of this process would be to develop the client's capacity to self-observe, understand how their psychosis may be linked to their patterns of relating, and help them reconnect to parts of themselves. Below is an overview of how CAT aims to do this.

The structure, process, and practical aspects of CAT

CAT is commonly used in many clinical settings (Calvert & Kellett, 2014). CAT has been developed as a time limited therapy, traditionally involving 16, weekly, hour-long sessions. Longer offers of therapy usually indicate an additional level of complexity. CAT aims to be collaborative and transparent in its application. As with many other therapeutic approaches, engaging in CAT can be emotionally unsettling. The therapist will aim to anticipate this and pace the therapy accordingly. CAT has its own set of terms and jargon (e.g. reciprocal roles, procedures) but how much these are used with a client will be determined by the therapist. The therapist may, for example, avoid using jargon that could create barriers for the client.

There are three recognised sequential phases to CAT: **reformulation, recognition**, and **revision**. The initial **reformulation phase** commonly involves identifying the dominant RRs and RRPs related to current difficulties, and developing an understanding of how an individual's historical life experiences have influenced the development of these patterns. CAT therapists may use a number of tools during the reformulation process. A paper based self-reflective questionnaire has been developed (The Psychotherapy File; Ryle & Kerr, 2002) to indicate a client's personal experience of a number of common problematic relational patterns. A 'reformulation letter' capturing a narrative of the information gathered is provided. In addition, a pictorial representation would be developed highlighting the key RRs and RRPs. Within CAT terminology, this pictorial representation is referred to as a Sequential Diagrammatic Reformulation (SDR). However, it is also commonly referred to as the therapy map, and it is often used as a point of reference throughout the therapy.

Figure 5.2 provides an example of a map. The RRs are captured in the rectangular boxes and the RRPs are the appraisals, emotions, and actions that result from the RRs. It captures a core RR of not feeling good enough and feeling criticised, in relation to a critical other who is giving conditional love. The leads to a RRP whereby, despite the individual's desire to be loved, her belief that others will

COGNITIVE ANALYTIC THERAPY (CAT)

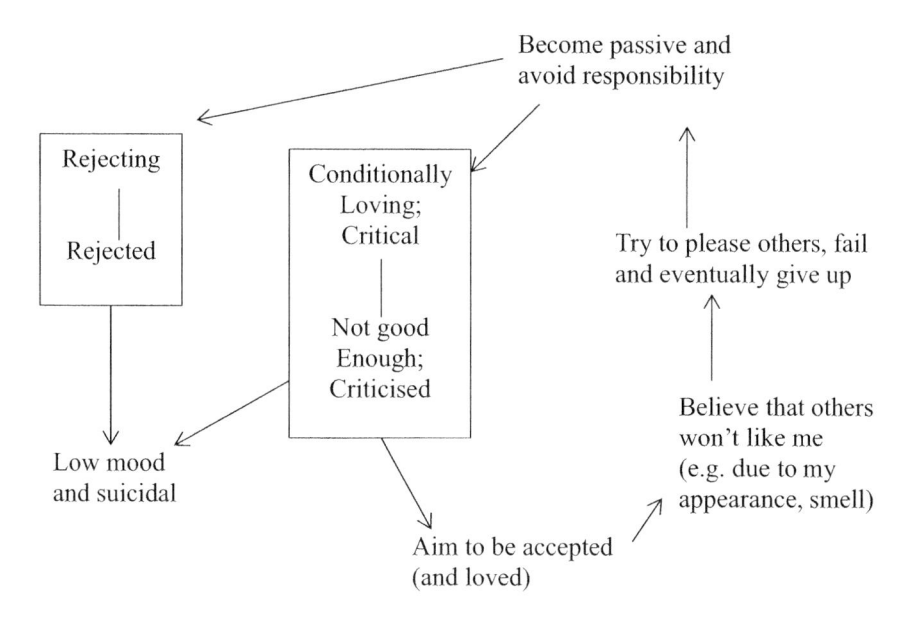

```
Rejecting              Become passive and
  |                    avoid responsibility
Rejected       Conditionally
               Loving;
               Critical        Try to please others, fail
                               and eventually give up
               Not good
               Enough;
               Criticised      Believe that others
                               won't like me
Low mood                       (e.g. due to my
and suicidal                   appearance, smell)

               Aim to be accepted
               (and loved)
```

Figure 5.2 Example of SDR (Therapy Map)

reject her, alongside her experience of not taking responsibility, is leading her to be passive which in turn leads her (and at times others) to become self-critical and rejecting. This in turn leads to low mood and feelings of suicide.

Noticing the ways a client reacts to the therapist (known as transference), and the pull to respond in a certain way that the therapist feels (known as counter-transference), are commonly used in CAT to complement the developing reformulation. For example, when working with an individual who struggles to take responsibility due to low self-esteem, the therapist may experience a pull to be more active in the therapy and take greater responsibility. The therapist will judge how much to share these observations, in order to support the client in feeling safe to notice, reflect, and learn from this. This can be a sensitive, challenging process. The reformulation letter will often comment on how dominant RRs and RRPs could negatively impact on the therapy relationship to aid the therapist and client in collaboratively monitoring for these patterns. Both client and therapist can experience ruptures in the therapy relationship when there is a mismatch between how one reacts and the expected or anticipated reaction. The therapist will encourage reflection at these times, drawing on the therapy map to repair the relationship.

The **recognition phase** of therapy works on developing self-awareness of the occurrence of problematic RRPs in daily life, including within the therapy relationship. This process of self-awareness development is referred to in CAT as developing an 'observing I' (Denman, 2001). The client will often be encouraged to actively self-monitor to contribute to this process. The recognition phase is essential to enable a client to identify times when their actions are contributing to the maintenance of problematic RRPs.

In the final **revision phase** of therapy, the aim is to develop exits from the otherwise cyclic, maintaining nature of problematic RRPs. Exits can involve a wide range of different strategies. Examples include revising one's inner-speech to develop a more compassionate inner-voice, which may involve practice and role-plays to learn this new skill. Alternatively, learning assertiveness skills can lead to behaviour change around responding to others who are bullying. For somebody troubled by attacking voices, they could work on understanding the fear behind the voices and learn to negotiate with the voices in order to manage feeling safe. Intervention strategies developed from other approaches are often applied in the revision phase of CAT, for example, cognitive behaviour therapy (see Chapter 2) or Compassion-Focused Therapy (see Chapter 8).

Conversations around the ending of therapy should take place throughout the therapy process to prepare the client. The ending of therapy will be marked by the invitation of letter sharing to reflect on the therapy journey, review the changes that have occurred, and identify how the client can maintain and build on their progress as they move forward.

Evidence

The evidence base around CAT for psychosis is limited to a number of small case studies (Graham & Thavasotby, 1995; Perry, 2012) and case series (Kerr, 2001; Glesson et al., 2012). These suggest that CAT can be acceptable to clients with experiences of psychosis and provide anecdotal evidence that some people benefit from this approach. There is an increasing application of CAT with individuals experiencing psychosis, leading to a greater drive to further assess the safety and acceptability of CAT with psychosis (Taylor, Perry, Hutton, Seddon, & Tan, 2015; Taylor & Seddon, 2017). Larger-scale trials will be needed to confirm that CAT can lead to improvements for those with experiences of psychosis. However, the indications from small scale research, and studies in other areas of mental health difficulty suggest that CAT has promise as an intervention for psychosis.

Taylor, Jones, Huntley, and Seddon (2017) questioned CAT therapists to explore how best to adapt CAT when working with individuals presenting with psychosis. Many key aspects around the application and use of CAT were seen as relevant and appropriate for individuals who have experienced psychosis, implying further training in the application of CAT with psychosis is not required beyond standard CAT training.

Further considerations

The application of CAT therapy can and should be adapted to meet the client's ability to engage in the process, and it is essential that all clients who agree to engage in CAT therapy have an understanding of what the process will involve before the therapy begins. As with all psychological interventions, the process of CAT therapy can be emotionally unsettling for the client. It can be difficult and upsetting at times; it can feel exposing and scary. However it can also be an enlightening process and feel empowering.

All trained CAT practitioners providing CAT therapy should be receiving clinical supervision. This provides a confidential space to support the practitioner to identify transference and countertransference issues within the therapy and to help guide their practice and provide a governance arrangement. To be a CAT practitioner, the therapist must have completed a two year post-graduate diploma in CAT, which will have included 16 sessions of their own therapy. For further information about CAT, visit www.acat.org.uk.

Conclusion

There are many psychological approaches that are applied to psychosis. CAT offers a developmental theory that emphasises the relational nature of humans and a clear framework for therapy. The application of CAT with psychosis provides an understanding of psychosis-type experiences from a relational perspective. This allows individuals to develop an understanding of how their experience of psychosis relates to and reflects their own intrapersonal (within themselves) and interpersonal (with others) patterns. This can be particularly important in challenging narratives that psychosis-type experiences are not understandable.

Note

1 The author has preferred to remain anonymous and use a pseudonym.

References

Bakhtin, M. (1984). *Problems of Dostoevsky's poetics*. Manchester: Manchester University Press.
Calvert, R., & Kellett, S. (2014). Cognitive analytic therapy: A review of the outcome evidence base for treatment. *Psychology & Psychotherapy: Theory, Research & Practice, 87*, 253–277. doi:10.1111/papt.12020
Denman, C. (2001). Cognitive – analytic therapy. *Advances in Psychiatric Treatment, 7*(4), 243–252. doi:10.1192/apt.7.4.243
Gleeson, J. F. M., Chanen, A., Cotton, S. M., Pearce, T., Newman, B., & McCutcheon, L. (2012). Treating co-occurring first-episode psychosis and borderline personality: A pilot randomized controlled trial. *Early Intervention in Psychiatry, 6*(1), 21–29. doi:10.1111/j.1751-7893.2011.00306
Graham, C., & Thavasotby, R. (1995). Dissociative psychosis: An atypical presentation and response to cognitive-analytic therapy. *Irish Journal of Psychological Medicine, 12*(03), 109–111. doi:10.1017/S0790966700014555
Kelly, G. A. (1955). *The psychology of personal constructs*. New York: Norton.

Kerr, I. B. (2001). Brief cognitive analytic therapy for post-acute manic psychosis on a psychiatric intensive care unit. *Clinical Psychology & Psychotherapy*, 8(2), 117–129. doi:10.1002/cpp.251

Kerr, I. B., Birkett, P. B. L., & Chanen, A. (2003). Clinical and service implications of a cognitive analytic therapy model of psychosis. *Australian and New Zealand Journal of Psychiatry*, 37, 515–523.

Kerr, I. B., Crowley, V., & Beard, H. (2006). A cognitive analytic therapy-based approach to psychotic disorder. In J. O. Johannessen (Ed.), *Evolving psychosis: Different stages, different treatments*. London: Routledge.

Longden, E., & Read, J. (2016). Social adversity in the etiology of psychosis: A review of the evidence. *American Journal of Psychotherapy*, 70, 5–33.

Mind. (2016). *Understanding hypomania and mania*. London: Mind. Retrieved from www.mind.org.uk/information-support/types-of-mental-health-problems/hypomania-and-mania/#.WKB-539dDbk

Perry, A. (2012). CAT with people who hear distressing voices. *Reformulation*, 38, 16–22.

Ryle, A. (1990). *Cognitive-analytic therapy: Active participation in change*. Chichester: Wiley Blackwell.

Ryle, A. (1997). *Cognitive analytic therapy and borderline personality disorder: The model and the method*. Oxford: John Wiley & Sons.

Ryle, A., & Bennett, D. (1997). Case formulation in cognitive analytic therapy. In T. D. Eells (Ed.), *Handbook of psychotherapy case formulation*. New York: Guilford Press.

Ryle, A., & Kerr, I. B. (2002). *Introducing cognitive analytic therapy: Principles and practice*. Oxford: Wiley Blackwell.

Taylor, P. J., Jones, S., Huntley, C. D., & Seddon, C. (2017). CAT for psychosis Delphi: What are the key elements of cognitive analytic therapy for psychosis? A Delphi study. *Psychology and Psychotherapy: Theory, Research and Practice*, 90, 511–529.

Taylor, P. J., Perry, A., Hutton, P., Seddon, C., & Tan, R. (2015). Curiosity and the CAT: Considering cognitive analytic therapy as an intervention for psychosis. *Psychosis*, 7. doi:10.1080/17522439.2014.956785

Taylor, P. J., & Seddon, C. (2017) Cognitive Analytic Therapy (CAT) for psychosis: Contrasts and parallels with attachment theory and implications for practice. In K. Berry, S. Bucci, & A. Danquah (Eds.), *Attachment theory and psychosis*. London: Routledge.

Varese, F., Smeets, F., Drukker, M., Ritsaert, L., Lataster, T., Viechtbauer, W., . . . Bentall, R. (2012). Childhood adversities increase the risk of psychosis: A meta-analysis of patient-control, prospective- and cross-sectional cohort studies. *Schizophrenia Bulletin*, 38, 661–671.

Vygotsky, L. S. (1962). *Thought and language*. Cambridge, MA: MIT Press.

Vygotsky, L. S. (1978). *Mind in society*. Cambridge, MA: Harvard University Press.

Winnicott, D. W. (1973). *The child, the family, and the outside world*. London: Penguin.

6

TRAUMA-FOCUSED THERAPY USING COGNITIVE-BEHAVIOURAL AND EMDR APPROACHES

Client's perspective

Rebecca[1] and Joanna Ward-Brown

> It is increasingly being recognised that early experiences of trauma are a potential cause of experiences of psychosis. Historically, the link between psychosis and trauma has been under-recognised, possibly because of the emphasis on finding biological causes of psychosis. This chapter focuses on an innovative trauma-focused approach to therapy, that uses therapeutic techniques that we already know can be helpful for people facing trauma.
> – Peter Taylor

Introduction

I am Rebecca. I am 24 years old and live in the North West of England where I was born. I have been interested in British Sign Language since high school and can do basic signs. I also like football and used to be goalie in a local team. I have been working at a care home for the past seven years. I have some friends whom I like to go out drinking and having a laugh with, and one good friend who has been there for me through the tough times.

How I came to receive therapy

My first contact with mental health services was when I went into hospital after hearing a voice that others could not. This was a really scary and upsetting experience for me, and other people were worried about me and about others' safety and welfare. This happened when I was 21 going on 22 years old. Things had got to the point where I wanted to hurt myself as a way of managing what I was going through, and the voice was telling me to do it.

A few years before this, at the age of 16, I was sexually assaulted by a family member who I thought I could trust. I started to recognise that the voice I was hearing sounded like him. I was really angry at him for what he had done and was having really strong urges to hurt him and make him suffer for what he did. I was experiencing nightmares and flashbacks about what had happened and kept trying to bottle all of this up and not talk about it to anyone else. I told a friend about what had happened and this pushed me to a very bad place. I was feeling really low and was worried about the urges to hurt myself and wanting to harm my abuser; these events led to my hospital admission.

After having been in hospital for three weeks, during which time I was transferred to a different hospital so I could be nearer to family, I was picked up by the local crisis team. After I was discharged, I would meet with them for a few sessions each week. Crisis teams (Crisis Resolution and Home Treatment Teams) are a service in the UK that provide support to those experiencing a mental health crisis. Despite this contact with the crisis team, I went back into a different hospital after feeling suicidal again, and this time I felt even worse. After I had been discharged again, I was referred into the Early Intervention for Psychosis Service (EIPS). This is a different mental health service that works specifically with people who are having experiences of psychosis, such as hearing voices. The early intervention for psychosis service came to talk to me about how I was feeling and how the voices were affecting me. My case manager suggested that it might be helpful to talk to someone at the local trauma service about what I had been through. She gave me a questionnaire to fill in that looked at how traumatic things that had happened in the past were affecting me now. The questionnaire was called 'The impact of events scale' and I had to rate, on a scale from 0 to 4, how much I was experiencing certain difficulties such as: "I avoided letting myself get upset when I thought about it or was reminded of it (the trauma)", "I had dreams about it", and "pictures about it popped into my mind".

The start of therapy

I was feeling really nervous and anxious about meeting my therapist, who worked at the trauma service, to talk about the therapy. I had many thoughts in my mind about the therapy: 'will it work?', 'will it make me worse?', 'how much depth will I have to go into?' It is hard to remember how I felt as it feels like such a long time ago. We agreed to start our sessions in the New Year. I felt excited but also anxious.

I was sent questionnaires in the post before starting therapy. I do not particularly like filling in questionnaires. It felt like some of the questionnaires had trick questions and I worried that the answers to some questions could be misinterpreted. However, when the questionnaires came in the post it made me think, "This is real now, I'm actually going through with it". I felt a sense of relief that I would have the chance to talk. At the same time, it felt weird that I had been offered help because I had struggled for so long on my own that I thought I was coping.

Before the start of my first session at the trauma service, I was concerned about what the therapist would think of me when I told her about my experiences, and especially about what my abuser had said to me during the incident. I was worried she might judge me or see me differently. I was worried about getting anxious and embarrassed when talking about what had happened to me. I was scared that I would lose control of my feelings and end up back in hospital. When I first met with my therapist it initially felt weird. I was thinking, 'what am I doing?' I knew why I was there, but I am not the kind of person to ask for help. I knew I needed it, but it was hard. The first session is a bit of a blur to me now. I remember feeling relieved when it had finished, as I felt that I had started to get the help I needed, but at the same time I felt like I had let myself down by going as I felt I should have been able to control my own emotions. I was dreading coming back for the second session and it took a lot of motivation to get myself there.

The therapy began with assessment sessions, which focused on finding out more about my problems, gathering information, and completing questionnaires. In these early sessions, my therapist started to draw up a 'formulation' on the whiteboard. This was a diagram that outlined the understanding we were forming together, which explored my difficulties and what had caused them. The formulation looked at my experiences of trauma and how they were affecting me now. These sessions were hard work! It was difficult drawing out my timeline and getting everything right where it should be on the line (which included mapping out all the difficult things I had been through in order and how these experiences had affected the way I saw myself and others). We completed many different questionnaires looking at the voices I experienced, my day-to-day living, my mood, the flashbacks I struggled with, and my sleep. I found that these questionnaires helped to structure the sessions. It was weird to see my problems written down on the board, in my formulation. It helped me to understand why I was feeling the way I did – feeling down, angry, not sleeping, and having nightmares – and why I had started to hear voices, which were linked to the trauma.

The formulation we came up with is presented in Figure 6.1, and is based on a psychological theory of how people react to trauma (Ehlers & Clark, 2000). The diagram shows how certain triggers or reminders of the trauma (e.g. reports of abuse in the news) could trigger a feeling of threat, as if the trauma was happening again at that moment, and experiences such as flashbacks, hearing a voice (which sounded like the abuser), and nightmares relating to the memory of the trauma. The diagram outlines some of the ways I had tried to cope with or control these symptoms or experiences, such as hiding feelings or avoiding certain places. The formulation then explains how these ways of coping actually kept the problems going by stopping me from fully working through the memory of the trauma, and by confirming the negative way I had come to see the world (e.g. seeing others as dangerous). Outside of the box are some factors that help explain the way I reacted to the trauma, including my past experiences and the way my brain (particularly a part called the amygdala that deals with emotions) tried to make sense of the trauma as it happened.

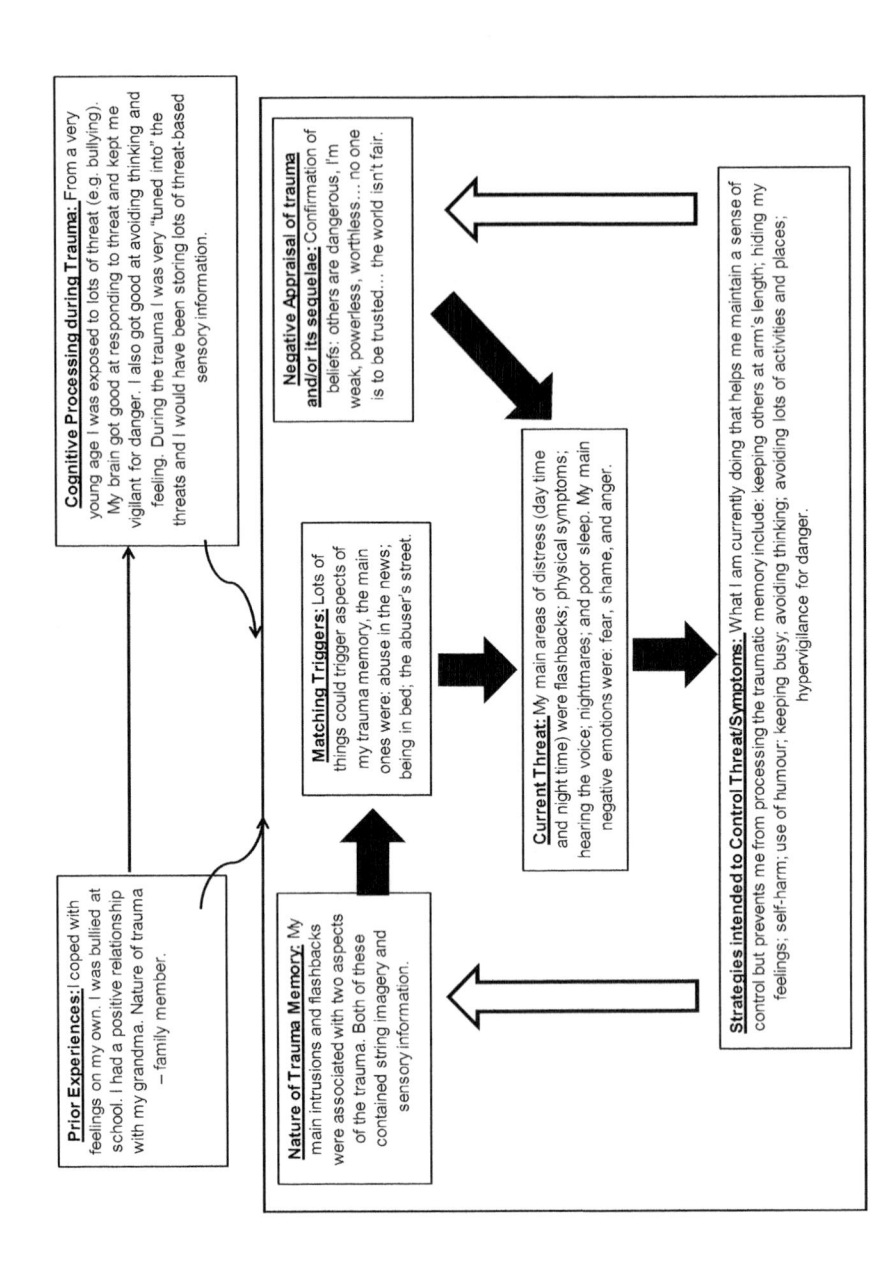

Prior Experiences: I coped with feelings on my own. I was bullied at school. I had a positive relationship with my grandma. Nature of trauma – family member.

Cognitive Processing during Trauma: From a very young age I was exposed to lots of threat (e.g. bullying). My brain got good at responding to threat and kept me vigilant for danger. I also got good at avoiding thinking and feeling. During the trauma I was very "tuned into" the threats and I would have been storing lots of threat-based sensory information.

Negative Appraisal of trauma and/or its sequelae: Confirmation of beliefs: others are dangerous, I'm weak, powerless, worthless... no one is to be trusted... the world isn't fair.

Matching Triggers: Lots of things could trigger aspects of my trauma memory, the main ones were: abuse in the news; being in bed; the abuser's street.

Current Threat: My main areas of distress (day time and night time) were flashbacks; physical symptoms; hearing the voice; nightmares; and poor sleep. My main negative emotions were: fear, shame, and anger.

Nature of Trauma Memory: My main intrusions and flashbacks were associated with two aspects of the trauma. Both of these contained string imagery and sensory information.

Strategies intended to Control Threat/Symptoms: What I am currently doing that helps me maintain a sense of control but prevents me from processing the traumatic memory include: keeping others at arm's length; hiding my feelings; self-harm; use of humour; keeping busy; avoiding thinking; avoiding lots of activities and places; hypervigilance for danger.

Figure 6.1 My formulation using the Ehlers and Clark (2000) model. Thin black arrows indicate where one process or event influences another. Thick black arrows indicate where one process leads to another. The thick white arrows indicate where one process prevents a change elsewhere.

The challenges of therapy: going back into hospital

Not long after my assessment phase of therapy, I started to feel really low and the voice was taking over. I was starting to feel very suicidal, and I ended up in hospital for two weeks. I did not have a very good experience on the ward, as it was a mixed ward and some of the men were behaving really strangely. I did not find this time on the ward very helpful. The staff decided to discharge me as they felt I was doing a bit better, and I ended up coming back for therapy. I was a bit dubious about continuing therapy because of this setback, but I decided to come back as I felt there was still time for the therapy to help.

My therapist and I talked about what had happened and what might have triggered my return to hospital. We considered if the therapy had brought back difficult feelings about what had happened to me in the past. We also talked about me letting my therapist know when I am struggling in the future. We agreed to start our work on emotional coping skills to help me manage my feelings before talking about what had happened to me in more detail.

Emotion, coping, sleep, and nightmares

We started some work on ways to cope so that I felt more ready to talk about what had happened to me in the past. We developed a safe place image, where I imagined a beach in Cornwall and all the sights, sounds, smells, and feelings in my body that went along with being there. I felt calm and more relaxed when I imagined being in this place. We used the word 'relaxed' as a cue to help me bring myself back to this place when I needed to. We also focused on a memory I had of feeling proud, when I stood up in front of an audience and gave a speech about my experiences at The Prince's Trust, a charity in the UK which supports young people. The most important part of this memory was of my mum and dad's proud faces. This reminded me that there are other people out there who do care about me. My mum has recently told me that she is proud of me, and hearing this makes me feel loved. Recalling this memory of giving the speech helped me to reduce some of the negative thoughts and feelings I had about myself, such as not feeling good enough.

My favourite technique was the 'poisoned parrot'. The idea is to imagine that your negative thoughts are coming from a parrot, who has been trained to recite these negative or hurtful words back at you. The goal of this technique is to learn to see these negative comments as just words ('it's just that parrot again') which we do not have to believe or pay attention to. We looked at my thoughts and my memories of the assault I had experienced and saw that my abuser's words were not as hurtful as his actions. We looked at my own negative thoughts about myself, and we worked on ways to let these go rather than accepting them as facts.

We also looked at my sleep routine and if there was anything that could be changed to help improve my sleep (for example, changing things in my bedroom, diet, exercise, and routine). We then worked on a strict sleep routine to help me to spend less time in bed awake. The idea was that bed would become a place I associated more strongly with sleeping. This meant I had to get out of bed if I could not sleep within 15 minutes or so, and do something relaxing before going back to bed when I felt sleepy again. I have recently become interested in adult colouring which is really relaxing, and I would do this at times when I could not sleep. It took a while to get the balance right, and it was hard work as I needed to stay up really late sometimes until I felt tired enough to go to bed and go to sleep. With time, my sleep started to get better and has been pretty good ever since.

We then started to work on my nightmares, which involved me reliving the trauma I had experienced. We wrote out my nightmare on the board and then changed the ending so that Basil Brush (a UK television character that is a talking fox) came in, shrank down the abuser, and then threw him in the bin and said his catchphrase, 'boom boom!' It was not violent; it was a way of getting rid of the rubbish. I felt better in myself doing this, although it did not work the first couple of times, so we changed it a bit and I read this new story before I went to bed every night for about three weeks. As a result, the nightmares started to bother me less. At the same time as this work, I was put on Prazosin (a medicine that is sometimes used for people with nightmares related to trauma) and this also helped with my nightmares. I was on Prazosin until the end of therapy.

Using Eye Movement Desensitisation and Reprocessing (EMDR) to process the trauma

EMDR started with me thinking about the worst part of the trauma. I was asked to focus on where I felt any difficult emotions in my body as well the negative belief I had about myself linked to the trauma (e.g. that I'm worthless). I then had to follow my therapist's hand with my eyes as she moved it from side to side, and every now and then see what came up for me in terms of thoughts, images, or feelings. This was really hard work, probably the hardest part of therapy. It went into lots of depth and detail about the trauma I had experienced. I was worried about what my therapist would think of me if I told her exactly what had happened, what was said to me during the incident, the words that were used. I felt a huge sense of shame, guilt, and embarrassment. EMDR brought out a mixture of emotions, thoughts, and memories. I did not expect to experience the emotions in that way and they felt overwhelming at times. The main emotion I felt was anger, which was still there at the end of the sessions. My therapist asked me to imagine the anger as a coloured shape in my stomach, where I felt it, and asked me to imagine a light beam coming in and dissolving the imaginary shape and my feelings of anger. We then imagined my safe place of the beach, which helped me to feel calm and like I had no worries. Doing the eye movements felt weird at first, but it felt like it was helping me to get things off my chest and to be able to talk about things that I had never been able to talk about with anyone before, not even family. Sometimes it was hard to concentrate on the eye movements as my therapist was sitting on a squeaky chair. She also had a rumbling stomach a couple of times! We ended up giggling about this and it took us away from the more difficult stuff.

I felt exhausted after each session, and then had to go to work. I had mixed feelings about coming back for these sessions because they were so difficult. I told myself that if I did not go back, I would not know if it really worked. I thought to myself 'what have I got to lose?', and even though I did not feel better at this point, it felt like it was getting some of the difficult stuff out in the open.

We got to a point where I kept getting stuck on the worst part of the trauma, and we talked about what to do next. My therapist gave me the option of doing some reliving work to help me talk through what had happened in the right order. I felt a bit nervous about this plan, but I thought it might help to get stuff out.

Cognitive Behavioural Therapy and reliving work

My therapist asked me to stand up and draw a bird's-eye view of a good memory and a bad memory, and asked me to spend some time talking about one of these memories and then moving on to the other memory for a couple of minutes. This taught me that I had more good memories than bad memories. I managed to move between the memories and the different feelings quite quickly. My therapist then asked me to draw the full bird's-eye view of the memory of the trauma, and asked me to talk through the different parts of the scene, talking through what happened in which part (the house, the garden) in some detail. This helped me to get more details of the memory and put things in the right order. It was hard doing this, and I found it upsetting.

I then had to talk through what had happened to me during the trauma in the past tense. Looking back, this was easier than talking about it in the present tense. I got stuck again on the worst part of the trauma, which was something the abuser had said to me during the attack. We spent some time waiting for me to feel able to say these horrible things out loud. We talked about needing to get the 'poison' out or to 'rip the plaster off', and with time I was able to tell my therapist what he said to me. Unfortunately, while I was doing this, there was an interruption to the session, which was really difficult and upsetting. Talking through the worst part was emotional, I cried in the session, and then I cried after the session while sitting in my car in the car park at work. I felt guilty and ashamed about what had happened to me.

I made myself come back to therapy the week after to talk through what had happened to me again, this time in the present tense. It felt harder, as I was talking as if it was all happening again. It still took me a while to say the worst bit again, but I had to pretend I was peeling the plaster off. I ended up telling my therapist more details this time. I felt embarrassed again, but I also felt quite proud that I had actually said it. I had never told anyone what he said to me. I still have not told anyone else these kinds of details.

Working on recovery

We talked about any positives that had come out of surviving this trauma. I think it has made me stronger and I worry about other people going through what I have been through, whether it is abuse or psychosis. I want to help people who have been through similar things.

During therapy, I was pushing myself to get back into full time work, and I was able to get fit and get back into sports. I became a lot more sociable; I was seeing friends, DJing, volunteering at a play-scheme, and going to karaoke.

We looked at how I would like to see myself and what I needed to say to myself to feel more positive about myself. I wrote down the statements 'I have nothing to be ashamed of', 'I am worthy', and 'I am loved'. These were the opposite of how I had felt and thought when I first came into therapy. I put these statements in my work drawer, and every day I pulled them out of my drawer and read them to myself. This helped me to feel proud of myself. It was hard to believe at first, but they gradually became more believable, and now I do not need to look at the paper, because they are in my head.

The therapeutic relationship

At first, my relationship with my therapist felt lop-sided as I was doing most of the talking and sharing details about myself, whilst my therapist shared few details about herself. I found it hard that I was talking about me and my therapist was not talking about herself in these ways. This made me worry more about how she would take it when I told her the worst parts of the trauma. The relationship felt stronger after I had told my therapist the worst bit about what happened to me. It helped that we both had a sense of humour, and we were both patient. The distractions and funny moments did help a little bit as they broke things up a bit, and eased the tension from talking about difficult things. The other staff at the trauma service were really helpful and supportive.

Ending therapy

I had mixed emotions about ending the therapy. I felt proud that I had done it and did not need it anymore, but I also felt sad that I did not have someone to talk to anymore. The therapy had become part of my weekly routine. It felt good to look at my scores on the questionnaires about hearing voices, symptoms of Post-Traumatic Stress Disorder, mood, recovery goals, coping with emotions, and my day-to-day functioning (e.g. work, activities, socialising) before and after therapy and see how far I had come.

Where I am now

I would like to tell others that if they are thinking about trying this therapy, they should stick with it. Even though it is a lot of commitment and hard work, it pays off.

I no longer have nightmares about what happened. I am now living on my own. I moved in with my friends for a year which went really well, though there were five of us living under one roof, so it did start to feel a bit cramped! I like living on my own, it is the freedom to do what you want when you want. It can get a bit lonely sometimes, but I have friends down the road. I carried on using some of the coping skills I learned in therapy, such as the safe place, poisoned parrot, distraction techniques, and positive self-statements, but I have not been using them as much recently as I have not felt the need. I use an adult colouring book and listen to music to cope with anxiety and voices, although the voices are not as bad nowadays.

I managed to get back into full time work and got a promotion to the position of senior carer in a care home, where I first worked as a carer, and then an administration assistant. I have just found out I have got a new job as a personal assistant carer. I am quite anxious to start, but I am feeling happy and proud that I got the job. I never thought I would be able to get through an interview outside of my current job, where I have been working for the past seven years.

I have also spoken at two conferences and been involved in teaching at a University about working with trauma and psychosis. I stood up and told my recovery story. I was really nervous at first, but I did it, and all the compliments I got from those listening were overwhelming.

Practitioner's perspective

David Keane

Introduction

Over the last decade, researchers have increasingly investigated the link between traumatic life events and the development of psychotic experiences. In doing so they have revealed a number of thought-provoking results:

- Results suggest an estimated 50% to 98% of individuals who have experienced psychotic symptoms have also experienced trauma (Read, van Os, Morrison, & Ross, 2005).
- Results suggest a 'Dose-Related Response' between the experience of trauma and the severity of mental health difficulty. Namely, the more frequent and substantial the experience of trauma, the more significant difficulties there are likely to be (Bentall, Wickham, Shevlin, & Varese, 2012; Varese et al., 2012).
- Results suggest a link between certain childhood traumas and specific psychotic experiences or, in other words, individuals who experience certain types of trauma may be at higher risk of certain types of distress. For example, childhood sexual abuse is related to a greater risk of voice hearing, whilst physical abuse is related to a greater risk of paranoia (Bentall et al., 2012; Varese et al., 2012; Morrison, Frame, & Larkin, 2003).

Likewise, mental health services within the UK National Health Service (NHS) have increasingly focused their attention on the relationship between trauma and psychosis. This has created increased confidence and optimism for therapists when providing trauma therapy to people with more complex mental health needs.

This section begins by highlighting why it is often crucial to offer individuals an opportunity to talk and think about adverse and traumatic life events, and help individuals identify the link between these events and the development of their difficulties. This section will then progress to offer an overview of the theory that underpins clinical practice and introduce the 'modular treatment programme', concluding with a review of the current evidence base and offering the therapist's personal reflections.

Why it may be important to think and talk about past adversity and trauma

Imagine that whilst driving to meet a friend at the cinema, a car pulled into your path, causing you to swerve, slam on your brakes, and stop only an inch or two away from impact. Take a moment to close your eyes and picture that scene. After recomposing yourself, it is likely that you would continue your journey to the cinema. Now, reflect on the following questions:

1   When you got to the cinema and saw your friend, what would you do?
2   When you told them about what happened, how would you feel?
3   When you were watching the film, what might be happening in your mind?
4   That night, would you be likely to dream about it?
5   How long would you keep thinking and talking about this experience?
6   Why would you stop dwelling on it?

When we experience any unpleasant life event, it is intuitive to talk, think, and possibly even dream about our experience. Of note though, at first, when we do any of these things, we are likely to re-experience the emotions felt at the time of the incident to the same or similar intensity.

For example, your answers to the above questions may have sounded something like this:

> *When I met with my friend at the cinema, I would tell them what had just happened. Whilst telling them, I would feel 'flustered'. During the film, I would possibly unintentionally think about the near miss. That night I may dream about the event or a similar experience, and after a day or two I'd probably stop talking and thinking about it. I guess that would mean I had now dealt with it.*

Figure 6.2 illustrates the likely process that you have been through. Re-experiencing emotions during the course of talking, thinking, and dreaming about our life experiences is a fundamental part of helping us deal with and move on from what has just happened. In fact, it is these very things that help our brain 'process' the new information. This 'processing' involves the individual understanding the event, attaching meaning, and ultimately storing the new information for future reference.

Talking, thinking, dreaming, and re-experiencing the emotions associated with the incident highlighted in the scenario may have led to the following conclusions:

> *I was driving safely at the time. The other driver wasn't concentrating and that's why he pulled out on me. I guess we've all done this at some stage. My safe driving protected me from a more serious incident. I guess if I keep driving in this way then I can avoid most dangers on the road.*

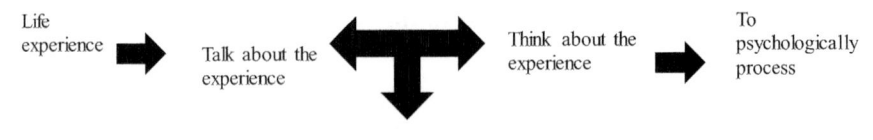

```
Life                                              To
experience  →  Talk about the  ⟵  Think about the  →  psychologically
               experience         experience           process
                              ⟱
          Re-experience the associated physiological emotional responses
                              ⇅

          Whist the brain checks this new information against your assumptive
          world (core views of self, others and the world)
```

Figure 6.2 Diagram illustrating the process that is gone through following a life event or trauma

If you did make sense of it in this way, then you would likely stop dwelling on it after a short period of time. The speed at which you move on or 'process' the situation is likely to relate to the fact that the conclusion drawn is not likely to conflict with what you already believe to be true about your driving and that of the other person, alongside more general views about road safety.

Unfortunately, for many individuals, life experiences can be so significant or disturbing that this intuitive process gets interrupted, and as such the memory of the event gets 'stuck', poorly integrated, and not fully psychologically processed.

Conceptual understanding and theory

There are a number of conceptual theories and models that help us further understand how traumatic life events can, at times, lead to psychological difficulties. This chapter will briefly introduce one: "The Adaptive Information Processing Model (AIP)" (Shapiro & Laliotis, 2011; Shapiro, 2001, 2002). Whilst the AIP model is associated to Eye Movement Desensitisation and Reprocessing (EMDR) literature, it is this author's belief that its relevance reaches across the range of psychological interventions aimed at the management of trauma related difficulties.

Shapiro, in her adaptive information processing model, suggests that all humans are assumed to have an intuitive system that enables them to psychologically process life experiences, which she calls the Information Processing System (IPS). She suggests that all the sensory information gained from life experience (what we see, hear, smell, feel, and taste) is 'processed' by our IPS. The IPS's job is to 'digest' new sensory information, keep and store relevant aspects for future reference, and disregard irrelevant information. It is suggested that the IPS does this by processing all the new important sensory information and storing it in memory networks that contain related thoughts, images, emotions, and sensations (Shapiro, 2001). As such, new learning occurs when new associations are connected with information already stored in memory. For example, think about the previous scenario, the near miss in your car. Your IPS stores new information and new associations, including the visual image of a car at a junction and the new learning in regard to the potential of a car pulling out into your path. When driving down the road and approaching a junction next time, you may find yourself being reminded of this association and as such you slow down.

Shapiro goes on to propose that when a traumatic or very negative event occurs, the IPS can get overwhelmed and information processing may therefore be incomplete. This results in the new sensory information not being connected with more adaptive information that is held in other memory networks. For example, a survivor of childhood sexual abuse may have decontextualised (non-connected) memories of the abuser saying repulsive things during the abuse, alongside what this meant to them at the time and how they felt at the time. Therefore, the memory of the abuse remains detached from other memories and many sensory elements will remain unprocessed. The magnitude of this may be felt when the individual intentionally or unintentionally thinks about their childhood, and experiences any of the following:

- Hearing a voice echoing the words said during the abuse.
- Re-experiencing the emotion felt at the time of the abuse at a similar intensity in the present.
- Temporarily feeling like they are back in childhood.
- Experiencing a strong sense of being damaged and to blame.

Shapiro highlights that it is not only major traumatic events that can cause psychological disturbance. Sometimes a comparatively minor event from childhood or adulthood, such as being bullied by peers, criticised by a parent, or rejected by a partner may also not be adequately processed.

Working with trauma and psychosis using a modular approach to treatment

In recognition of current theoretical understanding of trauma and psychosis, Lancashire Traumatic Stress Service (LTSS) have developed a treatment programme designed to meet the needs of individuals presenting with both trauma and psychosis experiences. This approach provides a clear, structured, six module treatment programme that helps promote a sense of safety and control, and enables the therapist to tailor treatment specifically to the needs of the individual, working incrementally towards asking them to think and talk about past adversity and trauma. (For further information on this approach, please see www.lancashiretraumaticstressservice.nhs.uk/ltss-treatment-programme.html).

The best way of understanding a modular approach is through the use of a metaphor. Imagine that the journey of recovery is like walking across a rickety bridge over a canyon, and the view of the bridge is hidden behind a number of 'obstacles' or 'blocks'. You may be reluctant to make this journey at first, and to cross the bridge safely and with relative confidence, you must first identify where you are trying to get to, then identify the obstacles in the way and clear the path. In other words, it is the individual's responsibility to identify and articulate what goals for therapy are meaningful to them, and it is the therapist's and individual's responsibility to identify the barriers to getting there. For therapists, this means treating the problem rather than the diagnosis, and keeping interventions simple and carefully linked to their intended mechanisms, current research evidence, and the client-defined goal.

Each module focuses on different aspects of theory and clinical practice and as such represents a comprehensive treatment programme that has flexibility to meet a diverse range of difficulties. In brief, each module's focus is as follows:

Module 1 – Introduction, assessment, and formulation: In this module, we establish priorities and goals, and make sense of difficulties through the development of a personalised treatment plan.

Module 2 – Pharmacological treatment: In this module, we ensure that if medication is prescribed, this medication is agreed by the client, and as far as possible by the therapist and prescriber, to be the most helpful medication at the most helpful dose, and tailored to both the demands of therapy and the individual's current difficulties.

Module 3 – Safety, stabilisation, building resources, behavioural activation, and education: In this module, we target strategies that promote a sense of control over life, encourage engagement in activities that support 'reclaiming a life and building a future', and ask the client to start to consider what a future that offers meaning, purpose, hope, and direction may look like. In conjunction with this, we provide personalised education to promote understanding of what might have triggered, and what may maintain, the client's difficulties.

Module 4 – Sleep and nightmare management: In this module, we target any associated sleep and nightmare difficulties. When appropriate, we combine psychological and pharmacological approaches such as behavioural sleep management and Imagery Rehearsal Therapy (IRT; Krakow & Zadra, 2006). IRT is designed to reduce the number and intensity of nightmares among people with trauma related difficulties. Whilst there can be differences in the way in which this therapy is provided, there are generally a number of steps involved (see Table 6.1).

Module 5 – Focusing on the trauma: In this module, we offer interventions that focus directly on traumatic life events. The opinion of LTSS is that treatments that are in line with the guidance produced by the National Institute for Health and Care Excellence should be considered (National Institute for Health and Care Excellence, Clinical Guideline 26). This guidance suggests that Trauma Focused Cognitive Behavioural Therapy (TF-CBT) and Eye Movement Desensitisation and Reprocessing (EMDR) are the appropriate

Table 6.1 Image rehearsal therapy steps

Step 1 – The first step is to start by looking at the disturbing dream or nightmare directly, getting it out of the shadows so to speak. Talking it through clearly and writing it down is often a good start.

For some people this can almost immediately help to reduce the 'power' of the nightmare, helping them to remember that this is an event from the past and that they are now safe.

Step 2 – The second step then involves imagining an alternative ending for the nightmare; this will become clearer in the example below.

Step 3 – The third step involves rehearsing the new version of the nightmare in your imagination each day and at night just before falling to sleep.

---

treatment approaches (a brief summary of these two approaches will be offered shortly).

Module 6 – Relapse prevention and preparing for the future: Finally, in this module, we identify strategies for staying well and coping with setback.

Trauma Focused CBT (TF-CBT)

TF-CBT works on principles to assist a client to intentionally think about traumatic events in a contained and safe way. In TF-CBT, this is achieved by prolonging exposure to an unprocessed memory (see protocol by Foa, Hembree, & Rothbaum, 2007).

TF-CBT involves initially telling your traumatic story, with eyes open, in the past tense and with a third person perspective, but then moving on to re-telling or reliving the story with eyes closed, in the present tense, and with a first person perspective. Recordings of reliving sessions are made and these recordings are then listened to between sessions. Time is taken to name and at times restructure specific beliefs that lead to distress, for example, "I was not to blame for that horrible thing that happened in childhood . . . I was only eight, just a child, I cannot hold myself at all responsible for what happened"; and new beliefs are then held in mind at the same time as reliving the most distressing parts of the memory.

Eye Movement Desensitisation and Reprocessing (EMDR)

EMDR again works on the principles of assisting a client to intentionally think about a traumatic event, but, unlike with TF-CBT, where the client needs to relive the whole memory, in EMDR the client is initially asked to only focus on worst moment of the experience. EMDR is based on the idea that negative thoughts, feelings, and behaviours are the result of unprocessed memories. The treatment involves standardised procedures that include focusing simultaneously on (a) an image that represents the worst moment of the traumatic event, the associated negative belief about oneself, emotions and bodily sensations, and (b) bilateral stimulation that is most commonly in the form of repeated eye movements. Unlike CBT with a trauma focus, EMDR does not involve (a) detailed descriptions of the event, (b) direct challenging of beliefs, (c) extended exposure, or (d) homework.

Further information on the EMDR 8 Stage Protocol can be accessed via Shapiro's work (Shapiro, 1995).

Evidence base for trauma focused interventions for people with psychosis

Statistical analysis of clinical trials shows that, generally speaking, TF-CBT and EMDR are safe and effective, and NICE recommends that these treatments should be the first-line psychological treatment for Post-Traumatic Stress Disorder (PTSD). (Bisson et al., 2007; Bisson & Andrew, 2009) More recently there have been a number of important studies looking at the applicability of TF-CBT and EMDR in clients with psychosis. These studies highlighted a number of important findings, including:

- A treatment protocol that consisted of 12 to 16 sessions of combined TF-CBT interventions, a crisis plan, psycho-education, breathing exercises, and cognitive restructuring, proved to be safe and effective in reducing PTSD symptoms in people with psychosis (Mueser et al., 2008).
- Prolonged exposure (PE) techniques, as found in TF-CBT, generated no adverse events and result in significant reductions of PTSD symptoms. These results suggest that PE is effective and safe (Frueh et al., 2009).
- EMDR and TF-CBT were equally effective in reducing PTSD symptoms (van den Berg & van der Gaag, 2012).
- Both EMDR and TF-CBT were effective in significantly reducing symptom severity of PTSD symptoms, delusions, hallucinations, depression, and anxiety. They were also found to increase self-esteem, alongside other improvements in general distress, and triggered no adverse events or symptom exacerbation (De Bont, Van Minnen, & De Jongh, 2013).

This said, one must also highlight here that whilst the research clearly suggests that some individuals with psychotic experiences do well with these approaches, the evidence base is still quite limited.

Personal reflections

It is increasingly evident that for many who experience psychosis, traumatic life events are at the source of their difficulties (de Bont et al., 2016). This chapter was written not to promote the idea that everyone with psychosis should receive trauma informed therapy, rather it has aimed to highlight the range of difficulties that may be addressed via a "trauma informed modular approach". To work out whether an approach like this is suitable for a particular individual, it may be of benefit to ask the following three questions:

1 How do you feel right now? Try to name the emotions or the areas of distress (e.g. "Feeling ashamed and flawed as a person").
2 Have you ever felt these before? Try to float back through memories and identify an earlier time in life when you felt the same or similar.
3 Do current symptoms have a relationship to this past event? For example, do the voices sound like personal meaning associated with the traumatic event or other's words at the time of the event?

This chapter focuses on two psychological interventions: TF-CBT and EMDR. This is in recognition to the standard operating procedures at LTSS and its NHS setting, current national clinical practice guidelines for PTSD, and the current research evidence base. The LTSS modular approach offers further flexibility to clinicians to incorporate psychological interventions from other areas of psychotherapy when needed in line with individual's goals. It is beyond the scope of this chapter to detail these psychotherapies, just to recognise that TF-CBT and EMDR do fit within a wider landscape of trauma therapy.

Whilst the LTSS modular treatment programme offers flexibility to the individual and therapist, one must recognise that there are potential disadvantages to this approach. Some individuals discover ways to 'contain' traumatic memories and would find an approach like this destabilising. Others develop beliefs about themselves, others, and the world that serve a protective function in minimising the emotional discomfort associated with living with unprocessed memories. For example, imagine you are faced with the tragic death of your partner and children in a road traffic collision. Rather than accepting the painful reality of this, you may wish to believe that the government had conspired with local hospitals to kidnap your family. One must carefully consider the advantages and disadvantages of engagement with an approach like this, and importantly, as Rebecca eloquently described in the first part of this chapter, recognise that therapy is not a painless exercise.

The benefits of a comprehensive modular treatment approach are captured by the personal reflection of the two therapists who have contributed to this chapter:

> *We started this journey engaging with two young women who had experienced trauma in their lives and gone onto develop psychotic experiences. Both of these young women had been in hospital and under the care of mental health crisis teams on a number of occasions, and both had struggled to sustain a period of recovery. By the end of therapy, both stood in front of an audience of more than a hundred to powerfully and articulately tell their recovery stories. It is with thanks to these two courageous young women that we have gone on to treat others with similar difficulties, offering them a treatment response that incorporates an*

opportunity to talk and think about past trauma and, most importantly, enables individuals to engage with a meaningful and enduring recovery.

Note

1 Rebecca has given consent to publication of her account in this form. Joanna Ward-Brown is Rebecca's therapist, and has worked alongside Rebecca to record her account of her experience of having therapy.

References

Bentall, R. P., Wickham, S., Shevlin, M., & Varese, F. (2012). Do specific early-life adversities lead to specific symptoms of psychosis? *Schizophrenia Bulletin, 38*, 734–740.

Bisson, J., & Andrew M. (2009). Psychological treatment of post-traumatic stress disorder (PTSD). *The Cochrane Database of Systematic Reviews, 18*.

Bisson, J. I., Ehlers, A., Matthews, R., Pilling, S., Richards, D., & Turner, S. (2007). Psychological treatments for chronic post-traumatic stress disorder: Systematic review and meta-analysis. *British Journal of Psychiatry, 190*, 97–104.

de Bont, P. A., Van Minnen, A., & De Jongh, A. (2013). Treating PTSD in patients with psychosis: A within-group controlled feasibility study examining the efficacy and safety of evidence based PE and EMDR. *Behavior Therapy, 44*, 717–730. doi: 10.1016/j.beth.2013.07.002

de Bont, P. A., van den Berg, D. P., Van der Vleugel, B. M., de Roos, C., de Jongh, A., van der Gaag, M., & van Minnen, A. M. (2016). Prolonged exposure and EMDR for PTSD v. a PTSD waiting-list condition: Effects on symptoms of psychosis, depression and social functioning in patients with chronic psychotic disorders. *Psychological Medicine, 46*, 2411–2421.

Ehlers, A., & Clark, D. M. (2000). A cognitive model of posttraumatic stress disorder. *Behaviour Research and Therapy, 38*, 319–345.

Foa, E. B., Hembree, E. A., & Rothbaum, B. O. (2007). *Prolonged exposure therapy for PTSD: Emotional processing of traumatic experiences: Therapist guide*. Oxford: Oxford University Press.

Frueh, B. C., Grubaugh, A. L., Cusack, K. J., Kimble, M. O., Elhai, J. D., & Knapp, R. G. (2009). Exposure-based cognitive-behavioral treatment of PTSD in adults with schizophrenia or schizoaffective disorder: A pilot study. *Journal of Anxiety Disorder, 23*, 665–675.

Krakow, B., & Zadra, A. (2006). Introduced information relating to the clinical management of chronic nightmares: Imagery rehearsal therapy (IRT). *Behavioral Sleep Medicine, 4*, 45–70.

Morrison, A. P., Frame, L., & Larkin, W. (2003). Relationships between trauma and psychosis: A review and integration. *British Journal of Clinical Psychology, 42*, 331–353.

Mueser, K. T., Rosenbergm, S. D., Xie, H., Jankowski, M. K., Bolton, E. E., Lu, W., & Wolfe, R. (2008). A randomized controlled trial of cognitive behavioral treatment for posttraumatic stress disorder in severe mental illness. *Journal of Consulting & Clinical Psychology, 76*, 259–271.

National Institute for Health and Care Excellence (NICE). (2005). *Post-traumatic stress disorder: Management*. Retrieved from www.nice.org.uk/guidance/CG26?UNLID=921488020157423290

Read, J., van Os, J., Morrison, A. P., & Ross, C. A. (2005). Childhood trauma, psychosis and schizophrenia: A literature review with theoretical and clinical implications. *Acta Psychiatrica Scandinavica, 112*, 330–350.

Shapiro, F. (1995). *Eye movement desensitization and reprocessing: Basic principles, protocols and procedures*. New York: Guilford Press.

Shapiro, F. (2001). *Eye movement desensitization and reprocessing: Basic principles, protocols and procedures* (2nd ed.). New York: Guilford Press.

Shapiro, F. (2002). Paradigms, processing, and personality development. In F. Shapiro (Ed.), *EMDR as an integrative psychotherapy approach: Experts of diverse orientations explore the paradigm prism*. Washington, DC: American Psychological Association Books.

Shapiro, F., & Laliotis, D. (2011). EMDR and the adaptive information processing model: Integrative treatment and case conceptualization. *Clinical Social Work Journal, 39*, 191–200.

van den Berg, D. P., & van der Gaag, M. (2012). Treating trauma in psychosis with EMDR: A pilot study. *Journal of Behavioral Therapy & Experimental Psychiatry, 43*, 664–671.

Varese, F., Smeets, F., Drukker, M., Lieverse, R., Lataster, T., Viechtbauer, W., . . . Bentall, R. (2012). Childhood adversities increase the risk of psychosis: A meta-analysis of patient-control, prospective and cross-sectional cohort Studies. *Schizophrenia Bulletin, 38*, 661–671.

7

PSYCHODYNAMIC THERAPY

Client's perspective

Paul-Newell Reaves

This chapter really captures the openness, flexibility, and importance of building a strong therapeutic relationship that can make Psychodynamic therapy the right approach for some people. This chapter helps to question how we think about therapy and what we want out of it.
– Naomi Fisher

Introduction

My name is Paul-Newell. I have experienced psychosis, and I am involved in ongoing psychodynamic therapy. Psychodynamic therapy originated with a Freudian understanding of therapy, especially an emphasis on unconscious motivators, and reoccurring patterns developed in early childhood (Erwin, 2002). Aspects of this approach to therapy that apply to me and my work with my therapist, Dr. S., consist of free-association, the attention to psychological defences (that initially helped to protect from pain and trauma but have become problematic and limiting), a belief in bringing the most troublesome issues into the light, and the influence of the therapist-client relationship. I will discuss all these elements very soon. The work I did with Dr. S. was largely psychodynamic, but also made use of some techniques and elements that are outside of this tradition, including visualisation techniques. Another feature of the work I did with Dr. S., that is not part of psychodynamic therapy, is that Dr S. was also my psychiatrist. This is different from many other contexts where different people may take on these psychiatrist and therapist roles.

First, I will summarise the events that led me into therapy. Then, I will stress the importance of the first few moments and the first few sessions in the therapist-client relationship. Addressing the bulk of my therapy, I will discuss free-association, especially what, for me, makes for a productive and cathartic session. I will then cover the approach of the therapy. I will follow this with examples of how therapy has helped me understand the impact of my childhood experiences on my adult life. The most helpful aspects of my psychodynamic therapy will then be addressed, followed by the most challenging elements of this therapy.

Welcome to the world inside my head.

Yesterday

At 19 years old, I experienced a psychotic episode. I was hearing voices and experiencing the delusion that people could hear what I was thinking. At first I heard voices of people in my immediate vicinity, but soon from across the country, then from around the world. Intriguingly, all these voices I perceived as belonging to people I knew well; I have never created a fictional personality that speaks to me, it has always been someone already familiar to me. These psychotic experiences were coupled with an utter lack of functionality and extreme isolation. I slept in my closet in an effort to minimise the voices, and only left my dorm room to eat once a day.

Within two months, I recognised I needed help. Most fortunately, I felt zero self-stigma or self-hatred. Paranoia was ceaseless, fear and terror were daily emotions, but shame about having these experiences was not present in my life. I believe this is due to my growing-up straddling the Generation-X and Millennial generations; when I grew up, we all thought madness and imaginary voices were kind of cool.

At 25 years old, fresh out of a four-month inpatient stay at a psychiatric hospital, the Austin Riggs Centre, I began my psychodynamic therapy work with Dr. S.

Come together

As important as the man and his character were to my ultimate choice of Dr. S. as my long-term therapist, it is the way he surrounded himself in his practice that made the most immediate impression. At that early stage in our therapeutic relationship, his cosmopolitan and sun-lit office appealed to me a great deal. The urban location mattered to me, as well, four blocks from a downtown Metro train stop. Degree certificates were hung, but out of the way, behind the client chair; not overtly displayed for impact or boast, but available for inspection. The therapist's chair was positioned in the centre of the room by a wall-length window, on the far side of the chair, a stiff couch. A low bookshelf was directly in the line of vision of both the client chair and couch, and featured biographies of artists and playwrights. These shelves also featured three-dimensional art – two wooden fish, and a Venetian Gondola oar mount.

Dr. S. worked in 45-minute sessions. I had become accustomed to the 50-minute or 70-minute session at the Austin Riggs Centre, which also focused on therapy and free-association, and I distinctly noticed the shorter time period. Before I adjusted to it, the catharsis that I usually experienced from therapy seemed dramatically interrupted by the shorter session. Catharsis is, for me, one of the great benefits of therapy. It is the experience of an unweighting of troubles by talking through them. This is not necessarily a universal characteristic of psychodynamic therapy, but something I have found beneficial. I found that the more frequent the therapy, the more often I experienced catharsis. We at first met three times a week, and this frequency would soon become an important issue for me in terms of stepping down my care, linked in my head to my level of recovery.

I've just seen a face

My experiences prior to therapy have had an important influence on what occurred in the first few sessions and even in the first few moments of the initial session. First came the presumptions, expectations, and baggage that I brought with me into the office. This soon evolved into one of the most important elements of my psychodynamic therapy, the relationship between therapist and client. After flip-flopping through seven psychological professionals in the first year after my breakdown, I was slow to develop my relationship with Dr. S. I find it a major chore to develop these relationships, and it took a while to determine if he was the right therapist for me. But after I made that decision I was quick to trust Dr. S., partially due to his character, but as much due to mine. I like to think I read people well, and so trust certain people very easily. Additionally, my previous experience with therapy had made me quite comfortable talking in the office, so once a sufficient level of trust was built, our relationship grew rapidly.

I had chosen to work with a male therapist, believing that sexuality and organ functioning would be easier to discuss with someone of my own gender. Surprisingly, the emotional side of my personal history, concerning romantic partners, frequent and prolonged lack thereof, and romantic relationships more generally, have played a far more dynamic role in our psychodynamic work than explicit sexuality. Certainly, psycho-pharmaceutical side-effects related to sexual functioning have been a recurrent concern of mine, but discussions of repressed sexuality, as well as the build-up and release of sexual tensions have been virtually non-existent in our sessions. Certainly not what I was expecting in this type of therapy.

As for the therapist, himself, the very first moments of our interaction spoke volumes. He opened the door from the waiting room to the office and waved hello. This amiability defines his character, as I know him. When I entered, he offered his hand to shake.

Important to the early development of our relationship, on one occasion in the first few months I became extremely worked-up, and stormed out of the office early in the session. I smoked a cigarette, debating whether to return, during which time Dr. S. called my cell phone, once – a call that I ignored. Within 10 minutes I did decide to return. He expressed gratitude that I had returned, and may have even been relieved about this. I view this as a major turning point in our relationship, bringing into focus both of our limits, but also our reactions to the pushing of those limits. Soon after, the hard work began.

I want to tell you

Psychodynamic therapy traditionally involves inviting the client to engage in free-association. Free-association involves a stream of consciousness, a sharing of whatever thoughts or ideas come to mind, a flow of speaking from the client, with links between this flow of words which say something about what is going on in the client's mind that the therapist is, hopefully, able to make sense of. Dr. S. stressed the importance of my speaking about anything I wanted, and everything on my mind. Again, when growing up, this type of therapy was very much on the public radar, and so this sort of exercise seemed natural to me. Our discussions usually involved school, friendly and romantic relationships, my goals, my poems, and occasionally, my dreams. This raises the issue of productive therapy verses more conversational sessions. What I experience as our most productive, cathartic sessions involved deep psychological work, probing my emotions and personal history, and ultimately a cleansing of mental wounds. However, often our sessions were less productive, composed of more casual conversations, intellectual discussions, and talking about movies, books, or art. These less productive sessions could arise from anything from my own upcoming deadlines and school due dates, to not being in the mood or not being ready to discuss an issue, to illnesses, and even hangovers. These less productive sessions may not feel as good, but as Dr. S. would say, they keep me in practice.

Dr. S. has a laid back style of analysis. Though frequent with his clarifying questions and input to maintain the conversation, he is perfectly comfortable allowing lengthy silences. His suggestions and profound analyses come infrequently, and when they do come, he rarely speaks for more than a few minutes. However, his insights, suggestions and analyses are often extremely helpful, both in the long-term and short-term. One of his most frequent comments, when I identified troubling emotions or experiences, was to suggest that I stay with that emotion. What he calls staying with the emotion involves feeling it fully, allowing time to process the emotion. Hopefully, this emotional processing will enable an understanding of the emotion, perhaps easing the feeling in the future. Staying with these emotions feels like an important part of the catharsis that comes from our sessions.

We can work it out

Two major issues that Dr S. had profound ideas about, early on, were what we referred to as my weak interpersonal boundaries and my flagellatory self-judgement. Dr. S. suggested that I seem to absorb the emotions of others, with the result of extreme emotional overwhelm. This could be seen as an inability to know where my own Self ended and where another person's Self began; in psycho-jargon, weak interpersonal boundaries. One example of this effect was when a woman boarded a bus I was riding while involved in a loud, protracted argument on her cell phone. I remember feeling extremely uncomfortable as soon as I heard the tone of her voice, and I began to feel an undirected anger soon after, not directed at the person on the phone, not directed at myself, but undirected.

Whilst Dr. S. made use of psychodynamic principles and ideas, he also introduced some techniques that are not part of the psychodynamic approach, but that nonetheless were extremely helpful. We worked on defining this interpersonal boundary by visualising a physical barrier around myself, to keep the emotions of others outside of my own self. I chose to imagine a walled fortress, and would physically bring my fists together in front of my abdomen, visualising gates closing, in an effort to seal this barrier. The difficulty in such a method lay in remembering to enact this visualisation. When swept up in an emotional state, it was difficult to remember that this coping method was available to me. However, it gradually became easier to remember, and eventually automatic. Not only did this technique strengthen my emotional boundaries in the moment, it began to build up my interpersonal boundaries more substantially, so that I needed the visualisation less and less. Aiding this long-term recovery, I began taking notes when my interpersonal boundaries were overcome, allowing me to recall these moments in the therapy sessions. The combination of visualising a strong seal around myself, along with talking about moments of weak boundaries, has created a vast difference in emotional overwhelm. I now need this visualisation barely at all.

The issue of flagellatory self-judgement was equally severe for me. Though rarely judgemental of other people, I was extremely critical of myself. Again departing from a purely psychodynamic approach, Dr. S. proposed a simple coping method, consisting of recognising my self-judgement, and telling myself that I do not deserve such a judgement. The difficulty in this strategy was the first half, recognising my self-judgement in the moment. Like the interpersonal boundaries issue, once swept up in the emotional overwhelm of self-criticism, it became very difficult to remember to enact the coping method. Again, over time this method came more naturally, eventually becoming reflexive. I raised an issue in the therapy, "what about when I do deserve judgement for something I have done, and must I tell myself I do not deserve this?" Dr. S.'s reply became, "you do not deserve flagellatory judgement, you do not deserve to be overly punished for any judgement".

Within psychodynamic theory early childhood experiences are seen as important in shaping one's future life. From a psychodynamic point of view all of the issues discussed (including the two just outlined) would be seen as potentially having roots in childhood experience even though the relevant experience may not be explicitly identified. One issue where we have discussed some early experiences linked to a current problem is that of my difficulty with sitting at traffic lights. In this situation, I stress out and it feels like my blood pressure skyrockets. Through our work, Dr. S. suggested this stress might link back to earlier childhood experiences. We were able to see a pattern, through my childhood and into adulthood, around the need to control. For example we discussed how, as a child, I would force out my excrement every time, instead of allowing my bowels to work naturally. For me, identifying these patterns from childhood and into adulthood helped me to understand and make sense of my difficulties.

Here comes the sun

For strong, effective therapy, one must understand just how difficult the work will be. The psychodynamic therapy I have received is time consuming work, emotionally draining work, and I feel that one must work at it hard. But understanding that work level is how to get the most out of this kind of therapy, and understanding makes it easier.

Most importantly, I like Dr. S. When I am unable to see him, I feel a hole in my day-to-day life. When I am able to see him, I generally feel better for several days. Crucial to the psychodynamic approach, this relationship has worked very well for me. His suggestion that I stay with each emotion, allowing myself to fully process it, is of frequent benefit. Understanding more about the way childhood experiences can shape future life has helped as well.

Dr. S. has also been willing to conduct sessions by phone and video chat, which has been immensely helpful when I miss sessions – still a frequent occurrence. However, long-distance therapy has the disadvantage of finding somewhere other than the office for therapy. It needs to be quiet, but more importantly, somewhere no-one else can hear.

Activities that are not part of the psychodynamic approach, but were still helpful in my therapy with Dr S. include my work with visualisations, and taking notes on moments of emotional overwhelm and psychological vulnerability, followed by bringing up these issues in the sessions.

Help!

On the other end of the spectrum, my therapy has its difficulties and challenges as well. I understand therapy as a peeling back of emotional scabs, followed by a scrubbing or cauterising of psychological wounds, followed by a long length of time to allow these wounds to form calluses, maybe even heal. However, this idea is more than mere metaphor; if there are deep psychological wounds, then one's mind forms defensive scabs to protect from continued infection. And all wounds, especially psychological ones, require time to heal, often a long time. This process was extremely draining for me. I found that most often the early part of my therapy involved crying the entire length of every session; I understand this as peeling back the scabs, always a painful experience. Though tears may always be an element of therapy – as it should be, crying is a natural reaction to intense emotions – eventually the amount of crying eventually lessened for me. Then came the scrubbing of the wounds, a deep, psychological, working through of my emotions and revelations about childhood experiences. My experience has been that this lasts the entire length of therapy, though my self-awareness has substantially increased, easing the difficulty of such work. In time, even the most violent psychological damage has formed calluses, and has begun to hurt much less. I believe that some conditions will never go away, will never completely heal. But I believe that the harder I work, and the more I understand about the nature of this work, the faster the pain and difficulties ease.

I often feel immensely vulnerable in the work with Dr S., though the level of this vulnerability has risen and faded, repeatedly. This was for me the greatest difficulty in the psychodynamic therapeutic experience. Since my teens, my emotions had been buried, and I barely felt anything at all. This distancing of emotions, followed by such intense and prolonged feelings of vulnerability resulted in me feeling extremely overwhelmed. It was this flooding of emotions that has proved especially difficult for me. However, it has aided in long-term recovery, putting me in touch with my emotions.

My relationship with my therapist has proved troublesome at times, as well. Dr. S., of course has his own life to live, and his own flaws, but I find it annoying when he does not remember issues or facts from my life that I have mentioned in previous sessions. He can also be quite insistent on issues that I dismiss. He has often repeated the notion that I might be feeling emotions of jealousy toward my sister, who is steadily succeeding in her career. I have repeatedly rejected that idea; I am simply not a jealous person, and I would also hate doing her job. Eventually, I got annoyed and asked him to stop bringing it up – a request that he has so far honoured. Finally, Dr. S. takes too many vacations for my liking. Sometimes up to two weeks, several weeks every summer, and many long weekends throughout the rest of the year. He is perfectly entitled to such leave, but his vacations can leave a void in my life. Structure is an extremely important element in my recovery, and without our twice weekly morning sessions, I am left with nothing to do two mornings a week. Without rigorous awareness of this lack of structure, I easily slip back into habits of non-functionality. Additionally, losing a week of therapy sessions sets back the therapy in the immediate future, and the feeling of catharsis is substantially reduced. I find that it takes a few unproductive sessions to then rebound from this void.

Another challenge that took a great deal of trust building and testing of limits to overcome is that I have often been worried that Dr. S. would fire me and end our work together. When I was missing substantial numbers of appointments consecutively, I was convinced he would insist on parting ways. The threat becomes building a relationship with another therapist, or having to forgo therapy altogether. However, once this limit was reached, and the result was not as I expected, I began to trust that he would not do so, and was able to overcome this fear. I suspect that he has had a similar fear that I will fire him, although he has given me no substantial cause to do so.

Getting better

As I have undergone therapy, the greatest change has been my ownership of my psychotic experiences and hallucinations. At the point of my initial breakdown, I had no idea what was happening. Now, through intensive therapy and my work with Dr. S., I am not afraid of my hallucinations and delusions. Much of this change is due to understanding what is going on in my head, and also talking through these issues. But I have also learned about Mad Pride communities, and draw a great deal of strength from that. This change is crucial to my well-being and lack of self-stigma – by knowing and owning these psychoses, I am able to maintain a healthy self-respect and self-esteem. Instead of labelling myself as a 'patient', or 'mentally ill', I choose to call myself a 'client' of psychiatrists, and a 'consumer' of psychiatric treatment. Though these changes in language may seem inconsequential or petty, they create a major difference in my ownership of my condition. Something as simple as the language labelling all mental health conditions as disorders constructs us as a social caste that is distinctly worse than being 'normal'. I do not mind being misunderstood, and do not mind too much being stared at; I do mind being devalued and stigmatised.

Self-care has remained a challenge. Bathing, brushing teeth, cleaning up for myself: all of these have remained challenging for me. Combine this with the ongoing difficulty of oversleeping, and continuing to miss appointments regularly, and my functionality can be very low, indeed. Dr. S. has proposed that not caring for myself is indicative of not caring about myself. As I continue to wash my psychological wounds, hopefully these challenges will lessen.

With therapy specifically, I have become far more aware of my emotions and mental states. Again, a crucial development in my ownership of my condition. But this self-awareness itself also aids my therapy, easing the level of emotional draining and psychological strain. The goals I set myself have also changed. Though I have achieved most of the long-term goals I set, the short-term goals have been significantly more difficult to make progress towards, with the goal of self-care having wavered on a month-to-month basis. I still experience lack of functionality and struggle with self-care, but I am optimistic about my future as a person experiencing psychosis.

Thanks for letting me share.

Practitioner's perspective

Alison Summers

What is psychodynamic therapy?

A brief definition

Psychodynamic therapies are talking therapies where therapist and client work together to try to understand the client and their relationships, with the therapist using psychodynamic ideas about the mind and about the practice of therapy. They are therapies that attend to unconscious factors that may underlie unwanted patterns of feeling, thinking and behaving, and which aim to help people feel less trapped by these. In using the word 'psychodynamic' I am treating it as interchangeable with the word 'psychoanalytic' and in this section will discuss what it means in relation both to the nature of therapy and the ideas behind this.

Psychodynamic ideas about the mind

Understanding psychodynamic ideas about the mind is complicated by the fact that there is no single psychodynamic theory, but rather various inter-related theories (e.g. object relations, self-psychology, relational, Lacanian), and many psychodynamic therapists draw on more than one. This section provides an overview of ideas that are in line with a particular branch of psychodynamic theory known as object relations theory, ideas which I see as sufficiently general to apply to a large extent in most other models. I have selected object relations as a theory in widespread use, and the one with which I am most familiar. More detail about aspects of psychodynamic therapy discussed in this section is provided by Lemma (2003) and I have provided additional references only for material not covered there.

A central idea in psychodynamic thinking is that crucial parts of our emotional life happen outside our conscious awareness. The word 'psychodynamic' itself has been defined as "the interrelation of the unconscious and conscious mental and emotional forces that determine personality and motivation" (https://en.oxforddictionaries.com/definition/psychodynamics).

Psychodynamic theory is also concerned with how our minds develop, and sees this happening through an interplay of innate biological characteristics and life experience, particularly experiences of relationships from infancy onwards. This development happens through unconscious learning processes (referred to as 'procedural learning') and leads to us having an 'inner world' of habitual ways of experiencing ourselves and others, with associated habits of feeling and behaving, which can continue to evolve throughout life.

Much of our mental life is unconscious, but from a psychodynamic perspective, some aspects are also *dynamically* unconscious, that is, they are kept from conscious awareness in order to protect us from emotional pain. Psychodynamic theory describes the processes through which this happens as 'defences'. For example, a pattern of overestimating our own abilities and seeing others as less able may be a defence against unconscious feelings of inadequacy and vulnerability. Defences are universal and essential to enable us to live our lives without being overwhelmed by feelings, but they can also be problematic when they are extreme or inflexible. To continue the example above, overestimating our abilities in certain circumstances may be helpful, perhaps making a daunting situation feel manageable. However, if this pattern is extreme and inflexible, it may cause problems of its own, such as an arrogant attitude that repeatedly alienates others.

From a psychodynamic perspective, our experience is continually shaped and sometimes distorted by our unconscious inner worlds. Clues to such distortions constantly emerge in our choice of words, our patterns of speech, the content of dreams or psychotic experiences, and in the patterns in our relationships. For example, when someone's narrative changes from seeming articulate and coherent, to seeming disjointed and harder to follow, this may be a clue that the topic being discussed is something associated with difficult emotions.

Psychodynamic ideas have developed over decades, through therapists listening to and trying to understand people. More recently, many longstanding psychodynamic ideas have begun to be supported by contemporary research. For example, infant development research, particularly around attachment, supports many psychodynamic ideas on how our minds develop within early relationships with caregivers (Berry, Bucci, & Danquah, 2019).

Psychodynamic ideas about psychosis

Psychodynamic theory argues that a psychotic state can arise in anyone, though some people are more prone to this than others. Psychosis is seen as emerging through the interaction of life experiences, psychological processes, and biological factors, with the relative contribution of different factors differing between individuals.

Psychodynamic theory offers a model for understanding psychological and social contributions to psychotic states. It suggests that our inner worlds shape our capacities to tolerate ('contain') painful mental experience, our habitual patterns of defences, and our liabilities to difficulties in challenging areas such as maintaining a stable sense of self, developing independence, and managing aggression and self-criticism. They also determine the meaning of life events and how stressful these feel. A psychotic state may develop when stresses cannot be handled through non-psychotic strategies. For example, someone's feelings of inferiority may become manageable only through development of fixed beliefs about having superhuman powers.

Thus, from a psychodynamic perspective, psychotic states, at least in some individuals, are understood as arising, in whole or in part, as a response to unbearable mental experience, and as having a possible self-protective function in relation to this. Whatever the cause of a psychotic experience, a psychodynamic view is that the *content* is always meaningful, as this stems from aspects of a person's inner world. Meanings may not necessarily be straightforward to untangle, however, particularly as psychotic processes may themselves make it hard for the person to reflect on the painful underlying issues.

Aims of psychodynamic therapy

Psychodynamic therapy aims to help people change problematic patterns in their emotions and relationships, so that they can feel, think, and relate to others more freely, and be less troubled by symptoms or distress. Particularly in its more intensive forms, it can be seen as aiming at deep-seated change.

When psychodynamic therapy is offered to people who experience psychosis it may sometimes also aim for deep-seated changes, such as integrating difficult aspects of mental experience. However, aims are often less comprehensive and depend in part on the severity of psychosis, the stage of recovery (Fuller, 2013), and how long therapy can be continued. They might include coping better, avoiding secondary effects on relationships, or reducing liability to relapse.

How does psychodynamic therapy work?

As for other therapies, the process of change in psychodynamic therapy is likely to involve a combination of elements, rather than one individual mechanism.

The experience of the relationship with the therapist is always central. It may contribute to change through aspects of what the therapist actually offers, such as their reliable empathic responsiveness. This may allow internalisation of a helpful, more compassionate relationship, and more self-acceptance. It may also contribute through the client's experiencing the therapist in ways that are distorted by the conscious and unconscious patterns of their inner world (a phenomenon known as 'transference'). The live emotional experience of interacting with the therapist, and together with the therapist considering the meaning of this experience, may be a crucial route towards increased capacity for self-understanding and change.

One route to change may be through the client consciously learning about patterns in their thinking, feeling, and ways of relating to others. They may become more aware of areas of difficulty and thus better able to manage these, or may develop enriched narratives about themselves, something which may itself be therapeutic.

Change may also occur through unconscious (procedural) learning leading to new patterns in the client's internal world, such as subtle changes in the ways they experience themselves in relation to others, and in their ability to tolerate emotions which had previously felt unmanageable. An example: a client felt that anger and criticism towards people he depended on, including the therapist, was unacceptable and would lead to rejection, but was troubled by violent hallucinations and unfounded fears about others being angry towards him. He thought sometimes that he had reasons to feel angry and was puzzled that he never actually felt so. Over time, repeatedly experiencing the therapist's openness to considering negative feelings towards herself, and her empathic non-judgemental responses when he was able eventually to express some of these, led to his feeling more accepting and aware of this aspect of his emotional life, and less troubled by hallucinations and paranoia. In other words, the experience of being with the therapist may be as important, or more important, than any conscious intellectual learning that takes place.

Psychodynamic therapy is generally not, as is sometimes thought, focused on uncovering childhood memories. However, exploring links between past and present experience may help self-understanding, and therapy may lead to the present feeling more clearly distinct from the past.

What happens in psychodynamic therapy?

An overview

In psychodynamic therapy, arrangements for sessions are intended to be very regular, predictable, and reliable for the client. As far as possible, time and place are always the same, and sessions start and finish on time. Compared with other therapies, particular care is given to these things.

Within sessions, there is no pre-planned structure or agenda. The client can speak about anything they wish, though the therapist's contributions help shape the session. Leading up to the ending of therapy, feelings about the ending itself usually become an important focus.

The therapist listens carefully to the client and may ask for clarification, or make comments, often focusing on feelings. Comments might be about the content of the client's words, about what the therapist notices, or about possible ways of understanding aspects of the client's experience ('interpretations'). They will not usually include advice.

Between sessions, clients may find themselves thinking about what has happened within sessions, or experience feelings stirred up by this. However, there are no formal homework tasks.

Before settling into therapy, there will generally be an assessment, to help therapist and client decide if the approach seems likely to help, and to begin a process of trying to understand the client's difficulties. At this stage, the therapist may sometimes ask more questions and direct the conversation more than they do subsequently.

Different people may have different experiences of therapy in part because of personal qualities of both therapist and client, and the consequently unique characteristics of every therapist-client relationship. This seems to be true even for the most strictly protocol-driven therapies (Firth, Barkham, Kellett, & Saxon, 2015), but may be more so still for psychodynamic therapy. Psychodynamic therapy experiences also vary according to the theoretical ideas the therapist uses.

The therapist's role

In psychodynamic therapy, the aim is to create a space where client and therapist can reflect on emotional experience and its meaning. The reliability of the setting is considered important to this, and in addition the therapist aspires to be trustworthy, non-judgemental, and non-retaliating, regardless of what is communicated by the client.

Above all, the therapist aspires to be open to moment-to-moment experience throughout each session. This means being receptive not just to the client's words, but to what they communicate unconsciously, perhaps through tone, hesitations and pauses, through the structure of a narrative or through feelings, facial expression, and shifts in breathing and posture. When a client's way of relating in therapy parallels recurrent patterns in their relationships elsewhere, the therapist will consider the possibility that this is because it reflects the client's inner world.

Being open to experience means for the therapist to be receptive also to their own moment-to-moment experience, such as their feelings and the ways they may feel drawn to respond to the client (often called their 'countertransference'). Aspects of this are thought to offer vital clues to what is happening for the client and in the interaction.

The therapist moves continually between a position of empathy and experiencing, and one of thinking and trying to understand. They consider especially the client's emotional experience, and possible unconscious meanings. What they say to the client is guided by their understanding of what comments they feel the client may be able to make use of.

There is clearly scope in any therapy for a therapist's perceptions, understanding, and comments to be influenced by their own inner world. This can contribute to empathic understanding but can have unhelpful effects too if the therapist's own anxieties and defences have undue influence. An instance of this might be when an emotional issue causing difficulty for the client, for example, the therapist seeming not to care enough, is not discussed because the therapist also has difficulty with the same issue. Measures to identify and minimise these unhelpful effects are integral to psychodynamic therapy. They include not just ongoing supervision, as is common in many therapies, but also the requirement for all psychodynamic therapists to undergo lengthy personal therapy as a central part of their training.

Classical approaches

In a classical psychodynamic approach, sessions are unstructured and the therapist's comments include interpretations about possible unconscious motivations. The therapist gives relatively little information about themselves, and behaves less like a friend or coach than in many other therapies. They refrain from responses intended primarily to relieve tension or satisfy the client's wishes, for example they will usually not engage in small talk, offer reassurance, or see it as their role to relieve uncomfortable silences.

These ways of working are intended to assist the process of understanding and change. The therapist's relative anonymity and neutrality mean that what happens in sessions is shaped more by the client's patterns of thinking, feeling, and relating, and less by those of the therapist. The therapist's refraining from actions to relieve tension means that difficult states of mind (such as frustration and disappointment) are experienced rather than avoided. There is thus more opportunity for therapist and client to explore difficult feelings together as they arise.

Modified approaches

Many contemporary psychodynamic therapists believe that, when working with clients prone to psychosis, they need to be prepared to modify their approach using supportive techniques.

Modifications include presenting a clear explanation of therapy, participating actively with an ordinary conversational style, helping the client to anchor themselves in a shared view of reality, avoiding undue escalation of anxiety, limiting the extent of free-association, and avoiding undermining adaptive defences such as a positive transference. The aim is an optimum balance between techniques intended to assist deeper psychological change and techniques which are supportive and make therapy achievable.

For some clients, such modifications mean that therapy is very different from a traditional approach, although the theory guiding the therapist's thinking will still be psychodynamic. The extent to which the therapist uses modifications depends on their judgement of what will be helpful at a particular time. It might vary within a single session and some therapies might begin with a supportive approach and move over time towards a more classical one. An example: In the early stages of a therapy, a therapist avoided leaving lengthy silences as she was aware that these simply strengthened the client's belief that she disliked him and was not going to help him. A year into the therapy, however, he had begun to confidently recognise such beliefs as coming from his own mind. Now, when a silence prompted such feelings, he and the therapist were able to use this as an opportunity to explore together what was happening between them.

How does psychodynamic therapy affect clients prone to psychosis?

Some clients find that psychodynamic therapy feels supportive and stabilising. However, it can evoke intense feelings, and even when the ultimate outcome is beneficial, some people also feel worse during the process. Sometimes feelings are overwhelming, and lead to therapy ending or to psychotic states emerging or worsening. Modified therapy approaches are designed to reduce the chances of this happening.

Some practicalities

Generally psychodynamic therapies tend to last longer than others. Six months would often be regarded as too brief to be helpful for someone prone to psychosis. A year might be seen as a minimum, two years as desirable, and longer therapies as often worthwhile, and capable of achieving more profound benefits. Psychodynamic therapy is typically offered weekly. More frequent sessions may be judged helpful for some people, for example when aiming for more profound change or when needs for support are greater. For people prone to psychosis, it is generally considered most helpful for therapist and client to sit face to face, in contrast to the classic image of therapy with the client lying on a couch. This chapter has focused on individual (one to one) therapy, though many psychodynamic therapists also work with couples, families, or groups.

Is psychodynamic therapy a useful option?

The evidence

The evidence available supports the view that, for some people who experience psychosis, psychodynamic therapy may be an effective intervention (Summers & Rosenbaum, 2013). This evidence consists largely of observational studies, and therapists' and clients' accounts of individual therapies.

Psychodynamic therapists have not traditionally used randomised controlled trials (RCTs). The six existing RCTs of psychodynamic therapy for psychosis offer conflicting findings, and as all have significant design flaws, they do not tell us whether psychodynamic therapy is effective or how it compares to other therapies (Summers & Rosenbaum, 2013).

One Danish study, although not an RCT, used a strong research design (Rosenbaum et al., 2012). This found that people with recently diagnosed psychosis who received supportive psychodynamic therapy plus usual treatment had significantly better average outcomes two years after starting therapy than a control group having usual treatment only

People prone to psychosis frequently have problems that can be categorised under more than one diagnosis. It is thus worth noting that there is considerable evidence for effectiveness of psychodynamic therapy with other diagnoses (Shedler, 2010).

As for all therapies, there has also been little research into adverse outcomes. One study (covering a range of diagnoses) found that on average 5% of clients reported lasting adverse effects, with no significant difference between different types of therapy (Crawford et al., 2016).

Should psychodynamic therapy be on offer to people who experience psychosis?

Regardless of therapy type, focusing on individual treatment risks distracting attention from societal contributions to mental health problems. Also, any therapy brings a particular world view, and thus possibly contributes to erosion of alternative cultural understandings.

For psychodynamic therapy, one specific disadvantage is that it is costly because of the relatively long therapy duration and therapist training. Training is typically around four years, with a requirement for lengthy personal therapy of at least this duration. Psychodynamic therapy also demands of clients a considerable time commitment. If it has additional benefits over cheaper therapies, these could justify additional costs, but research that would answer this question does not exist at present.

One argument for making psychodynamic therapy available to people who experience psychosis is that different therapies have effects on different aspects of psychological functioning and so may meet different needs (Adshead & Fonagy, 2012). Features specific to psychodynamic therapy that might give it unique value include its attention to emotion, relationships, and unconscious underlying factors, and its flexibility to adapt to individual needs. The relative length of therapy may be an advantage if longer therapies are needed to enable deep-seated, lasting change.

Lastly, there are arguments for offering people choice. This is clearly wanted by many who seek help, and may in itself, be therapeutic through supporting people's sense of personal agency.

Who should be offered therapy?

There are no simple criteria that indicate when psychodynamic therapy is a good choice. Psychiatric diagnosis is a poor guide, as people with the same diagnosis have different needs and preferences. Meeting with a therapist for assessment cannot confirm with any certainty if psychodynamic therapy will help but can at least allow therapist and client to gain some idea of whether they want to work together and what problems may be anticipated. For someone in an extreme state, who perhaps finds just being with another person unbearable, psychodynamic therapy is unlikely to be a first choice. However, even here, a period of carefully adapted contacts (Prouty, 2002) may make therapy possible at a later stage

What may affect the outcome?

For someone who has experienced psychosis, any therapy is likely to be more helpful if adequate attention is given to what the person needs apart from therapy. Some people in psychodynamic therapy may need support between sessions to allow exacerbations of distress to be weathered safely, and sometimes therapy only feels possible in a therapeutic community or inpatient setting. Many people have needs which can never be met by any therapy, for example for housing or employment. For some, support from family and friends plays a crucial part, and peer support may be very important. For some, medication may make therapy manageable, whereas for others it may be a hindrance.

Whether therapy is helpful will depend greatly on the particular therapist, their skills, their experience with psychosis, their personal qualities, and the quality of the client-therapist relationship. Good outcomes seem linked to a good early therapeutic relationship, where the client feels hopeful that the therapist is likely to help, but does not have excessive unrealistic expectations (Goldsmith, Lewis, Dunn, & Bentall, 2015). Before embarking on therapy, to be sure the therapist has at least a minimal level of skill, clients can check they are registered with a professional body, and have experience with psychosis.

The extent to which therapy helps is also likely to depend on its duration. Generally, for severe and complex problems, longer therapies seem more effective (Leichsenring & Rabung, 2011).

Current guidelines

UK guidelines (National Institute for Health and Clinical Excellence, 2014) do not recommend psychodynamic therapy for psychosis, though do support the use of supportive therapy and of psychodynamic principles to understand people's experience. Where research evidence is limited, as in this case, the usefulness of guidelines is correspondingly limited. There is also likely to be less consensus about what is appropriate to recommend. Norwegian guidelines, for example, suggest that supportive psychodynamic psychotherapy can be offered in to individuals with a history of past but not current psychotic experiences (Helsedirektoratet, 2013).

All guidelines based on a diagnosis of psychosis carry the additional disadvantages that diagnostic category may not be the main determinant of a person's capacity to benefit from therapy. The category 'psychosis' encompasses very different problems and needs.

Psychodynamic therapy or a mix of therapies?

A therapist who is familiar with more than one type of therapy may sometimes choose to offer a therapy which includes elements of different therapy approaches. They might give the 'hybrid' therapy a different name which reflects that it includes different elements, or they might simply use the name of their main therapeutic approach. This could happen with any type of therapy. This section has described psychodynamic therapy without such additional elements and so contrasts with the personal experience that Paul-Newell Reaves has shared in the previous section where the therapist has described the therapy as psychodynamic, but has added other non-psychodynamic elements, for example suggestions on coping techniques.

Conclusion

There are clearly unanswered questions around psychodynamic therapy for people who experience psychosis, and limitations to this chapter as a comprehensive summary of the range of theory and practice. I hope, however, that I have been able to convey something of the qualities that may lead people to value it, and to leave an overall impression of a therapeutic approach that, for some, is likely to be well worth considering.

References

Adshead, G., & Fonagy, P. (2012). How does psychotherapy work: The self and its disorders. *Advances in Psychiatric Treatment, 18,* 242–249. doi:https://doi.org/10.1192/apt.bp.111.009274

Berry, K., Bucci, S., & Danquah, A. (2019). *Attachment and psychosis.* Hove: Routledge.

Crawford, M. J., Thana, L., Farquharson, L., Palmer, L., Hancock, E., Bassett, P., . . . Parry, G. D. (2016). Patient experience of negative effects of psychological treatment: Results of a national survey. *The British Journal of Psychiatry, 208,* 260–265. doi:10.1192/bjp.bp.114.162628

Erwin, E. (2002). *The Freud encyclopedia: Theory, therapy, and culture.* New York: Routledge.

Firth, N., Barkham, M., Kellett, S., & Saxon, D. (2015). Therapist effects and moderators of effectiveness and efficiency in psychological wellbeing practitioners: A multilevel modelling analysis. *Behaviour Research and Therapy, 69,* 54–62. doi:10.1016/j.brat.2015.04.001

Fuller, P. (2013). *Surviving, existing, or living: Phase-specific therapy for severe psychosis.* Hove: Routledge.

Goldsmith, L. P., Lewis, S. P., Dunn, G., & Bentall, R. P. (2015). Psychological treatments for early psychosis can be beneficial or harmful, depending on the therapeutic alliance: An instrumental variable analysis. *Psychological Medicine, 45,* 2365–2373. doi:10.1017/S003329171500032X

Leichsenring, F., & Rabung, S. (2011). Long-term psychodynamic psychotherapy in complex mental disorders: Update of a meta-analysis. *British Journal of Psychiatry, 199,* 15–22. doi:10.1192/bjp.bp.110.082776

Lemma, A. (2003). *Introduction to the practice of psychoanalytic psychotherapy.* Chichester: Wiley Blackwell.

National Institute for Health and Clinical Excellence. (2014). *Psychosis and schizophrenia in adults: Prevention and management* (NICE guideline (CG178)). London: National Institute for Health and Clinical Excellence.

Norwegian Directorate of Health. (2013). *Nasjonal faglig retningslinje for utredning, behandling og oppfølging av personer med psykoselidelse (English summary: National guideline for assessment, treatment and follow-up for persons with psychosis)*. Retrieved from www.helsedirektoratet.no

Prouty, G. (2002). *Pre-therapy: Reaching contact impaired clients*. Ross-on-Wye: PCCS Books.

Rosenbaum, B., Harder, S., Knudsen, P., Køster, A., Lindhardt, A., Lajer, M., . . . Winther, G. (2012). Supportive psychodynamic psychotherapy versus treatment as usual for first-episode psychosis: Two-year outcome. *Psychiatry, 75*, 331–341. doi:10.1521/psyc.2012.75.4.331

Shedler, J. (2010). The efficacy of psychodynamic psychotherapy. *American Psychologist, 65*, 98–109. doi:10.1037/a0018378

Summers, A., & Rosenbaum, B. (2013). Psychodynamic therapy for psychosis: Empirical evidence. In J. Read & J. Dillon (Eds.), *Models of madness: Psychological, social and biological approaches to psychosis* (pp. 336–344). Hove: Routledge.

8

COMPASSION FOCUSED THERAPY (CFT)

Client's perspective

Mystic Leaf[1]

> I find compassion focused therapy a really interesting approach to working with the difficulties that can be presented by psychosis. It recognises the importance of the way we relate to or communicate with ourselves (e.g. with compassion or with criticism) in influencing our mental health. We live in a world dominated by competition and achievement, and so I can see the value of the ideas in compassion focused approaches.
>
> – Peter Taylor

What led me to receive therapy?

I am a 31 year old woman who had her first experience of psychosis at the age of 27. For much of my 20s, I was preoccupied with finding a romantic partner, with my search for love eventually delivering me into psychosis. My account, which comprises the first part of this chapter, focuses on the cultural influences and the sequence of events that culminated in that episode of psychosis, and the therapy that I received to help me.

Throughout this section, I refer to the framework of emotions put forward by Gilbert (2010). This suggests that we all have three emotional systems which govern the way we work towards our goals and feel about ourselves; the threat, drive, and contentment systems (see Figure 8.1). It is thought that when these three systems are out of balance, all sorts of problems can develop, including psychosis. The drive system is the human drive for status, relationships, or resources. When we achieve these things, we feel good about ourselves. If something has happened which restricts this drive system, for example losing a job, or culturally feeling unable to approach the opposite sex and initiate relationships, then the threat system is activated. This makes us feel stressed and unable to cope with the position we are in. In extreme circumstances this can lead to the development of psychosis. There is a rescue system that can help us cope with the threats we face, which is called the contentment system. When we feel stressed, if we can intervene with self-compassion and soothing, we are activating the contentment system. It has been suggested that this can prevent psychosis or reduce the severity of it.

My story begins when I was 24 years old. As a newly qualified doctor, I was about to embark on my career in medicine and felt I just needed a husband for life to be complete. I was led to believe that a highly eligible young man had shown an interest in me and would be introduced to me at the local Eid celebrations. When he did not show up, I was left feeling disappointed and angry. I was anxious to have a serious relationship that would definitely progress to marriage. I had been brought up to strongly believe that the man had to make the first move, either by texting, emailing, or approaching at a gathering and making conversation. These were the rigid rules of courtship that had been taught to me in little snippets throughout my life. So I started to follow the man from the Eid celebrations on Facebook, with the hope that he would eventually call or text. I became aware of his 'status updates' and his 'likes', and I started to feel like I was having a virtual Facebook friendship with him. As time progressed, I became more and more dissatisfied with being single and increasingly felt the need for mental and physical intimacy. The more dissatisfied I became, the more addicted and fixated I became to my virtual Facebook relationship with this man.

My medical career started to hold less and less importance in my life, and my need to find a life partner was slowly taking over. I was losing concentration at work, and I was spending long periods of time alone in my room, avoiding contact with colleagues and friends in favour of my Facebook life. My social circle diminished rapidly. It was around this time that I decided to leave my career in medicine.

I started to develop a belief in 'human angels'; specifically two people whom I followed on Facebook, whom I believed were there to look after me. Looking back, I can see that this was my first psychotic belief, but it seemed rational to me at the time. The first angel was a previous teacher from my time at university, who I had always admired and had a crush on. The second angel was one of his female friends on Facebook. She was a woman that I had never met, but I imagined to be a clever, compassionate mother figure who had achieved a lot professionally. Both these 'angels' were Indian and doctors, making them people that I held in high esteem. I believed that their job was to help me, and in particular to help me romantically secure the man from the Eid celebrations. I thought that simple actions like changing their profile pictures, adding friends, or 'liking' pages were intended to send me messages. They were the best friends I never had.

Around the same time, I developed a belief that my mother was putting my younger sister forward for the attentions of the man from the Eid celebrations. I viewed her as real competition as she was a doctor and therefore still had a lucrative job, whereas I was jobless and having to start my career from scratch again. I found this terrifying because it further eroded my sense of control over my life. The more I felt threatened by the competition from my sister, the closer I felt to the human angels emotionally. They were companion substitutes, particularly now that I had lost trust in the two people previously closest to me, my mother and my sister. The angels were now my closest support group and my main source of external compassion and soothing. Nobody else knew about the angels, only me.

As this psychotic belief intensified, other odd beliefs also developed. I started to believe that my father, through simple actions such as switching the lights on and off or drinking his tea, was trying to evoke sexual feelings in me so that I would only be attracted to Indian people. I was frightened when I had these thoughts. Following an outburst in which I woke up and shouted at him for trying to do this to me, my mother called the general practitioner who referred me to the Early Intervention for Psychosis Service (EIPS). It was then that I had my first experience with mental health services.

My experiences of other therapies

There was a psychology department within the EIPS, which provided therapy to help people make sense of their experience of psychosis. I was initially offered cognitive behavioural therapy with a clinical psychologist (see Chapter 2) but found this approach unhelpful. The approach came across to me as cold, factual, and objective, and I started to learn the correct and incorrect answers to give in therapy. For example, I knew that the correct thing to say was that "my thoughts about the man from the Eid celebrations are less strong when I spend more time socialising with friends", even though this was not true. I felt the psychologist was not connecting with my inner world, and was struggling to make sense of the psychotic ideas and tendencies I was experiencing.

My experiences of Compassion Focused Therapy

After a while there was a change in staff and I began to see another clinical psychologist who practised Compassion Focused Therapy (CFT). We had weekly morning sessions, which lasted one hour. I felt this to be about the right length of time, as I managed to say and explore everything I needed to in that period. Throughout therapy, the setting was the living room in my parents' house. I initially had about eight months of CBT. I almost felt I did not deserve this as I come from a background where counselling and therapy is seen as soft or for weak people, rather than a direct solution to fix a problem. Eight months seemed very generous, as I was aware of how much a session with a clinical psychologist would cost ordinarily! When they offered me another clinical psychologist for CFT, I moved the therapy to the 'indulgence' box in my mind, rather than seeing it as something I really needed. I did not have full insight into my problems at this time and I truly believed the paranoid thoughts, such as my sister being put forward for the man from the Eid celebrations. This made it hard to see the therapy as anything more than an indulgence.

Nevertheless, I felt I could open up during CFT, because of the way the psychologist related to me. She was very close to me in age, possibly a few years younger. She seemed gentler, and her voice was softer and more soothing. I emotionally took to her like a duck to water. In this psychologist, I saw a woman in a parallel world; single, just like me, and dreaming of getting married one day and 'having it all'; but it had not happened for her yet either. Maybe it was just that she was very professional, but she seemed to be coping admirably with it. Because she was not Indian, I did not feel embarrassed or ashamed to talk about these feelings openly.

This psychologist was also more receptive to material that was obviously very psychotic in nature, such as the 'human angels'. I never detected any shock or barriers to me discussing this material; the more I told her, the more comfortable I felt. The fact that she knew all aspects of my thoughts, from the human angels to the virtual Facebook world, meant there were no barriers. If I mentioned the paranoid thoughts that my mum was putting my sister forward for the man from the Eid celebrations, it was accepted without question. I think for clinical psychologists and other psychological therapists, the importance of being non-judgemental and really listening to a client talk about their 'psychotic symptoms' is a powerful, healing thing to do. Opening up about these issues made a huge difference.

I cannot remember exactly how the psychologist suggested CFT to me. I do remember that much of my conversation with her was focused on how low in mood I was feeling about not having a job or a partner. At the time, I thought that the goal of the CFT was to lift my mood, and it was only later that I learned that CFT was a treatment for the psychosis itself. I thought it was very kind of her to try to make me feel better about not having a partner or a job, but I wondered if this therapy would actually solve either of these problems, let alone the psychosis. I had my doubts, but I just went along with the sessions. I knew that I believed in angels, and I was convinced at the time that this was not psychosis and instead I was very spiritually developed.

Embarking on CFT involved using compassionate imagery. This was not straightforward, as I initially found the idea of self-compassion alien. The thought that other people are naturally nice to themselves was a real surprise to me. The second psychologist recognised my hesitation in this area, and rather than asking me to think of new compassionate images, she started to work with the images that I already had. She realised that the human angels were actually powerful, soothing images that helped me to deal with the daily blows of life and my feelings about myself. So rather than rejecting my psychotic belief in the human angels, she encouraged me to keep it as part of this process of using compassionate images. The psychologist explicitly and bravely said in therapy, "They seem to be a good thing, why don't we keep them and use them as a tool?" She was not judgemental and did not lead me to feel ashamed of these experiences. She emotionally engaged with my story and was sympathetic to my feelings and needs.

This process of asking about the human angels and encouraging me to keep focusing on them allowed me to continue to use the one area where I was actually being kind to myself. I would imagine the human angels saying soothing, comforting, and uplifting things to me. They would help me cope with being rejected from a job, feeling hopeless about my romantic situation, or having a fight with my mum. As well as encouraging me to listen to the human angels, the psychologist did also ask questions and help me think whether the human angels were actually looking out for me, or if they were just responding to information on Facebook. I gradually realised that they were not actively helping me, and although this discovery was disappointing and left me feeling more alone, the psychologist encouraged me to keep using them as images. I have continued to use the human angels as a tool to be more compassionate to myself until very recently, as the other psychotic beliefs that I had developed gradually disappeared. Looking back now, I can see the human angels were a way of engaging my contentment system; they were something that helped me cope or deal with the challenges I was facing in my life in the absence of other coping strategies.

We then started letter writing as the next part of CFT. This was more self-directed, in that I was not given any examples to follow. The goal was for me to write to myself in a compassionate and consoling voice about the challenges I was facing, and then to look at the letter in the sessions. I chose the content and usually it was heavily focused on not having a partner or a job. I would try to make the letters kind and consoling to myself about these things. This felt a bit uncomfortable, because I did not have the ability at this time to be compassionate to myself. I also did not believe, at an emotional level, the things I was saying to myself. I believed the negative and critical thoughts in my own head more than this new compassionate way of thinking. I would look at my psychologist's expression in the sessions and wonder if she even believed the more uplifting alternatives I came up with in the letters, or if deep down she saw what I saw in myself; a professional and personal failure with no job, no husband, no kids, and the label of 'psychosis'.

As part of the process of CFT, I wrote about 15 compassionate letters to myself. I initially felt that this was a tedious, time consuming, and 'soft' practice. I believed that it would not solve my more concrete problems of finding a job and a partner. On writing the first few letters, I noticed that whilst on the surface they sounded compassionate, I was not left feeling soothed. The psychologist and I examined the letters together and realised that I still had a critical voice coming through in the letters. This critical voice was the result of a lifetime of experiences, which pushed me to think certain thoughts and behave in certain ways. For example, my mother had always told me that whenever something bad happened, I should put it down to fate and destiny. So, in my letters, I was harshly telling myself "you must believe that the reason that you have not got a job is because of your destiny". I realised this was not the compassionate and understanding voice I was supposed to be aiming for in the letters, as I was telling myself to just get over my disappointments and carry on. We would therefore comb through the letters in our therapy sessions, and alter phrases to make them more soothing. For example, we changed the above to "I understand that you feel sad that you have not got a job. That feeling is normal and OK". This helped me to gradually start writing letters that identified my feelings and were accepting of them, although it still did not feel totally natural.

As time went on and we practised letter writing more, I became aware that the psychologist had a different internal climate to me. She was kind to herself and cut herself slack. She believed it was OK to have feelings, whatever those feelings were, and just to sit with them and let them pass. No ifs or buts, no analysis, it was fine to just let them come and go like clouds.

The psychologist would ask me how I was feeling, as an icebreaker at the start of the therapy session. I would fall into a slump, describing how low in emotion I was because of not having a partner or a job. I would look for an expression in her face that would confirm that things were indeed very grave for me. However, she would look light-hearted, positive, and maybe even amused. I wondered if she dealt with not being married in the same way she was encouraging me to, by sitting with her feelings, letting them pass and waiting until she felt better. Did she then move on with her life, rather than getting into a mad flurry, trying to desperately do something about not being married? Did she not feel the need to actually fix the problem, if she even perceived there to be one? That is when I realised I really wanted an internal climate like the psychologist's: one that automatically cushions you when you are low; one that helps you to keep perspective when things are sad and serious. This answered some of my doubts about CFT and motivated me to learn to be more compassionate to myself, so that I could have her outlook on problems.

We did hit the nail on the head at one point in our sessions, when we discussed whether I could approach the man romantically instead of the other way around. The psychologist said something that still sticks in my mind: "Sometimes you have to ask to get something good". That was a moment I really connected with her on a personal level. I imagined that if she liked a man, she would follow the philosophy in her head and 'ask for something good'. I became aware that being compassionate to myself could mean asking for good things for myself, not just accepting every bad thing as 'fate'.

As the psychologist encouraged me, I gradually became more comfortable to 'just sit' with the feelings. This is a technique called 'mindfulness'; instead of forcing negative thoughts away from my mind, I would sit with the thoughts and allow them to pass naturally. This was something I gleaned from the letter writing. One way of making the letters more soothing was to first identify the feeling and then to accept it, rather than analysing the feeling any further. I tried to do this at different times by anchoring my thoughts to the present moment, through concentrating on my heartbeat or breathing (e.g. by imagining a balloon filling my lungs). Then I simply waited for the feeling to pass without fighting the feeling at all. This meant that if I felt 'in a slump', I stayed 'in a slump', and just let it pass. I felt like I was teaching myself laboriously to do something that the psychologist did naturally, possibly even at an unconscious level. This technique was an amalgamation of the techniques I learned from the CBT sessions, CBT handouts, and the CFT.

Since the therapy ended, I have not sat down and written any more compassionate letters to myself, as I find it time consuming and depressing to see my dark thoughts on paper. I do however internally reword my thoughts, to make them more accepting of my feelings and more compassionate to myself. In my mind I also practise the above mentioned mindfulness techniques. Mostly when I am 'in a slump', thinking about my ever dwindling chances of finding a partner, I will use mindfulness techniques. I was already familiar with some mindfulness exercises that I had come across when I was 19 years old, in a book called *The Little Book of Happiness* by Patrick Whiteside (2000). The ideas that were introduced in therapy built on that prior knowledge and were not too alien to me.

When I finished the CFT, I felt that I had connected with the psychologist and almost made a friend. I say 'almost', because the professional line still remained. With my first experience of therapy, my contentment system, the system of soothing and calming that counteracts an overactive threat system, was not developed. It did not allow me to think about the psychotic ideas and intuitions I experienced. My way of being compassionate to myself was not identified and nurtured. With CFT, I was allowed to keep these compassionate images and also encouraged to write compassionate letters to myself to develop my contentment system. This helped me reach the point where I could find a job and start to rebuild my life.

Reflections on the Compassion Focused Therapy model

It was after the therapy that I was introduced to Gilbert's (2010) three system model, through a teaching session I was part of and a talk I gave with a clinical psychologist at a conference. I had no idea about this model during the therapy. I understand the drive system to be the energy and motivation to achieve the good things in life. Most of us are motivated to achieve the things in life which make us feel happy about ourselves and lead to internal thoughts such as 'I am successful'. In my case, I expected a good job would make me feel successful. In turn, I thought a good job would help me to get a partner, which would also lead me to feel successful and happy. However, I was struggling to get a job, which meant the thoughts in my head were not thoughts of success. Without a job, I felt that I had less chance of finding a partner, again leading to anxiety rather than happy thoughts. CFT suggests that people with a well-developed contentment system are able to ward off this anxiety by accepting difficult feelings and saying kind, uplifting things to themselves. I had not learned how to be kind to myself and so did not have this natural immunity or defence against these negative thoughts, and they were able to dominate my mental life.

My understanding now is that this imbalance ultimately led to the psychosis I experienced. Culturally, I believed that in order for a man to marry me, I would have to be a virgin and I would have to be young. These were qualities required to gain the good things in life: a partner, children, and happiness. I had neither quality, and my drive system was unable to change this. Without these two things, I could not compete effectively with the girls in my culture for a mate. This caused me a lot of anxiety, and again I was not counteracting this anxiety with a protective contentment system, and so the psychosis developed.

Conclusion

Since the therapy, I have found work as an assistant manager of a charity shop and I am focused on building my career. I am building up my hobbies and activities to expand my friendship group, keep myself psychologically healthy, and increase my chance of stumbling upon a 'Mr. Right'. My thoughts are now naturally more compassionate and I still use mindfulness techniques and internal rewording of thoughts to make them more compassionate. I have stopped visiting the angels on Facebook as I now see them as the gateway into my psychosis, something I no longer want in my life. However, as part of my therapy journey, I found the human angels helped me greatly as a tool. I am eternally grateful for the two psychologists that worked with me and the care that I received from the EIPS team. I am also grateful for the opportunity to write about my experience in this book.

Practitioner's perspective

Jon Crossley

Introduction

Compassion Focused Therapy (CFT) is a relatively new therapeutic intervention, which seeks to help people change the way they respond when they feel threatened or distressed. It builds on other therapeutic approaches and has been influenced by both scientific knowledge about the way the brain processes emotion, and spiritual traditions which emphasise the value of compassion (Gilbert, 2014a). It was developed to help people who frequently encounter shame and self-criticism, and has been found to be beneficial for a range of mental health difficulties including psychosis.

The key concepts

Two concepts in particular can be useful for understanding CFT. First there is the concept of the evolving human brain, which joins together the 'old brain' and 'new brain' (Gilbert, 2009a). The 'old brain' is the part of the human brain that is shared with mammals and other animals and has been active for millions of years. It developed in such a way as to optimise our chances of survival, and so is concerned with watching for threat and guiding us towards relationships, connectedness, and social status. Affirming emotions such as elation and contentment are effortlessly produced by success in these areas, while distressing emotions such as shame and fear are readily evoked by failure. The 'new brain' by contrast is only evident in humans. It evolved in such a way as to allow the use of symbols, a unique and distinctive characteristic of humans, which then enabled the development of language and other complex skills such as reflecting and imagining (Hayes, Wilson, Gifford, Follette, & Strosahl, 1996; Langer, 1967).

The joining of old and new brains has allowed our traditional abilities of navigating threat and connecting with others to be integrated with sophisticated communication and reasoning skills. This creates enormous potential for creative and adaptive behaviour and may in part explain our dominance as a species. However, the evolving brain also creates the conditions for a range of emotional problems unique to humans. Complex 'new' abilities such as imagination and reflection allow threat to be attended to long after it has passed. 'Old' emotions such as anxiety, which would previously have quickly dissipated as threat disappeared, can now be maintained by 'new' neurological activity. Humans can therefore continue to feel anxious long after a particular threat has moved away. This applies both to threats to physical safety, such as being attacked, and threats to social position, such as being criticised and overlooked. Other mammals do not have this same capacity, as they have not acquired the 'new brain'. A cat, for example, which has been locked out overnight will quickly settle on a chair, rather than agonising about the injustice of being left outside and who was to blame. This capacity for enduring and troublesome emotional states, due to new processing systems being overlaid on an old structure, is described as the 'tricky brain' (Gilbert, 2009a).

The second concept that helps to explain CFT is the three system model of emotion (Gilbert, 2014b). This framework, which is supported by research within the field of neuroscience (Panksepp, 2010), is a helpful simplification of the complex process of emotion. The model suggests that there are three systems that work together to regulate emotions; the *threat, drive* and *contentment systems* (see Figure 8.1). The *threat system* is the dominant system, which alerts us to danger by generating distressing feelings such as anxiety, anger, and disgust. This sense of unease prompts us to react in ways that generate more benign feelings, thereby regulating emotion. There are two contrasting paths for this regulation of emotion; via the *drive system* and via the *contentment system*. The *drive system*

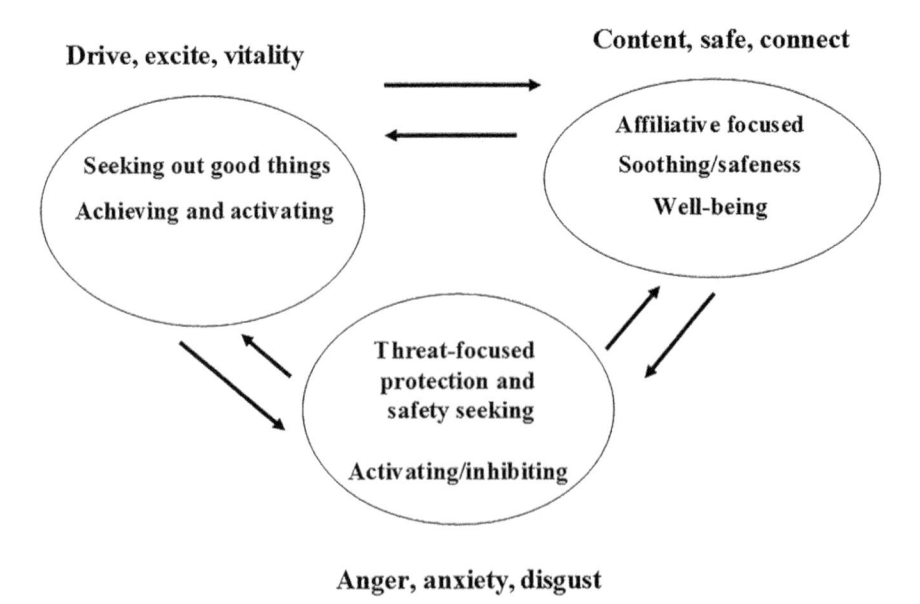

Drive, excite, vitality — **Content, safe, connect**

Seeking out good things
Achieving and activating

Affiliative focused
Soothing/safeness
Well-being

Threat-focused
protection and
safety seeking

Activating/inhibiting

Anger, anxiety, disgust

Figure 8.1 Emotion regulation systems. From P. Gilbert. (2009). *The Compassionate Mind*. With kind permission from Little, Brown Book Group

is concerned with attainment and achievement, which establishes emotional well-being by evoking excitement and stimulation. The *contentment system* in contrast seeks social connection and soothing to establish feelings of containment and safety.

Emotional difficulties arise when the three systems are not balanced. This can occur for a variety of reasons. It may be that the drive system is overactive in its management of threat due to being continually stimulated. Individuals are arguably vulnerable to an overstimulated drive system in the advertisement saturated environment of Western society, which is constantly communicating the need to be different (e.g. to acquire more possessions, to have better relationships; Holmes, 2006). Alternatively, the contentment system may not be active due to a lack of development. This might happen in cases of childhood neglect for example, where the contentment system is not nurtured in infancy by repeated calming and soothing from a parent or caregiver.

In such circumstances, when threat is regulated predominantly by the drive system, a relentless determination to overcome or avoid threat can result (Gilbert, 2009b). This determination can take on different appearances, depending on the nature of the threat, and the corresponding actions that are available to the individual. In the instance of the threat of inferiority for example, the individual may respond with an unremitting pursuit of achievement, or an incessant search for material possessions. By contrast, engagement of the contentment system would involve a softer and more consoling approach that tolerates the feelings of inferiority. This would reduce the sense of danger and relieve the need for unceasing accomplishment, thereby bringing balance to the three systems. This restoration of harmony across the systems is the aim of compassion focused therapy.

Psychosis: systems out of balance

The notion of psychosis is contested, with a lack of consensus in academic and clinical settings. There are a number of contrasting theories about the causes of what is known as psychosis, and also about how services and society should respond, as well as controversy over whether psychosis actually has validity as a concept (Coles, Keenan, & Diamond, 2013; British Psychological Society [BPS], 2014). A strong argument has been made that overwhelming feelings are critical to the onset of psychosis (Cromby, 2015; Garfield, 1995), and this is the position that will be taken in this part of the chapter. This theory is supported by different forms of evidence, for example research into the anomalous experience of hearing voices, which suggests thematic links between the content of voices and the emotionally overwhelming events that individuals have experienced (McCarthy-Jones & Longden, 2015).

Regarding feeling as central to psychosis is particularly helpful when considering CFT, with its focus on the regulation of emotions. Within the three system model, unbearable emotion represents a level of perceived threat that the individual is unable to regulate using the drive and contentment systems. The threat instead is expressed as 'out-of-the-ordinary' or anomalous experiences that we understand as psychosis, such as hearing voices or holding paranoid beliefs. These anomalous experiences may add to the level of threat the person senses. The experiences can be frightening in themselves, for example hearing voices that are critical and derogatory. Other people's responses, such as suspicion, avoidance, or ridicule, may cause further feelings of shame and self-criticism. Such feelings can interact with anomalous experiences in a self-perpetuating maintenance cycle that leads to an inflated and overstimulated threat system (Waite, Knight, & Lee, 2015). For example, an individual may feel threatened by derogatory voices and shout back, leading to rejection from friends, which results in further criticism from the voices, enhancing the sense of inadequacy. In this way the dysfunctional regulation of feelings, in response to social threats in particular, is understood to be at the heart of the development and maintenance of psychosis (Braehler et al., 2013; Cromby & Harper, 2009).

Compassion Focused Therapy for psychosis: theory

The goal of CFT is to cultivate the capacity for self-compassion, in order to allow the three systems to be balanced. Several different definitions of compassion exist, which differ slightly in nuance and content. CFT draws on a Buddhist informed definition of compassion that emphasises two elements (Gilbert, 2014b).

The first element is noticing, turning towards, and tolerating suffering, rather than avoiding or denying it (Epstein, 1995). Within CFT for psychosis, this involves turning compassionately towards threats such as anomalous experiences (e.g. voices) and self-critical thoughts rather than pushing these away. Turning towards the difficult parts of oneself that evoke shame and are typically avoided is in itself a threatening process, which therefore needs to be done carefully and gradually in order not to further inflate the threat system.

The aim in turning towards suffering is not to embrace this state of discomfort but to encourage change, the second principle of compassion. By recognising the suffering that is present, it is possible to foster skills and wisdom that provide different ways to respond to threat (Batchelor, 1997). Individuals sometimes have difficulty using their contentment system to regulate their threat system because of negative views that they hold about the value of soothing and compassion (e.g. it is a sign of weakness to show compassion). It is important therefore to draw attention to the value of self-compassion. This sets the foundation for shifting from shame-based self-criticism to compassion-based self-correction.

Compassion focused therapy for psychosis: practice

The practice of CFT for psychosis has several phases that do not necessarily follow a particular order. The different therapeutic techniques may be applied at various points during the intervention, depending on suitability and the preferences of the client. A useful place to start however is with psycho-education, which includes sharing the concepts of the tricky brain and the three system model. These concepts help to explain the persistence of difficult thoughts, emotions, and experiences, by highlighting that we interact with a threatening social environment using an emotional system that is ill-equipped for the task. This knowledge by itself can help to reduce self-criticism and shame, as well as providing a map for navigating a more self-compassionate path going forwards (Gilbert, 2014b). There is a five minute animated film 'Compassion for Voices' (Heriot-Maitland & Anderson, 2015) available online which helpfully illustrates these ideas and the process of CFT for psychosis.

Another early part of the work should be formulation, where the individual considers how their current and earlier experiences fit into the three systems model. By linking emotional experiences with the three system model, the person starts to recognise the ways that they are alert to threat and how their contentment system might be compromised or underused. An important part of this process is to help the individual to understand their relationship with compassion including any negative views they have of this. CFT research studies have identified that fear of compassion is common (Leaviss & Uttley, 2015) and it can be helpful to explore this anxiety.

This understanding paves the way for the important practical elements of CFT, which develop the capacity of the contentment system. Mindfulness, or attending to the present moment rather than being occupied with past worries or future uncertainties, can be a helpful state of mind to foster. There are a wide range of mindfulness exercises that may be employed to cultivate this attitude of attending to the moment, such as observing the body's posture or pattern of breathing, considering specific actions like eating or drawing, or noticing specific aspects of the environment such as particular colours, sounds, or objects (Bays, 2011). These exercises encourage observation of the body and mind without evaluation (Williams, Teasdale, Segal, & Kabat-Zinn, 2007). The therapist engages in the exercises with the client, to both model the approach and to demonstrate that mindfulness and self-compassion require ongoing practice and nurturing. The aim is for the client to practise the exercises between sessions, and materials such online audio-clips and mobile phone applications (or 'apps') can help establish this routine. This approach can initially be very challenging to the client, who may have learnt to be afraid of the flow of the mind, and these fears will need to be addressed during the therapy.

The use of imagery can also be very helpful at this stage. This can include imagining a familiar and special place or recalling someone who was caring and calm. The individual is encouraged to cultivate these images in detail, to evoke feelings of warmth and safety. Despite psycho-education about the value of compassion, it may only be when actually trying to generate a warm and supportive image that the individual realises how difficult it is. Research investigating CFT for psychosis found that many participants struggled to generate compassionate images, as they felt afraid of, or could not relate to, personal experiences of compassion (Laithwaite et al., 2009; Mayhew & Gilbert, 2008). A flexible approach is therefore needed, that does not rush this process and allows time to play with imagery. It may be helpful to focus on kind voices or faces as a starting point if imagining a compassionate figure is too difficult, or to use plants or animals as compassionate objects if human images are too threatening. The aim is to gradually develop an image which has the qualities of wisdom, strength, warmth, and acceptance (Gilbert, 2009a).

These exercises, involving mindfulness and imagery, serve as preparation for engaging with the two elements of compassion; turning towards anomalous experiences such as voices or paranoid beliefs that evoke shame and self-criticism, and responding differently to them. Mindfulness can gradually allow voices and overwhelming thoughts to be attended to and tolerated rather than avoided, and compassionate images can be drawn upon to prompt self-compassion when distressed.

There are several other techniques that can also be employed in CFT, for example chairwork and compassionate letter writing (Gilbert, 2009a). Chairwork allows the individual to occupy different chairs when acting out different systems or parts of themselves, thereby allowing the different aspects to talk to each other. The therapist initially encourages the client to express anxieties and concerns, which verbalises the threat system. The client then moves to a different chair and speaks for the contentment system by talking kindly and warmly to the original, now empty chair, that they were sitting in. This approach can be extended by having the client speak compassionately to their voices. The therapist asks the client to provide the perspective of the voices in the first chair, before directing the client to respond compassionately from the other chair. This opens a new dialogue with the voices, not characterised by fear, anger, or frustration.

The aim of letter writing is similar, with the client taking a compassionate position from which to write to themselves. They are encouraged to express understanding and acceptance of their situation, distressing feelings, and anomalous experiences, rather than being critical. It is important that these and other techniques are employed in a way that encourages a sense of warmth and connection, rather than inadequacy or failure that would further inflate the threat system (Gumley, Braehler, Laithwaite, MacBeth, & Gilbert, 2010). By engaging in these exercises, clients start to recognise the negative judgements they make of themselves, and begin to reshape these verdicts to be kinder and less critical.

The research evidence

As CFT is a relatively new intervention, there have been few formal research trials to date. Nevertheless there are different types of evidence suggesting that CFT holds clear potential for some specific presentations including psychosis. Firstly, there is support for the individual approaches included within CFT. Regarding mindfulness, there is a growing body of evidence suggesting its efficacy for a range of mental health difficulties. The research into mindfulness with psychosis is more limited (DiGiacomo, Moll, MacDermid, & Law, 2016), but preliminary evidence has indicated that mindfulness training can improve clinical functioning, increase mindfulness of distressing thoughts and images (Chadwick, Hughes, Russell, Russell, & Dagnan, 2009), and lessen paranoid beliefs (Ellett, 2012). The benefits of imagery-based interventions have similarly been established for a range of clinical presentations (Arntz, 2012), and there is initial evidence that positive imagery can reduce paranoia for those in the general population who have high levels of paranoid ideas (Bullock, Newman-Taylor, & Stopa, 2016). Chairwork with psychosis has received only very limited research attention (Chadwick, 2003), but wider research studies have suggested that chairwork is effective both as a standalone intervention and as an ingredient of psychotherapy (Pugh, 2017).

There have also been a limited number of research trials considering CFT as a specific intervention. A recent systematic review of the CFT research identified 14 well-designed studies (Leaviss & Uttley, 2015). This review concluded that CFT shows particular promise for individuals high in self-criticism, but the evidence is currently insufficient to show whether CFT is more effective than current standard treatments such as cognitive behavioural therapy (see Chapter 2).

There are few research studies at present considering CFT for psychosis; only three of the fourteen studies within the above review considered people with diagnoses that related specifically to psychosis. Braehler and colleagues (2013) conducted the first randomised controlled trial of CFT for psychosis, which systematically compared a 16-week group CFT programme to the usual treatment. It found that the group CFT programme led to greater clinical improvements, as rated by service users and clinicians, when compared to standard treatment. These improvements included an increase in compassion, and reductions in depression, negative beliefs about psychosis, and fear of relapse. The other two studies did not compare CFT with other interventions, but did find that CFT was well received by people who have experienced psychosis. Laithwaite and colleagues (2009) found that a therapy group based on CFT in a high security setting led to an improvement in self-image, and a reduction in experiences of depression and psychosis. Mayhew and Gilbert (2008) described three accounts where individual CFT led to hostile voices becoming less persecutory and more reassuring.

This summary of the evidence base emphasises that there is clearly more research to be done in this area, but the results to date are promising. It is important to recognise the challenge of engaging with CFT, however, for clients who experience psychosis. A qualitative study of the role of self-compassion in recovery found that the path to accepting psychosis as part of one's life experiences was particularly challenging (Waite et al., 2015). This emphasises the difficulty of turning towards suffering, as the typical response is to turn away. The study also identified how hard people found it to be kind to themselves when ill, which appears to be one of several potential obstacles to self-compassion identified within the literature (Leaviss & Uttley, 2015). Further research is therefore needed which investigates the process of CFT, and considers how these challenges are negotiated.

Final thoughts

Compassion Focused Therapy offers a unique blend of approaches and techniques, underpinned by a philosophy emphasising the inherent limitations with our emotional processing system, which allows distressing feelings to persist and expand. This understanding offers a more compassionate explanation of why mental health problems arise, and can serve to lessen self-recrimination and shame about the presence of such difficulties. The potential benefits of compassionate responses and validation from others is apparent in Mystic Leaf's account, and also in some recent research. Heriot-Maitland, Knight, and Peters (2012) found that anomalous experiences tend to be more manageable, less distressing, and less likely to lead to referral to mental health services if there is validation and acceptance by others. By contrast, individuals who have been referred to and accepted by services for anomalous experiences commonly feel trapped, marginalised, and subordinate in their relationships (Gumley, Braehler, & Macbeth, 2014). If mental health services are able to respond by offering validation and compassion, it is more likely that individuals will be able to develop a compassionate response themselves to the sense of threat that they are experiencing.

Note

1 The author has preferred to remain anonymous and use a pseudonym.

References

Arntz, A. (2012). Imagery rescripting as a therapeutic technique: Review of clinical trials, basic studies, and research agenda. *Journal of Experimental Psychopathology, 3*, 189–208.

Batchelor, S. (1997). *Buddhism without beliefs: A contemporary guide to awakening*. London: Bloomsbury.

Bays, J. C. (2011). *How to train a Wild Elephant, and other adventures in mindfulness*. Boston: Shambhala.

Braehler, C., Gumley, A., Harper, J., Wallace, S., Norrie, J., & Gilbert, P. (2013). Exploring change processes in compassion focused therapy in psychosis: Results of a feasibility randomized controlled trial. *British Journal of Clinical Psychology, 52*, 199–214. doi:10.1111/bjc.12009

British Psychological Society. (2014). *Understanding psychosis and schizophrenia. Division of clinical psychology*. Leicester: The British Psychological Society. Retrieved from www.bpsshop.org.uk

Bullock, G., Newman-Taylor, K., & Stopa, L. (2016). The role of mental imagery in non-clinical paranoia. *Journal of Behavior Therapy & Experimental Psychiatry, 50*, 264–268.

Chadwick, P. (2003). Two-chairs, self-schemata and a person based approach to psychosis. *Behavioural & Cognitive Psychotherapy, 31*, 439–449.

Chadwick, P. D. J., Hughes, S., Russell, I., Russell, D., & Dagnan, D. (2009). Mindfulness groups for distressing psychosis: A replication and feasibility study. *Behavioural & Cognitive Psychotherapy, 37*, 403–413.

Coles, S., Keenan, S., & Diamond, B. (2013). *Madness contested: Power and practice*. Ross-on-Wye: PCCS Books.

Cromby, J. (2015). *Feeling bodies: Embodying psychology*. Basingstoke: Palgrave Macmillan.

Cromby, J., & Harper, D. (2009). Paranoia: A social account. *Theory and Psychology, 19*, 335–361. doi:10.1177/0959354309104158

DiGiacomo, A., Moll, S., MacDermid, J., & Law, M. (2016). Mindfulness-based interventions in the treatment of psychosis: A narrative systematic review. *Canadian Journal of Counselling & Psychotherapy, 50*, 18–34.

Ellett, L. (2012). Mindfulness for paranoid beliefs: Evidence from two case studies. *Behavioural & Cognitive Psychotherapy, 41*, 238–242.

Epstein, M. (1995). *Thoughts without a thinker: Psychotherapy from a Buddhist perspective*. New York: Harper Collins.

Garfield, D. A. S. (1995). *Unbearable affect: A guide to the psychotherapy of psychosis*. New York: Wiley.

Gilbert, P. (2009a). *The compassionate mind*. London: Constable & Robinson.

Gilbert, P. (2009b). Introducing compassion-focused therapy. *Advances in Psychiatric Treatment, 15*, 199–208. doi:10.1192/apt.bp.107.005264

Gilbert, P. (2010). *The compassionate mind*. London: Constable-Robinson.

Gilbert, P. (2014a). Compassion-focused therapy: Preface and introduction for special edition. *British Journal of Clinical Psychology, 53*, 1–5. doi:10.1111/bjc.12045

Gilbert, P. (2014b). The origins and nature of compassion focused therapy. *British Journal of Clinical Psychology, 53*, 6–41. doi:10.1111/bjc.12043

Gumley, A., Braehler, C., Laithwaite, H., MacBeth, A., & Gilbert, P. (2010). A compassion focused model of recovery after psychosis. *International Journal of Cognitive Psychotherapy, 3*, 186–201. doi:10.1521/ijct.2010.3.2.186

Gumley, A., Braehler, C., & MacBeth, A. (2014). A meta-analysis and theoretical critique of oxytocin and psychosis: Prospects for attachment and compassion in promoting recovery. *British Journal of Clinical Psychology, 53*, 42–61. doi:10.1111/bjc.12041

Hayes, S. C., Wilson, K. G., Gifford, E. V., Follette, V. M., & Strosahl, K. (1996). Experiential avoidance and behavioral disorders: A functional dimensional approach to diagnosis and treatment. *Journal of Consulting and Clinical Psychology, 64*, 1152–1168. doi:10.1037/0022-006X.64.6.1152

Heriot-Maitland, C., & Anderson, K. (2015). *Compassion for voices: A tale of courage and hope*. Retrieved from http://compassionforvoices.com/videos/compassion-for-voices-film

Heriot-Maitland, C., Knight, M., & Peters, E. (2012). A qualitative comparison of psychotic-like phenomena in clinical and non-clinical populations. *British Journal of Clinical Psychology, 51*, 37–53. doi:10.1111/j.2044–8260.2011.02011.x

Holmes, G. (2006). Toxic mental environments. *Clinical Psychology Forum, 164*, 39–43.

Laithwaite, H., O'Hanlon, M., Collins, P., Doyle, P., Abraham, L., Porter, S., & Gumley, A. (2009). Recovery after psychosis (RAP): A compassion focused programme for individuals in high security settings. *Behavioural and Cognitive Psychotherapy, 37*, 511–526. doi:10.1017/S1352465809990233

Langer, S. K. (1967). *Mind: An essay on human feeling* (Vol. 1). Baltimore: The Johns Hopkins Press.

Leaviss, J., & Uttley, L. (2015). Psychotherapeutic benefits of compassion-focused therapy: An early systematic review. *Psychological Medicine, 45*, 927–945. doi:10.1017/S0033291714002141

Mayhew, S. L., & Gilbert, P. (2008). Compassionate mind training with people who hear malevolent voices: A case series report. *Clinical Psychology and Psychotherapy, 15*, 113–138. doi:10.1002/cpp.566

McCarthy-Jones, S., & Longden, E. (2015). Auditory verbal hallucinations in schizophrenia and post-traumatic stress disorder: Common phenomenology, common cause, common interventions? *Frontiers in Psychology, 6*, 1071. doi:10.3389/fpsyg.2015.01071

Panksepp, J. (2010). Affective neuroscience of the emotional brainmind: Evolutionary perspectives and implications for understanding depression. *Dialogues in Clinical Neuroscience, 12*, 383–399. Retrieved from www.ncbi.nlm.nih.gov/pmc/articles/PMC3181986/

Pugh, M. (2017). Chairwork in cognitive behavioural therapy: A narrative review. *Cognitive Therapy & Research, 41*, 16–30.

Waite, F., Knight, M. T. D., & Lee, D. (2015). Self-compassion and self-criticism in recovery in psychosis: An interpretive phenomenological analysis study. *Journal of Clinical Psychology, 71*, 1201–1217. doi:10.1002/jclp.22211

Williams, M. G., Teasdale, J. D., Segal, Z. V., & Kabat-Zinn, J. (2007). *The mindful way through depression: Freeing yourself from chronic unhappiness*. New York: Guilford.

Whiteside, P. (2000). *The little book of happiness*. Kansas City, MO: Andrews McMeel Publishing.

9

OPEN DIALOGUE (OD)

Client's perspective

Nick Hayes

> Most of the therapies described in this book happen on a one to one basis. Nick's account of Open Dialogue (OD) recognises that having those who are important in your life take an active role in therapy can create common ground to move forward together. Those who have experienced depression will recognise the effort it takes to find hope when it is lost. Such apparently simple shifts are often key events in the process of recovery.
>
> – Naomi Fisher

I have been seeing a team who use the psychological therapy approach called 'Open Dialogue' (OD) following a period of time in hospital due to difficulties with mania and low mood. In this chapter, I hope to explain how valuable and instrumental they have been in helping me get back to full health. I will begin by outlining my background, and what lead me to receive OD, before going on to discuss what this approach was like, including the benefits and challenges as I experienced them.

Background

Following a breakdown in 1997, I had enjoyed nearly 20 years of being completely healthy before my latest illness, and for much of that time I had been free from any medication. Although in 1997 I had a tentative diagnosis of bipolar and was treated with lithium, I was fortunate enough not to suffer from any depressive symptoms. I left hospital and went about my personal and professional life without really thinking of myself as bipolar or a manic depressive, or even as having any mental health issues. During this time I was never absent from work, neither high nor low, and just living through the normal challenges of ordinary life. The breakdown was simply a chapter in my past that had been closed.

That was until, in the summer of 2016, I had a second breakdown which was brought about through very particular stresses at work. In my original breakdown, I had been manic for a period of nearly six months, refusing medication and disputing any diagnosis before eventually responding to a second spell in hospital. On this occasion, my mania came upon me very suddenly over a weekend and I found myself in hospital by the Monday. At times during the breakdowns I have experienced, I have lost touch with the context of my behaviour and the appropriateness of my actions. During these periods of psychosis I have acted in a way that was unsettling and potentially frightening. Following the second breakdown I experienced, I was treated with Olanzapine (a medication often used for psychosis), stayed in hospital for two weeks, then left with the belief that history had repeated itself and this was just another chapter that I, again, could close.

It has been the most challenging aspect of my experience to accept that my condition is no longer one that I can simply turn the page on. Whereas in 1997, I had a prolonged mania and no low, at the end of the summer of 2016, I was stricken by a heavy bout of depression. Not only did this come as a huge blow and a great shock, but I found it much more difficult to cope with than any of the other aspects of my condition. I was barely able to sit down, not able to read, could not watch the television, lost my appetite, could hardly speak, and even struggled to find solace from sleep. I returned to the psychiatrist who offered Fluoxetine to balance the olanzapine. Later, when the depression continued to drag on, the doctors suggested lithium as it had been part of my treatment before. Those three drugs (lithium, Fluoxetine, and Olanzapine) now make up my medication. The depression continued to linger despite the drugs. While I was at my lowest, I was having daily visits from the crisis team, usually a pair of psychiatric nurses who would visit for a short period each day. I never met the same team twice, and the visits were largely just a checking in to make sure I had not slid towards self-harm or worse.

I was, and still am, grudgingly taking the medication, but have always sought alternative treatments beyond pharmaceuticals. During the summer of 2017, whilst still struggling with my low mood, I received Open Dialogue intervention. My depression has now largely lifted and my mania has not returned and that may be due to my regular medication. However, I have returned to a demanding job in an influential managerial role and I put the success of my recovery down in large part to the Open Dialogue treatment that I received from the autumn until the present. I have also seen a private therapist, had telephone counselling, and continue to see the counsellor at the school where I worked. It is therefore important to say that the combination of these treatments may have been what helped me. However, by far the strongest component has been that of the Open Dialogue sessions – it is those which have been a constant through the darkest days and those which have helped pull me through.

Content of the therapy

I have to thank my wife for introducing OD into my life. When I fell ill she was obsessed with finding solutions to my illness. It was she who found me therapists, she who researched medication on the internet, and ultimately she who found a contact for OD. At first it looked like a dead end as the project was only being piloted in our area, but with my wife's unfailing tenacity and charm, she managed to convince the social worker leading the pilot to take me on. I am forever thankful for her drive to make it happen. For those reading this chapter who are interested in OD, this approach has been developed in Finland, but is starting to be piloted and implemented in many new locations and health services, including the UK.

One of the key aspects of OD therapy is that it takes place wherever the client chooses. In my case this was at my home. As someone who has spent time in two psychiatric hospitals, I can see the value of using a safe space for the sessions – just having tea and water on hand has brought about a sense of calm and a willingness to disclose happily. It has meant that two or three members of the OD team come to visit me in my kitchen every two or three weeks or every week depending on my health. The sessions usually last about one to two hours. On occasions there has been a time limit, but often the discussion has developed at its own pace and I have been allowed to lead the debate to some kind of conclusion or resolution. The team of three included a social worker, a psychiatric nurse, and a peer mentor (i.e. someone who has suffered from mental health problems themselves). I have enjoyed the contributions from two peer mentors who have spoken frankly about their own experiences and willingly answered questions. There is nothing as vivid or startling as someone unpacking their own experiences.

I have been very fortunate in enjoying the contributions of two very different peer mentors. Due to a change in circumstances, the original mentor gave way to a new mentor and their contributions have been startlingly rich and relevant. As someone who suffered from the same kind of highs as myself, she brought with her some of the vocabulary that was previously lacking. When you are high you 'follow the signs', which is exactly what I felt during periods of mania, while she also spoke about the momentum of events taking hold by themselves and the challenge of knowing when to listen to the warning signs and to stop enjoying the ride!

The most uplifting element of her involvement has been her success in leaving behind medication and illness and her inspiring ability to move forward with her life and get involved in many exciting projects. As someone confronting the confusing crossroads of life after bipolar, I found her to be an authentic figure of inspiration.

There are two key features of the interaction which took place as part of the OD sessions I had. Firstly, there is a very open and frank disclosure of feelings and experiences. I am asked how I feel and how my week has been and I am free to open up. There is a supportive and sympathetic audience for my account – I do not feel the rush to summarise or edit, nor the need to conceal or overlook details. The pace of the sessions is led by me and my feelings. The sessions build over time since the same team members come to each session. This is the opposite of the crisis team meetings, mentioned above, which each involved different faces and the re-telling of the same story over consecutive days. I have grown to know and to trust the OD team and they have come to know my story. There seems to be huge power in sharing my feelings to those who are listening. I felt stronger and lighter and more hopeful after the early sessions. I found the language of the OD meetings to be very accessible, and it avoids clinical expressions. I was free to bring my own vocabulary, but often this was also questioned by the team – what do I mean by 'breakdown'? What do I mean by 'depression'? I am made to reflect on myself and my claims, to think more clearly about myself and to acknowledge the weight of words. Language is pivotal to the experience. Conventional clinical vocabulary can be alienating and value laden – the OD sessions encourage me to make my own sense of my symptoms and my own language. I barely recall using the term bipolar at all, but we did talk about feelings and emotions and hopes at great length.

The second key feature of the sessions are the moments of reflection. At spontaneous moments in the sessions, the team members would ask my permission to stop the discussion and reflect on what has taken place. This open review of events was incredibly powerful. I recall moments when the team reflected on my account of my breakdown. They reflected to each other about feeling my pain and frustration and that my breakdown was not random or something to feel guilty about but understandable and justifiable. It was remarkably liberating to talk about the situation at work, the pressures that had been building, the untenable place I found myself in, the lack of support, the crushing isolation of my position. More powerful still was the response of the OD team as they reflected on my story. They felt my pain. They shared their recognition of the weight that was upon me. They validated my breakdown – they made it OK to have broken in the face of so much unremitting pressure. This was a key point in launching my recovery. Within a group, with the three OD members, my wife, and my parents, to hear that validation and that acknowledgement was fantastically positive. I was in an environment in which my words were being heard, my journey was being shared, and my condition was no longer my problem.

Alongside the sessions, I have been to meetings with a counsellor and a therapist. These have proven useful, but in their intimacy and private contexts (just involving myself and the therapist in the room), they lack the power and weight of the social interaction of OD. I found that an important part of OD is that it demands that the testimony is not simply recounted but challenged as well. The team helped me to explore the meaning and values that lay behind the language and terms I used.

The voice of others is crucial to the experience. I had lost all my confidence and sense of self. I talked about myself in the past tense, for example 'I used to be a good teacher'. It was one of the team who stopped me short and said that I was still a good teacher. I said the words myself and they sounded like they might be true. What seemed to be impossible in my head now seemed possible – perhaps even likely when spoken out loud.

There is more to OD than simply talking and reflecting, but in essence, it is those acts which helped bring me out of my depression and looking forward to a healthier future.

A further way in which OD differs to other types of therapy and other types of mental health services is the active involvement of the people that know me (my wife, my parents) in the sessions. These others were encouraged to become an active part of the discussions and reflections that took place in those sessions. Having these others there was pivotal.

The sessions have always involved my wider family – most importantly my wife who has played a critical role in almost all of the sessions. It is easy for me to overlook just how grounding her presence has been and how she helped my confidence grow in the early exchanges. These were occasions where the darkest details of my feelings and experience were shared – it was empowering to share them with 'outsiders' while having the closest 'insider' at my shoulder and covering my back. She could see what the greatest problems were to those around me particularly when I was in a very closed-off and private world. Later in the treatment we even invited our two young children to the sessions, but they were happy to offer brief 'hellos' and disappear to have their tea!

Challenges

This is not a treatment that has helped me back to work and back to myself in an instant. It is something that has developed from autumn 2016 to the summer of 2017. Only in the early months of 2017 did I find that I was pulling free from the depression. Nonetheless, I remember the first meeting brought me a moment of joy – one of the team members insisted I had hope. Hope. It was a concept that had disappeared and now returned to me. I had nothing in the tank – no happiness, no job, no driving licence, and no future. But suddenly, in her insistence, she gave me hope, and that was how it started.

Working with a peer mentor has been incredibly fertile, but the challenge was overcoming my own prejudices. While I always thought of myself as someone who had a breakdown but not someone with a condition or ongoing mental health difficulty, I have had to re-evaluate that idea. I have had to connect with the peer mentor and appreciate that we share more than I might previously have wanted to accept. I remember the peer mentor talking about writing down her feelings each day – just a few words or even a picture. I have taken on that idea and now have an elaborate log of my days from September 2016 to the present. It has been invaluable in dealing with the darker days.

There are emotional challenges to confront in the sessions. We have had to talk about some very personal and painful events – there have been tears and sometimes people have felt like they did not want to continue. Certainly, my parents found the sessions heavy going and considered not coming back. There was an emotional weight to some of these sessions and the suggestion of some sort of blame. My mother's father suffered from depression and actually received Electro-Convulsive Therapy (ECT), so my mother feels a kind of responsibility for passing on those genes. This was brought up in discussion and found to be very sensitive area. Fortunately they reflected on their decision and returned.

It is remarkable just how involved my parents have become since OD has been part of my treatment. Twenty-one years ago, I had my only other episode and it was notable just how distant my parents were from the whole process. They found it impossible to understand what had driven their son to act and talk so out of character. My highs brought with them aggressive language and confrontational behaviour which they found hard to fathom. They responded by retreating from the situation and becoming less, not more, involved – the medical experts could be left to take charge.

The difference today could hardly be more stark. The OD team are greeted almost like extended members of the family, and despite that moment of stress noted before, my father and mother have been there at almost all the subsequent sessions. As the situation evolves, there has been talk of extending the sessions to include some other friends and family members. The atmosphere is so receptive and healing that this suggestion does not seem unnatural, but a logical extension of the work we have done so far.

My OD sessions have worked for me because everyone involved has been willing to listen, and to share, and to accept the disagreements. This might be disagreements between family members over how to return to work, how to manage stress, or how to reduce medication.

I have pushed to reduce medication and my wife has been more reluctant, but we have both voiced our opinions and found some common ground. The potential to have these sorts of discussions in the open, in a facilitative and supportive environment, with the important parties included as a part of the debate, is one of the strengths of OD. I have got the sense that the OD team are looking to put the emphasis back on the client – their role is to oversee, but it is up to the individual to lead and seek guidance rather than be led.

What I got from therapy

OD is a new therapy, particularly to the UK and, as noted, it was the persistence of my wife who eventually hounded the lead of the treatment to take on my case as part of a pilot study. I now suggest to my wife that in doing this she saved me. It seems to be that simple. Over the months of the treatment, I have returned to my professional position, started to regain my confidence and restored my faith in the future.

I have started on the path to coming off medication, my Olanzapine dose is now minimal, and I intend to withdraw from the other medications in the next year.

The members of the OD team have become much more than simply part of a medical team. I have a trust in them like no other human beings outside my family. From the very first meeting I felt I was in the hands of people who could help me. They made an instant connection and have held me ever since. They have enveloped me with their support and my debt to them is immense. In celebrating the success of OD, I have spoken at a conference about my experiences and taken part in a discussion group as part of the training for those learning about OD. The therapy has not only made me well but also presented me with opportunities to challenge myself and experience new things.

Latest news

More recently, I have suffered increased pressure on my return to work. This has not been normal everyday pressure, but the threat of suspension, losing my job, and destroying my career. It is almost exactly like the chaos which brought about my illness a year ago, and it is with a great feeling of regret that I have to admit to returning to hospital following a second manic period and breakdown in the face of these work related pressures. The OD team were not able to keep me out of hospital, but they were there to help me as my crisis grew, and maintained their links through my brief stay in hospital and now during the rebuilding. The familiarity of the faces involved and the fact they visited me in hospital, which can be the most stressful and disorientating of places, was invaluable. Since coming out of hospital, I am now working at moving forwards and possibly moving on, without the stresses of work to contend with. I have regular network sessions with the OD team and my family and have arranged to see a peer mentor independently, as she might be able to provide some more insight into my experiences. This is an opportunity and a freedom, which marks out OD as particularly helpful.

Going into hospital for a short time allowed me to see just how different the experience of more conventional psychiatric care can be, when compared to OD. In my two week stay, I was able to build relationships with only one nurse as the shift patterns revolved, there was no discussion about my life outside the hospital, and no talk of what would come next. Conversations with the psychiatrist were hurried and brief. The noisy patients received more care in an effort to keep them quiet, while the quiet ones were allowed to be happily sedated. There could be no greater contrast to the atmosphere and content of the OD sessions.

While I thought my journey with OD was coming to an end, I can see now that my relationship may just be opening up. During this most recent breakdown, I assert that it was the presence of two of the OD team at the moment of crisis that helped prevent the crisis from deepening into a more dramatic psychosis. The value of a familiar face amidst such internal and mental turmoil cannot be underestimated. Nonetheless, I have some disappointment that the support I was getting was not enough to see me successfully through my work troubles, but the team have not judged me in any way, and they continue to hold me through this difficult transition. Without their support, this latest breakdown could have been catastrophic. Instead, I am hopeful that it is just an opening up to bigger and better things. As we continue to meet, there is an acknowledgement that the teaching career as I knew it may be gone. However a life in higher education may suddenly be a reality which I never believed possible.

Practitioner's perspective

Niklas Granö

What is Open Dialogue: conceptual background and principles

Open Dialogue (OD) is a treatment approach for psychotic illness that has a long tradition in Finland and Scandinavia. OD is based on a need-adapted approach to the treatment of psychosis, which is the result of the Finnish national schizophrenia project in the 1980s (Alanen, Lehtinen, Räkköläinen, & Aaltonen, 1991). The need-adapted approach to treatment emphasises rapid intervention, the planning of treatment based on the specific needs of the client and their family, and carrying out assessment and treatment with a psychotherapeutic attitude (Alanen et al., 1991).

According to Professor Jaakko Seikkula and his group (Seikkula et al., 2003), the main idea in OD is that every client is treated using psychological therapy together with their own support systems (e.g. the existing supportive relationships they might have with friends or family). This is carried out through dialogical communication between the treatment team, the client, the client's family, and other members of their close social network. 'Dialogism' refers to a type of interaction where each participant feels heard and responded to, where every member of the network has his or her own 'voice' or points of view, which are separate, and equally valid, within the OD meetings. This acceptance of multiple different, unique perspectives is called 'polyphony' (Olson, Seikkula, & Ziedonis, 2014). 'Dialogical communication' in OD therefore means that everyone who is present in the care meeting can take part in the discussion regarding the client's treatment from their own viewpoint and expertise, as a spouse, as a parent, as a nurse or as a psychiatrist. Everyone in the meeting is equal and allowed to express themselves. This therapeutic conversation within these OD meeting, incorporating multiple perspectives, creates possibilities for a positive change. These joint meetings are arranged on the basis of the client's needs, with the frequency of the meetings depending on their preference. The choice of which other friends and family members are involved in the meetings is also tailored to the client's needs and preferences. As such, the aim is to help the client alongside their personal social support network, using a shared language, with the aim of creating a shared understanding of what is happening for the individual in their time of crisis.

The aim in OD is to support not only the client, but also their family and close social network. OD has its roots primarily in a type of therapy called Systemic Family Therapy (see Chapter 3) as well as in psychoanalytic traditions. In contrast to Systemic Family Therapy, however, OD is more like an overarching structure of how the treatment is arranged involving clients, therapists and network so that every 'voice' can be heard and responded to. In OD it is important to integrate different therapeutic methods into the treatment, based on the needs of the client. OD has its base in dialogism and the polyphony of voices within a network, which might lead to the use of different therapy forms. Within OD, meetings are often based on seven principles or elements, which are present in meetings and structuring the OD approach to care, but other specific treatment elements may be brought in depending on need. Hence, OD can be described more as an individually tailored treatment approach, rather than a rigid therapeutic framework. The seven original treatment principles of OD according to Seikkula et al. (2003) are as follows:

The provision of immediate help: The staff member at the clinic who first responds to the client's contact will arrange their initial meeting within 24 hours. The purpose of immediate response is not only to prevent any delay in care, but also to prevent potentially negative experiences such as hospitalisation in as many cases as possible. This is especially important for avoiding negative experiences for the client, such as the stress of involuntary referrals or compulsory admissions.

A social network perspective: As well as the client, their whole social network (including family members, friends, and other important members of the client's social life) are invited to the first meeting. The aim of inviting individuals that are close to the client both socially and emotionally is to allow the client and their family to feel safe and supported in their first meeting. A second purpose of this is to share the experience with family and friends to facilitate everyone's understanding of what is happening and what it means.

Flexibility and mobility: As the main component of OD is to tailor the methods of therapeutic intervention for each individual and their changing needs, this treatment aims to be as flexible as possible. The treatment is planned meeting by meeting, in accordance with the client's needs. Following the client's period of acute psychosis, treatment can be organised in a more structured form, for example, as one-to-one psychotherapy. In order to provide this kind of support, the mobility of the client's support team is a fundamental requirement in OD. Meetings can be arranged at home, at an outpatient clinic, or at inpatient unit at the hospital, to ensure that the narrative and dialogue between the client and their social network is continuing.

Responsibility: To ensure continuity, it is important that the original staff member who responded to the client's contact takes responsibility for organising the first meeting. This person will then become an important member of the client's specific support team, and will be responsible for inviting other staff to be involved in the client's support team.

Psychological continuity: The client's specific support team is responsible for the whole treatment process, regardless of whether the treatment takes place in a hospital or at an outpatient service. All different treatment methods, both psychosocial and pharmacological, are discussed in meetings and decided based on the client's needs. Ensuring psychological continuity helps keep a strong connection and ease of communication between the client, their social network, and the care team.

Tolerance of uncertainty: During a client's first experience of psychosis, when they are struggling to understand what is happening to them, there may be a heightened risk of the individual making poorly informed decisions. These kinds of situations may be worrisome, and lead to hasty treatment decisions. Tolerance of uncertainty means that, in OD, the focus is to create a secure feeling in the treatment by having daily meetings for the first 10–12 days. After this, the frequency of meetings is based on the needs of client, and their family and social network. Frequent meetings are needed to ensure that the client feels secure in the treatment, and to ensure that the dialogue between the client and the treatment team is an ongoing process. This helps to avoid premature decisions (e.g. compulsory admission, or to start medication when it would not be necessary). Tolerance of uncertainty can be seen as an active attitude among the therapists, to work together with the client and their social network, aiming for a collaborative approach, instead of the treatment simply being a reaction to what is happening for the client (Seikkula et al., 2003)

Dialogism: All of the principles in OD support the core idea of creating and promoting a dialogue between the client, their social network, and their support

Table 9.1 Seven original treatment principles of Open Dialogue (Seikkula et al., 2003).

Principle	Description
1. The provision of immediate help	The staff member at the clinic who first responds to the client's contact will arrange their initial meeting within 24 hours.
2. A social network perspective	The whole social network (including family members, friends, and other important members of the client's social life) are invited to the first meeting.
3. Flexibility and mobility	The main component of OD is to tailor the methods of therapeutic intervention for each individual and their changing needs, this treatment aims to be as flexible as possible.
4. Responsibility	To ensure continuity in this process, it is important that the original staff member who responded to the client's contact takes responsibility for organising the first meeting.
5. Psychological continuity	The client's specific support team is responsible for the whole treatment process, regardless of whether the treatment takes place in a hospital or at an outpatient service.
6. Tolerance of uncertainty	In OD, the focus is to create a secure feeling in the treatment by having daily meetings for first 10–12 days. This helps to avoid premature decisions.
7. Dialogism	OD support the core idea of creating and promoting a dialogue between the client, their social network, and their case-specific team.

team. The dialogical conversation is seen as a forum where families and clients have the opportunity to increase their sense of agency in their own lives by discussing the client's difficulties and problems (Haarakangas, 1997). Instead of having a specific interview procedure, the team's aim in constructing the dialogue is to follow the themes and the way of speaking that the family members are used to (Seikkula et al., 2003).

A video interview with Jaakko Seikkula about the principles of OD is available online (www.youtube.com/watch?v=Ph212sLDQd0).

What does OD look like in practice?

A fictional example may help to make the principles of OD more understandable. The example below is derived from experiences of an early intervention for psychosis team, in which OD was applied, focused on individuals deemed at high risk of psychosis (Granö et al., 2016).

Aino is a 15 year old girl who has started to have difficulties in school, and has unexplained absences. Aino has contacted the school nurse because she is having problems with sleeping. The nurse is worried about Aino as she looks depressed, and in a further meeting, Aino tells the nurse that she sometimes hears voices when she is alone. The nurse contacts the early intervention team, who work using the OD approach. A staff member on the team suggest that a network meeting could be organised. Staff from the clinic call Aino to discuss this with her, and ask for permission to contact her parents and invite them to the meeting. Both Aino and her parents think it would be best to arrange the meeting at Aino's home. The meeting is scheduled for the next day. In the meeting at Aino's home, Aino tells the group that she is anxious about the voices that she hears, because sometimes they say evil things, like "You are bad. You are a loser, Aino. Aino, I hate you". Aino does not understand where the voices are coming from, and she is afraid of being mad, which makes her very anxious. She has started to avoid going to bed in the evening, because she is scared of the voices. Instead, she listens to music through her headphones until late into the night, as she does not hear voices when she is listening to music. This means that she does not sleep enough, and then she is often late for school and cannot concentrate in lessons because she is so tired.

In the first meeting, treatment options are discussed with Aino, her parents, her care team, and the nurse. Even though the situation is concerning, everyone feels that Aino will be safe at home until the next day. A psychiatrist from the team prescribes an anti-anxiety medication to help Aino sleep. The next meeting at Aino's home is arranged for the following day. During that meeting, Aino says that she feels less anxious after she has had some sleep, and she is less afraid of the voices. Aino tells the group that she is being bullied at school, and that she has problems with her parents who divorced two years ago. Aino's parents have also been worried about their daughter since they divorced. First everything seemed everything to be OK with Aino, but after she moved to a new school, she became isolated. She struggled to make new friends, and she did not want to continue her hobby of dancing by joining a new group, due to the bullying she was experiencing. Aino grew up on the other side of country, and speaks a different dialect to the other children at her new school, which they find funny. Later, Aino feels able to tell the group that she had been worrying about her parents, as she knows that they have been struggling financially, and Aino did not want to add to their stress by asking for money for her dance classes.

During the meetings, Aino understood that she did not need to be worried about her parents' finances, and her parents understood that that they could talk more openly about their new life situations, and their new spouses. Aino came to understand in meetings that her parents' divorce was not her fault, and that her parents' earlier arguments were not because of her. Aino felt able to tell the group that the voices had told her that she is bad and evil and she felt relieved when she was able to tell her parents this. During the network discussions, Aino gradually built up an alternative understanding of her negative beliefs about herself (e.g. she is not bad and a loser). The group also discussed the experience of psychosis in more general terms, and it was a relief for Aino and her parents to understand how common it is to hear voices, and to understand that this is not always a sign of illness, as they had feared.

Aino's support team suggested that she should invite her teacher to a meeting to discuss how the school could help Aino. Her teacher suggested tailored school days, where Aino could start her day later by arranging an individual learning program, to avoid missing early lessons. Additionally, Aino received one-to-one support at school for mathematics. During the meetings, Aino's teacher gained a new understanding of Aino's behaviour. She had previously thought that Aino was lazy and defiant, but her teacher gradually developed a much more empathetic and supportive attitude, which made Aino feel better in school. The school nurse also suggested that an anti-bullying program could start to work with Aino. In discussions with Aino and the bullies, the bullies came to understand that Aino was not a snob, but shy and anxious. In turn, Aino understood that the bullies' behaviour in school did not originally have bad intentions, but was just their way of expressing their interest in Aino.

During the meetings, which took place mostly at Aino's home, Aino's anxiety and worry about the voices reduced, and hospital care could be avoided. Medication for psychosis was discussed, but as the situation quickly improved and Aino did not want medication, the medical treatment instead included anti-anxiety medication, and later some antidepressant medication. During the treatment, Aino reported that the intensity and frequency of the voices reduced. Aino did not worry as much about her parents, and the extra support she received at school helped Aino to keep up with her work and pass exams. The bullying stopped and Aino made some new friends. Aino was able to continue her old hobby of dancing. However, sometimes Aino still thinks about herself in negative ways, and tends to blame herself for a lot of things. Psychotherapy has been discussed for her future care. The frequency of meetings has now been reduced to twice a month.

Evaluation of Open Dialogue in the context of broader psychosis literature and clinical implications

OD has been shown to be more effective than if a person has standard treatment (Seikkula et al., 2003; Seikkula, Alakare, & Aaltonen, 2011), even though OD has not been studied in randomised trials. As OD can be described more as a way to organise care, rather than as a specific therapy method, it should be evaluated in this context. Even though OD was originally designed for people experiencing psychosis during a mental health crisis, these seven principles can be adapted partly or completely to other clinical settings (e.g. Granö et al., 2016). There are several reasons why the seven core principles behind OD may be helpful for people experiencing psychosis:

First, *the provision of immediate help* is essential during a mental health crisis. If a psychotic episode cannot be prevented, the aim is then to reduce the amount of time that a person is not receiving support for their difficulties as much as possible, as research has shown the benefits of early treatment (Melle et al., 2008). Second, the *social network perspective* is important because individuals are often young (Schulze-Lutter et al., 2015), living at home with their parents, and going to school, and so social networks will have so much influence over their lives. Hence, involving the family and network in care is essential. Third, *flexibility and mobility:* mobilising the family and social network to support the client gives much more opportunity and capacity for therapeutic input than standard therapy sessions at a psychiatric clinic, and tailored meetings at home or at school make it easier for the client to attend, and avoid the stigma associated with going to a mental health facility. Fourth, *tolerating uncertainty:* psychosis-like experiences are relatively common (Linscott & van Os, 2013) and do not automatically lead to psychosis, even though these experiences themselves can be distressing, and require the same kind of support (Lindgren et al., 2014). Psychotherapeutic methods are recommended as an initial treatment of choice for young people who are have psychosis-like experiences, and this can ensure that the individuals do not experience further or more extreme distress (Schmidt et al., 2015). In this sense, OD's principle of 'tolerating uncertainty' helps to avoid premature decisions (e.g. involuntary referrals, starting medication when it would not be necessary). Fifth, *psychological continuity and responsibility*: changes in social and occupational functioning (Schulze-Lutter et al., 2015), and neuro-cognition (Bora et al., 2014), as well as psychotic experiences in the early course of psychosis often make it difficult for clients to be able to attend appointments at clinics. To use same familiar therapeutic settings and clinicians throughout the care from the first contact may reduce the risk of leaving the service early. Sixth, *dialogism*: The sense that is made of a client's experiences can also be a cause of stress, particularly where pessimistic interpretations are made (e.g. assuming the young person will never recover). Working with both clients and their families, recognising their different voices and the sense they have made of the psychosis, and providing an alternative perspective (for example, normalising such experiences by sharing information on how common these experiences are) can make real changes in a client's life, both in reducing stress in the family and in increasing support.

In summary, OD can be seen as a core structure that can be used to organise psychiatric care. This structure can be added to, step-by-step and meeting-by-meeting, based on each individual and their circumstances, in order to include relevant therapeutic elements, and clinical evaluation in accordance with the therapeutic work.

References

Alanen, Y., Lehtinen, K., Räkköläinen, V., & Aaltonen, J. (1991). Need-adapted treatment of new schizophrenic patients: Experiences and results of the Turku Project. *Acta Psychiatrica Scandinavica, 83*, 363–372.

Bora, E., Lin, A., Wood, S., Yung, A., McGorry, P., & Pantelis, C. (2014). Cognitive deficits in youth with familial and clinical high risk to psychosis: A systematic review and meta-analysis. *Acta Psychiatrica Scandinavica, 130*(1), 1–15. doi:10.1111/acps.12261

Granö, N., Karjalainen, M., Ranta, K., Lindgren, M., Roine, M., & Therman, S. (2016). Community-oriented family-based intervention superior to standard treatment in improving depression, hopelessness and functioning among adolescents with any psychosis-risk symptoms. *Psychiatry Research, 30*, 9–16. doi:10.1016/j.psychres.2016.01.03

Haarakangas, K. (1997). The voices in the treatment meeting. A dialogical analysis of the treatment meeting conversations in family-centres psychiatric treatment process in regard to the team activity. *Jyväskylä Studies in Education, Psychology and Social Research, 130*, 119–126.

Lindgren, M., Manninen, M., Kalska, H., Mustonen, U., Laajasalo, T., Moilanen, K., . . . Therman, S. (2014). Predicting psychosis in a general adolescent psychiatric sample. *Schizophrenia Research, 158*(1–3), 1–6.

Linscott, J., & van Os, J. (2013). An updated and conservative systematic review and meta-analysis of epidemiological evidence on psychotic experiences in children and adults: On the pathway from proneness to persistence. *Psychological Medicine, 43*, 1133–1149.

Melle, I., Larsen, T. K., Haahr, U., Friis, S., Johannesen, J. O., Opjordsmoen, S., . . . McGlashan, T. (2008). Prevention of negative symptom psychopathologies in first-episode schizophrenia: Two-year effects of reducing the duration of untreated psychosis. *Archives of General Psychiatry, 65*, 634–640.

Olson, M., Seikkula, J., & Ziedonis, D. (2014). *The key elements of dialogic practice in open dialogue* (Version 1.1). Worcester, MA: The University of Massachusetts Medical School.

Schmidt, S. J., Schulze-Lutter, F., Schimmelmann, B. G., Maric, N. P., Salokangas, R. K., Riecher-Rössler, A., . . . Ruhrman, S. (2015). EPA guidance on the early intervention in clinical high risk states of psychoses European psychiatry. *European Psychiatry, 30*(3), 388–404. doi:10.1060/j.eurpsy.2015.01.013

Schultze-Lutter, F., Michel, C., Schmidt, S. J., Schimmelmann, B. G., Maric, N. P., Salokangas, R. K. R., . . . Klosterkötter, J. (2015). EPA guidance on the early detection of clinical high risk states of psychoses. *European Psychiatry, 30*, 405–416.

Seikkula, J., Alakare, B., & Aaltonen, J. (2011). The comprehensive open-dialogue approach in Western Lapland: II. Long-term stability of acute psychosis outcomes in advanced community care. *Psychosis, 3*, 192–204.

Seikkula, J., Alakare, B., Aaltonen, J., Holma, J., Rasinkangas, A., & Lehtinen, V. (2003). Open dialogue approach: Treatment principles and preliminary results of a two-year follow-up on first episode schizophrenia. *Ethical and Human Sciences and Services, 5*(3), 163–182.

10

PERSON-CENTRED THERAPY

Client's perspective

Jules Haley

In this chapter, Jules and Peter describe how the person-centred therapist aims to empathise with the client's inner world, and to support them in finding and using their innate resources to work towards recovery. In particular, I feel that Jules' account of therapy emphasises the importance of establishing and re-establishing the connection with her therapist, and of the validation that came with having someone sit alongside and witness her experiences. Jules also discusses the complications involved in communicating difficult experiences in a self-directed setting, and how flexibility in the therapy relationship can help to overcome such issues.

– Olympia Gianfrancesco

By the time I entered therapy I had a few attempted overdoses and 25 plus years of serious drinking under my belt. I was motivated to look at goal setting and wanted to sort out my low self-esteem and mild depression issues. I felt that if I could just fix these problems then I would be truly happy and all would be well. My first counsellor was a humanistic integrative therapist who I saw for 18 months. At that time, I was sober but empty, feeling deeply alone and purposeless. My world began to fragment; I was failing to reach an emotional balance. I was experiencing what I later learnt were flashbacks and hallucinations to previous experiences of trauma that I had buried. Beetles swarmed over and covered the floor, rooms contracted, rockets took off, and headless bodies appeared frequently in my dining room window. I was referred to the local mental health community team by my therapist who had unhelpfully decided that this was the time for her to withdraw her services and refer me on to others. I felt rejected, abandoned, and feared being labelled as psychotic. I know now but did not then that all these experiences were in an altered, highly anxious, and traumatised state. They all had their seeds in actual experiences of trauma or were symbolising that trauma. As my therapist seemed to be freaked out by it, this increased my distress further. Today I worry that there are not enough therapists willing to sit alongside trauma, to witness, touch, and hold the pain of others. When my experiences were perceived by health professionals through the lens of 'mental illness', I felt that sight and acceptance of me as a whole person was sadly withdrawn and lost.

Following withdrawal of my therapy and at the height of my distress, the community psychiatric nurse suggested that I 'voluntarily' present myself at the local hospital. The alternative solution offered was high doses of medication. In fact, my psychiatrist was about to prescribe a dose over the recommendations set out by the UK's National Institute for Health and Care Excellence (NICE). I suggested that he checked this, and I was meant to be the clueless one! I was declared too ill for any form of talking therapy and sent home to take the medication like a good patient. But my world still escalated out of control. I stopped going to work as advised by my GP. On reflection, this was not a great move as I lost all sense of routine, and any connection I had to the outside world died. I paid off my mortgage and planned my funeral. I even made suggestions to my partner about who I would approve of as my replacement once I had passed away. I did not want to die but I certainly did not know how to live.

I was referred to Jan by my previous therapist. I was told that 'she would know what to do' and was a 'genuinely nice person'. To be honest, at the time, I really did not care who Jan was, and it did not matter what she said in the first meeting. I would have seen anyone. On arrival for my first session, Jan offered me a hot drink. This meant that she had already passed my 'nice person' test, which at that time was my only criteria. I have heard later about the whole debate on whether offering a drink is crossing professional boundaries, but I find it comforting and welcoming, and it gives me something to hold onto when times are tough in therapy. She explained a bit about her person-centred approach, but what stayed with me was her explanation of how she believed in equalising power within the therapy relationship and taking a non-expert position.

Person-Centred Therapy is led by the client and is non-directive on the part of the therapist. However, it is the therapist's responsibility to create the right psychological environment; one of acceptance, empathy, and genuineness necessary for change to occur. In my experience, my therapy has been self-directed, as "it is the client who knows what hurts, what directions to go, what problems are crucial, what experiences have been deeply buried" (Rogers, 1961, p. 11). I had to learn how to get what I needed from Jan, but that meant finding out more about myself and my needs in order to articulate them. This may sound like progress. However, it was not easy and took years of hard inner work and painful reflection.

Establishing and maintaining psychological contact

For the first year, I saw Jan for an hour twice a week, and despite my desire to talk to someone, the progress was extremely slow. I found it incredibly difficult to identify and express my emotions and communicate anything that would indicate what was going on inside my busy head. I was afraid of being judged and felt that I somehow had to say the right things, but even this eluded me. Week after week we sat in silence as Jan left the session open, as Person-Centred Therapy is self-directed. It felt like I was drowning in my own isolation. Jan kept checking how the silence was for me, but even just replying to say that it was difficult felt out of reach for me at that time, so we struggled on. I felt re-traumatised at times and even more alone, until I realised that Jan was not going to rescue me and that I had to do something.

I eventually managed to break out of the habit of sitting in silence by emailing after the therapy session, usually out of sheer frustration. Jan had not suggested emailing; it was something that I initiated. I would write long emails going into detail about what was happening. I was able to process my emotions as I typed them after each session, then I held my breath and pressed send. Sometimes I would receive a detailed reply within 48 hours. At other times, I specifically asked her to just print the email and keep it for the next session. On rare occasions, I would panic and ask her to ignore the email, something that she was not able to do. She took it as a sign that the content was important and I was given the message back that I was not to be ignored. Emailing became an established way of working until I no longer needed it. I later learnt that this was not Jan's usual way of working, but that it seemed to her to be the only way of coming alongside my process and keeping any psychological contact with me. On reflection, this is true. If we had not established some form of dialogue outside of the sessions in those early fragile months, she would have lost me as a client and my life today would be very different. She took a risk supporting me in this way, and for that I am truly grateful, but I feel for others who do not have a therapist who is willing to meet them where they are.

Silence was not the only barrier to psychological contact that we had to battle early on in our therapeutic relationship. As well as having nightmares, flashbacks, and high anxiety, panic attacks and dissociation were also common. One of the first things that Jan taught me was how to breathe. It could be argued that this was not within the purist non-directive person-centred approach, but for me it was invaluable at keeping hyperventilation at bay and really helped build my trust in Jan's ability to keep me safe. I remember her asking me to describe times of emotional distress and asking what they looked like. She was really trying to understand what was happening for me. I gradually began to let her into my world, but struggled with feelings of embarrassment and shame. Over time I have been able to explore those younger parts of me that needed healing and support. I would often dissociate in our sessions but Jan was able to help keep me grounded. If we had a particularly difficult session, she would ask about my plans for dinner. She learnt early on that I was real foodie and so used this connection to bring me back to the here and now. She knew that this part of me could be relied on to get me home in one piece. Jan has always gone the extra mile to ensure that we keep psychological contact. In the early days when she went away, we would Skype, and this even included once when she was on holiday. Jan has always encouraged me to reach out for support and connect with others, something that was alien to me at that time.

Boundaries are flexible, not absent

Boundaries are really important to me as they help me feel safe, protected, and in control. Early on in therapy, Jan focused on creating an environment that felt safe. We talked about the room, and certain items were removed that I found triggering as they prompted old memories or feelings. They are still banned to this day! I remember once asking if we could light a candle at the beginning of each session so I could blow it out and symbolically leave my concerns in the room from one week to the next. The following week, Jan had bought a new glass candle holder, and some months later, when it was appropriate, she disclosed that the candle holder was not used by anyone else. It was mine. This was important and symbolic, as at the time I was dealing with issues of loss, choice, and ownership. We have joked that she would be in terrible trouble if she ever broke it as it is very precious to me. I remember the first time that she gave me a jar of homemade jam. It made me realise that maybe if I gave her a gift I would not be rejected.

I often feel her empathic understanding as we try to work together through my experiences. I value her expertise and her ability to hold me in all my complexity, but I now have also come to value her flaws, mistakes, and clumsiness. What I found helpful is taking bits of her willingness to share her humanity and 'way of being' into my life and making it my own. She is a great mirror of the person-centred core values of empathy, genuineness, and acceptance. This is in stark contrast to the hours I have spent in front of my own reflection shouting messages of hate. I have learnt from Jan through this mirroring to have more compassion and love for myself and for others.

There are other traditional boundaries within therapy that we cross, however these are always negotiated if any flexibility is required in advance. Examples include the length of session. I have a weekly 90 minute session, because the traditional 50 minutes does not work for me as my pace is slower. Occasionally this has been extended to two hours, but this is arranged in advance and usually with a specific reason. We actually stick to our fixed time and day, and only twice in the last five years have we run over, which was when I was in distress. We have an arrangement that if we ever go over by 15 minutes, my partner rings the bell. I usually see Jan at her home as she is in private practice, but occasionally, if there is a specific reason, Jan may make a home visit. This first happened when I had just moved house. As my family have never visited and friends were non-existent, I very nervously asked Jan if she would hold a session at my new house. She later said that it was a very moving request and that she knew it was important to me. She came with gifts for different aspects of me, a crystal glass window hanger to capture the light, a star tea-light holder because she said I am a star, and a soft polar bear for comfort. She was encouraging me to once again embrace and value all of me.

I remember once we sat in silence for 40 minutes and just held hands. That was all I needed at that time, just to be held and not questioned or talked to (and I did not want to talk either). I just needed a companion. For me, touch, the physical safe connection to another human being, has been very healing, but I realise this is controversial area within therapy. I remember watching a film where Carl Rogers held hands with a client and this somehow really validated my experience with Jan and helped me to process why it is so important. There have been various layers of need for touch, to keep me grounded and connected, to re-establish psychological contact when rupture occurred, or for comfort when distressed, which at times felt deeply spiritual and became a prayer. Occasionally I would physically become cold, almost frozen, so her physical passing of warmth through her hands helped me to thaw.

Self-directed sessions

I always find the start of each session difficult. Once the candle is lit, Jan will sit on her sofa opposite mine. Her opening is usually something like 'where are we starting today?' At this point I freeze because I know that it is now over to me. She will not lead, give advice, or even say very much. For someone who has felt out of control for most of their life, this is sometimes overwhelming. I have tried so many different strategies to overcome this fear. I usually arrive with a prepared list of things that I need to talk about and I get that out of my bag ready for this dreaded question. Due to the predictable freeze which descends on the room, I usually fail to offer the list, and if I am feeling particularly paralysed, deny all knowledge of the long list sitting next to me on the sofa, which usually has well over 90 minutes of content. Reviewing the week's activities is often a helpful starting place for the session. There have been sessions when I have managed to, with encouragement, work my way through the list of issues that I planned before the session, but there have also been many times when the notebook was left unopened. Progress has been slow and gradual, and not always linear. Five years on and sometimes we are back to emailing when times are tough.

One significant therapy session was when we read through a healing service written by the priest Jim Cotter (1990). It was my belief and trust in the strength of our therapeutic alliance that empowered me to bring my request to therapy in the hope that it would not be rejected. The session was simple, moving, and healing. It was so powerful and impactful that I had to re-read the liturgy when I got home as I knew that I had blanked parts of it. Jan spoke the words from the service, 'be in love with life', and these five words marked a significant shift in my thinking and helped end my relationship with suicide. I decided to commit to giving my life rather than taking it. Some may argue that perhaps this session was not Person-Centred Therapy because we used a structure from another approach, in this case a church liturgy. However, I would counter that it was client-led and it was not something that I would have been able to share with anyone other than Jan.

I have tried many ways to communicate in the sessions. Jan has gently encouraged me to write poems or my journal and to read various psychotherapy or recovery-focused books. There were times when I did read a particular book because she felt it would help me at that time, and it did encourage me to find my own answers, but some of her suggestions were not right for me and this took time to work out. I fell in love with writing as a way of healing, and I enrolled on a journaling course and a Gestalt freefall writing course, which encourages the use of writing as a creative therapy. I was able to go quite deeply within myself through writing and I established it as a routine. I would take my writings to therapy but again that paralysis would take hold. Jan and I found ingenious ways around this issue and came out the winners. One session involved reading the poem backwards, word by word, and line by line. It did not make sense but my words were out and witnessed. We once had an unusual evening when we agreed to use clay in the session. Jan threw the clay and the noise scared me half to death. We never did return to clay!

Trust – a two-way dynamic

Trust has been fundamental to our therapeutic relationship. My antenna has always been sensitive to trust and it is not something that comes easily to me. I was brought up to rely on myself and not to reach out to others. I have tested Jan on many occasions. Sometimes she has passed, and when she has failed, although it has been difficult, we have managed to work it through.

On one occasion, I had a difficult session, so we had agreed that she would email some changes to our planned appointments rather than discuss this in the session, because I was struggling to concentrate. One of her holiday dates had been extended, but the extension clashed with a session we had already rearranged. My partner protectively and sarcastically remarked that this was a 'great way to tell you'. I borrowed her anger and repeated this back at Jan via text and was assured by my partner that Jan could take anger.

We ended up in a situation that we now call 'appointment-gate'. Jan did not respond to my text so two days later I phoned her, mainly because I was worried that I had done something wrong by sending the angry text, but also because I was feeling mentally unwell. When Jan answered the phone, I was once again struck by muteness. She asked about my anger at her and I asked why she had not replied. She said that she had 'accepted' my anger but would not reply to 'that' message.

In a following session, I was about to tell her that she had used 'counselling bullshit'. I only got as far as say that "it was counselling . . ." and she interjected, "that is what you pay me for". I was so upset because I valued Jan for our therapeutic relationship, for her attitude, her way of being, everything that it felt like she was destroying. But the one thing that moved me was the fact that she admitted that she had been excited about her holiday but had not checked her diary. This excitement really resonated with me and showed her humanity. This is the only serious incident in five years that needed work on both sides to repair, but by this point we had a well-established relationship, so she had credit in the bank!

There was another period when I questioned her empathy. I desperately needed her to either agree or try to understand how and why I felt responsible for experiences in my past. I tried for weeks to get her to come alongside my point of view. I finally understood when she explained that her beliefs and values stopped her from agreeing with me, she point blankly refused to play ball. I am grateful for her stance on the issue of guilt and blame, and although difficult, it helped me to process and begin realigning my acquired false responsibilities.

I had been seeing Jan for about three years when someone asked me how I knew that my therapy was 'working'. There is a danger that the person-centred approach can be seen as just having a cosy chat and then feeling better afterwards. This has never been my experience. It is a completely different environment to what is usually experienced in day to day life. To have someone ready to truly hear and be accepting and willing to work alongside me, but who did not give advice, meant that it placed responsibility firmly on my shoulders to actually do the work. I changed because my experience was validated, not ignored or pathologised. Jan trusted that I was able to tap into my inner resources and guide my own healing process. In my darkest days, I was offered hope and love by another, and that sometimes felt uncomfortable or at worst overwhelming. Jan gave me hope that life could change. She encouraged me, knowing that I had been suicidal in the past, to let her know if I felt that way again. This was not so she could talk me out of it, but out of her concern that I do not sit with those feelings alone. I knew that she would hold hope, and occasionally, when despair began to rear its head, I would send a message asking her to light my candle. I often doubted that she would, but I now believe that she faithfully lit it every time. It was something that Jan once said in response to my wish to have a larger kitchen, a simple 'that would be great' that made me feel that change was possible. It planted a very deep seed.

Jan has encouraged me to embrace, trust, and value all parts of me, and when I have become frustrated with the most negative and destructive parts, it was her acceptance that helped stop my striving to eradicate them. I stopped fighting and began very gradually to have some compassion for myself. She was never judgemental or seemed surprised by any of the content that I brought into our sessions. She was encouraging even when I felt that my disclosures may result in a complete breakdown and the onset of madness. Instead she repetitively and reassuringly told me that I was 'going sane'.

Conclusion

So, why do I put myself through this on a weekly basis and how is it helpful? It is that struggle to speak where the work actually is. Jan sits and waits, I squirm, panic, get angry, want to be rescued, and want to run. But I do not bolt out of the door, although we have an arrangement that if I do suddenly leave, she will come with me, and so it has never happened. We find ways forward, always taking my lead and at my speed, which helps build my confidence. Sometimes I am able to focus and productively work through issues with her alongside, actively listening and checking her understanding.

I doubt that my life would be as fulfilling and that I would be fully functioning without this facilitative aspect which is fundamental to the person-centred approach. I feel empowered to find my own way and learn to trust and value my inner self, with my trusted companion encouraging me as I venture into dangerous ground. If outcome measures are needed, I would be able to submit a long list of achievements including many years of sobriety, a job that I actually like, and a place that I call home. However, it is not the 'doing' that means the most to me, it is the small things, such as noticing the morning birdsong and enjoying spontaneous laughter, or crying when it hurts. I am now free to experience and connect with others, as I connect more fully with myself and the world around me.

Practitioner's perspective

Peter Chatalos

Introduction

As a person-centred therapist, my goal is to treat each client as a unique human being and to see beyond any diagnosis to connect as much as possible to their inner world. I aim to see things from their perspective and stay present with them, willing to be affected by their experiences. I use diagnostic terms, like 'psychosis', reluctantly because many clients find them stigmatising and discriminatory. Nevertheless, this book usefully illustrates possible therapeutic options to potential clients, and I respect that there are those that may identify with 'psychosis' as part of their identity or recovery process. Although, like most person-centred therapists, I do not think in terms of diagnoses, I understand what is referred by the term 'psychosis' as follows: psychosis can be experienced with a range of phenomena over time or as an isolated, temporary condition. It is a complex psychological process with observable changes in behaviour, where a client can seem withdrawn from a reality shared with others; like one of my clients who saw 'strangers' that nobody else could. For many clients, psychotic episodes are frightening and confusing, bringing shame and isolation, while for others there are moments of enlightenment or pleasure, or some combination of these.

For this chapter on working in a person-centred way with psychosis, I start with an overview of its underlying concepts and theory; how it is a 'way of being' rather than a set of techniques. I outline what clients might expect, offer supporting evidence for Person-Centred Therapy, and discuss concerns about diagnoses from this perspective.

Underlying concepts and theory

Background

The non-directive, self-directive, Rogerian, or client-centred therapy emerged from the work of eminent American psychologist Carl Rogers (1902–87) in the 1950s. Now more commonly referred to as Person-Centred Therapy (PCT) or Approach (PCA), it continues to evolve into a diversity of practices. Rogers was hugely influential on the development of psychotherapy as a profession, and co-founded a 'third force' of psychology, humanism or humanistic psychology, to challenge the prevailing psychological traditions of psychoanalysis and behaviourism (Cooper, O'Hara, Schmid, & Wyatt, 2007). Where psychoanalysis emphasised unconscious dynamics and instinctual drives, humanistic psychologists wanted to support conscious growth. Where behaviourists investigated responses to external stimuli and observable behaviour, humanistic psychology advocated the study of the 'whole' person, including the influence of self-perceptions and personal meanings (i.e. how a person subjectively sees and interprets the world around them).

Humanistic psychology holds a positive view of human nature, validating the importance of subjective experience and personal development, despite any psychological, social, or biological limitations.

Positive view of human nature

Rogers' early training was psychoanalytic, but he found that these techniques were not helping those who were experiencing psychosis or other severe psychological difficulties. He rejected prevailing psychoanalytic ideas that he had learnt and experienced, which informed him that human nature should be kept under control because of innate destructive tendencies, and began developing his own approach.

Rogers replaced the term 'patient' with 'client', and came to believe in the major importance of relating to his clients respectfully as people of worth, despite their condition or behaviour. He emphasised how each person is a subjectively experiencing human organism at the centre of their perceptual world. Consequently, clients needed to be understood from their perspective, as 'experts' on their own lives.

Central to the person-centred approach is the understanding that people have one basic drive or motivational tendency, called the *actualising tendency*. This is a tendency for individuals to pursue life-enhancing activities, moving towards fulfilling their potential or maintaining stability. Likewise, people have an internal sense that can guide them towards this goal. From this perspective, people are not viewed as 'broken', but developing; moving towards becoming more fully functioning, with all the innate resources they need to choose. This tendency can be trusted to be a constructive, positive, and developmental resource for the individual, but it is affected by a need to belong.

Fundamental to survival is *positive regard*, a person-centred term for care, respect, affection, and love. If people only received Unconditional Positive Regard (UPR) from others, they would become psychologically adjusted: able to feel acceptance for themselves and open to all experiences.

Roots of psychological distress

The need to feel valued is interwoven with survival, but, as neuroscience is confirming, it is also crucial for its own sake (Gerhardt, 2004). From early childhood, individuals attempt to understand the relationships closest to them, because of their basic requirement for positive regard. As a person develops an idea of themselves (known as the *self-concept*) through these close relationships, this is influenced through what is approved and disapproved of by others. These norms or values become internalised as *conditions of worth* (i.e. how a person has to behave to be valued). The person tries to maintain a self-concept that can accommodate these conditions of worth, while making meaningful sense of their world.

Any experiences that conflict with the person's idea of how they 'should be' are *denied* or *distorted*. People become blocked from a part of themselves, learning to ignore the innate resources of their organism, their inner signals, or felt senses. This results in anxiety and feelings of vulnerability, which we call *incongruence*. For example, a young adult raised in a homophobic environment begins to feel attracted to members of the same sex. The feelings of arousal conflict with their self-concept, and innate feelings or signals are denied resulting in anxiety, or are distorted, perhaps resulting in homophobic behaviours.

In other words, individual's social experiences, upbringing and conditioning can obstruct or block the actualising tendency (the innate drive for self-enhancement), and this underpins psychological dysfunction, causing vulnerability and incongruence:

> When the incongruence between our experience and our view of ourselves becomes too great, we can no longer hold onto our sense of ourselves and, for some people, this leads to a chaotic disintegration of their lives.
>
> (Tolan & Wilkins, 2012, p. 98)

Rogers identified psychosis with such a state of disintegration. In such states, a person's attempts at denial or distortion of their true self become more severe and overwhelming, emerging as experiences such as hallucinations, paranoia, or catatonic behaviours, and their behaviour becomes considerably disorganised (Holdstock & Rogers, 1977; Joseph & Worsley, 2005).

A relational approach

In researching what worked therapeutically to bring about constructive personality change, Rogers identified six conditions as necessary, and concluded that *if* all these conditions existed, and persisted, *then* they would be sufficient for positive change to occur (Rogers, 1957, in Kirschenbaum & Henderson, 1989). He argued that these are *facilitative* conditions to aim for across all therapies and all diagnostic categories. The first two conditions acknowledge that:

1. The client and therapist must be in *psychological contact* (i.e. perceiving each other).
2. The client is feeling vulnerable, anxious, or in a state of incongruence.

The next three conditions emanate from the therapist. These together are the *core attitudinal qualities* of:

3   Congruence (or genuineness).
4   Acceptance (or Unconditional Positive Regard; UPR), and
5   Empathy (or empathic understanding).

Change is facilitated if the therapist is genuinely experiencing an empathic acceptance of the client and is also able to communicate this sufficiently to the client, as the last condition stipulates that:

6   The client is aware of, at least to a minimal degree, the Unconditional Positive Regard and the empathic understanding of the therapist.

Rather than a set of techniques, these core attitudinal qualities are intertwined as part of the person-centred therapist's *presence*, and become embedded as a '*way of being*' (Rogers, 1980). The therapist does not *try* to be empathic as a *tool* to change the client, but rather is dedicated to the process of supporting clients to feel accepted. This involves listening deeply to the whole client, from the parts that crave change to those that resist it.

There is a feedback loop, where the therapist and client are psychologically connected, (i.e. aware of each other) and the therapist's attitudinal qualities are being sufficiently experienced to create a facilitative environment. Hence the person-centred approach is fundamentally *relational*:

- It emphasises secure, accepting, and empathic relationships for the healthy development of the individual.
- Likewise, it stresses the therapeutic significance of a trustworthy and genuinely connective relationship between client and therapist.

Overall, person-centred therapists are aiming to facilitate their clients to trust in their actualising tendency and their internal, *organismic* sensing. As such, the therapy needs to remove obstacles to the person's ability to develop authentically and so must avoid triggering the client's conditions of worth. For example, a client may try to be more agreeable, because they believe that is what the therapist expects from them. Rogers appreciated that to facilitate this, it was also necessary to equalise power within the therapeutic relationship.

The non-directive attitude

Rogers challenged the traditional power of the expert-therapist, and worked towards a collaborative and egalitarian relationship (discussed in Proctor, 2002, pp. 84–103). A governing feature of the approach is that person-centred therapists aim to hold a *non-directive attitude*. This means that practitioners put aside any ideas they have of what direction should be taken, to follow the client's pace and direction. Some clients can find this lack of directiveness from the person-centred therapist challenging, especially if they have been used to receiving directions from 'authority' figures, or if they have had more directive therapies previously. In the first-hand account of person-centred therapy (see Part 1 of this chapter) the therapist does not lead but instead supports the client's connection to their inner resources and process of emerging autonomy, even when the client found the silences challenging and wanted to be 'rescued'. Furthermore, the therapist does not introduce techniques, interpretations, or specific psychological exercises although, as Part 1 exemplifies, some person-centred practitioners may give strategies when specifically requested.

This non-directive attitude reinforces respect for the client's autonomy, as experts of their experience, supporting their inner resources and sense of safety. It promotes the client's ability to shift and change, as they feel safer to take risks and explore themselves. The therapist will safeguard, manage boundaries, assess risks, and ensure that the therapy is ethically contained. Nevertheless, as Person-Centred Therapy provides a relationship where the therapist seeks to equalise power, some flexibility is possible to accommodate a client's circumstances.

What clients might expect

Boundaries and settings

Similar to other main psychotherapies, sessions will typically be in a quiet room with almost facing chairs. The therapist introduces their approach and boundaries, explains how the session is confidential, and invites the client to talk about their situation at their pace. Person-Centred Therapy is usually offered in hourly sessions (or a 50-minute therapeutic hour) at a regular weekly time and place. Some clients may need to make arrangements suited to their particular circumstances to make the therapy more accessible, so having differing length of sessions or working in a larger space can be negotiated. For example, in Part 1 of this chapter, flexible boundaries were negotiated in terms of time, place, and modes of communication that improved the client's access to therapy, and strengthened the therapeutic relationship. It is vital to have firm, reliable, but also permeable boundaries that can be adapted, so that the facilitative conditions can meet specific client needs. Some clients experiencing psychotic symptoms may not respond well to standard psychotherapy formats and may benefit from flexible, creative, and multi-disciplinary packages of care. In these settings, the person-centred therapist may be more directive than usual, working within their multi-disciplinary team to help clients utilise support from a variety of sources.

Empathic companions

In whatever setting, person-centred practitioners aim to be genuinely accepting, empathic companions on their client's journey. The therapist will check their understanding and experience of the therapeutic relationship, reflecting back the client's verbal and non-verbal communication. Therapists will be 'tuning into' their client's subjective experience, perspective, and way of communicating. Furthermore, practitioners will aim to be transparent about the therapeutic process and open to clients amending their reflections to achieve more accurate empathy.

One of the drawbacks of this approach is how the therapist's empathy can be misconstrued as tacit agreement with everything the client believes, including negative self-talk. For example, in Part 1, the therapist does not reinforce the client's negative self-beliefs, but rather empathises with the experience of holding such beliefs. While genuine empathy can help build trust, for some clients who have rarely received it, it can feel intrusive or even threatening. Trust within the relationship is hard to build or maintain but is easily broken, and staying fully present with the client is a constant challenge. A therapist's empathic error can rupture the therapeutic relationship, but if it is sensitively repaired, it can also be an opportunity to strengthen it.

When working with a client who is experiencing psychotic symptoms, there may be times when the therapist struggles to connect, or attune. If the therapist is figuring out a narrative that defies some 'shared' reality, then this can block their ability to offer the facilitative conditions required for therapeutic change. What helps me is an understanding that such symptoms can emanate from a profound human need to make sense of experience. As Warner (2005) describes, psychosis is one of several styles of what she calls, *difficult processing*. People will attempt to understand or *process* despite any physical or psychological impairment that impedes this:

> When clients have a psychotic style of processing, they have difficulty forming narratives about their experience that makes sense within the culture, or which offer a predictive value in relation to their environment. . . . Often such clients experience voices, hallucinations or delusions that are neither culturally accepted nor are easy to process.
> (Warner, 2005, pp. 94–95)

Warner reiterates how supportive relationships help support people with difficult processing. Moreover, for those experiencing psychotic processing, the person-centred way of respecting a client's reality *as their reality* can mitigate isolation and a need to defend, providing an opportunity through and out of psychosis. This incorporates listening carefully for idiosyncratic meanings and taking account of cultural differences.

Maintaining contact

The therapist must also be especially sensitive around whether the client is psychologically aware of, or engaged with, the therapist, as normal contact with 'self', 'other', and 'world' can be impaired when experiencing psychosis. To reinforce psychological contact, person-centred therapists may use 'pre-therapy' contact reflections, (e.g. Prouty, 1994). It is called 'pre-therapy' as it facilitates contact, a prerequisite for working therapeutically. With pre-therapy, the therapist attempts to connect with the client using some concrete and literal aspect of reality, usually something from the client's environment or situation, their facial expression, body language, words or sentence fragments, or to repeat a reflection that previously made contact. For example, if a client seems unengaged or unresponsive, the therapist may simply comment, 'you are clenching your hands'. This facilitates a re-connection with reality in a non-directive, non-judgemental, and non-interpretive way.

Research evidence

But is there scientific evidence that person-centred therapy is effective? The approach was actually founded on empirical observation. It has been suggested that Rogers was:

> the first person in history to record and publish complete cases of psychotherapy. He carried out and encouraged more scientific research on counselling and psychotherapy than had ever been undertaken anywhere
> (Kirschenbaum & Henderson, 1989, p. 11)

Psychosis was the subject of significant study and contributed to the approach's theoretical developments (e.g. Rogers, 1967). Nevertheless, reluctance to impose evaluation tools on clients limited the approach's subsequent engagement with research. Despite this reluctance, there has been significant re-engagement with research, leading to a growing body of evidence from studies supporting the efficacy of person-centred therapies (see Cooper, 2008; Cooper, Watson, & Hölldampf, 2010). The approach's underlying concepts have further been supported by findings from neuroscience, demonstrating the significant role of empathic or caring relationships in brain development (Gerhardt, 2004). In recent years however, scarce research has specifically looked at how helpful PCT is for psychosis.

One strength of the approach seems to be around supporting clients who ". . . tend to be experientially sensitive and often react very badly to interpretations and interventions" (Elliott, Greensberg, & Lietaer, 2004; cited in Cooper et al., 2007, p. 164). Likewise, 'pre-therapy' contact reflection work, within a supportive relationship, is associated with positive outcomes in social and interpersonal skills, helping clients to boost their self-worth and develop a more integrated sense of self (Traynor, Elliot, & Cooper, 2011). Nevertheless in my experience, some clients can feel uncomfortable with an empathic client-lead approach, preferring a more structured or therapist-led approach.

Overall, there remains a lack of research trials evaluating how helpful PCT is for people with experiences of psychosis. Perhaps a surprise finding from studies that have taken place is that they suggest that the main psychotherapeutic orientations are equally effective (see e.g. Cooper, 2008; Cooper et al., 2010; Wampold, 2001). This equality of effectiveness seems to span across a broad spectrum of psychological difficulties (Stiles, Barkham, Twigg, Mellor-Clark, & Cooper, 2006); although research has not explored how far this is the case for psychosis.

Instead, research indicates that the variances in treatment outcomes correlate with the quality of the therapeutic relationship, including factors that influence it, such as the therapist's characteristics and the client's desire for change (Cooper, 2008; Goldsmith, Lewis, Dunn, & Bentall, 2015). Those therapists that could instil trust and confidence were associated with more positive outcomes, and they tended to be accepting, reliable, and understanding (Wampold, 2001). Subsequently, research is validating the core attitudinal qualities as well as the importance of a robust therapeutic relationship. Further research evaluating how helpful PCT is for people with experiences of psychosis is still needed.

Diagnoses

While research supports the sorts of relationship-building qualities embraced in the person-centred 'way of being', there is a mixed message around diagnoses. Central to this 'way' is valuing a client's *unique* experience. Subsequently, many person-centred practitioners find diagnoses problematic and, for identifying a suitable 'treatment', irrelevant.

From its inception, the person-centred approach stayed clear of imposing prescriptive generalisations and assumptions that could undermine the client's perspective. Rogers was critical of the medical model, and how its pathway of diagnosis, treatment, and cure used with physical symptoms was applied similarly with psychological symptoms. He felt that something crucial was lost when human psychological distress was reduced to a physical process rather than being viewed holistically as a whole system. Rogers was concerned about the validity and abuses of diagnoses, in sentiments echoed by several psychiatrists, like his outspoken contemporary R. D. Laing (Johnstone, 2014).

There is still much concern in the person-centred world about the potential harm of labelling and diagnoses, triggering counter-therapeutic conditions of worth, or the dangers of misidentifying and mistreating symptoms (e.g. Hawkins, 2005). Diagnoses can prejudice the practitioner's openness to the real experience of the client and to their potential, negatively affecting the establishment of an authentic therapeutic relationship and placing the therapist in the expert-role. Indeed, when person-centred therapists were asked what they found particularly helpful for working with psychotic experiences, along with unconditional positive regard, they emphasised getting beyond labels and illness (Traynor et al., 2011).

Studies suggest that labels can be a source of stigma and negative judgement, but conversely, they can also bring benefits, for instance:

> The survey of people diagnosed with 'psychosis' found that it was both a means of access to treatment and support, and at the same time a cause

of disempowerment through messages about hopelessness and so on. Diagnosis helped by naming the problem and relieving people from self-blame, but hindered them by labelling them as a person leading to stigma and discrimination.

(Johnstone, 2014, p. 64)

Despite concerns, the person-centred community has recently made increasing efforts to build bridges, co-exist, and contribute its voice to the understanding of psychological difficulties (e.g. Joseph & Worsley, 2005). Accordingly, person-centred practitioners may make assessments, used to monitor the therapeutic process and work ethically, but this differs from a diagnosis. Rather than labelling, I prefer to describe what I see and attempt to understand how it is experienced or uniquely expressed within my client

Conclusion

Ultimately, I aim be fully accepting with *all* clients to support their actualising tendency and connection to their innate resources, including meeting the needs of clients experiencing psychotic symptoms. This means staying present and true to the core attitudinal qualities, as well as sensitive to the therapeutic relationship, which research associates with positive client outcomes.

Too frequently, individuals experiencing psychotic processes are socially rejected and labelled by mental health professionals. What the person-centred therapist can offer is sensitivity to each client as a unique human being. It is always my hope that working in a person-centred way can mitigate social exclusion by giving clients a sense of being genuinely seen and accepted, beyond any diagnosis.

References

Cooper, M. (2008). *Essential research findings in counselling and psychotherapy: The facts are friendly*. London: Sage.

Cooper, M., O'Hara, M., Schmid, P., & Wyatt, G. (2007). *The handbook of person- centred psychotherapy and counselling*. Basingstoke: Palgrave Macmillan.

Cooper, M., Watson, J. C., & Hölldampf, D. (2010). *Person-centered and experiential therapies work: A review of the research on counseling, psychotherapy and related practices*. Ross-on-Wye: PCCS Books.

Cotter, J. (1990). *Healing – more or less*. Sheffield: Cairns Publications.

Elliot, R., Greensberg, L. S., & Lietaer, G. (2004). Research on experiential psychotherapies. In M. J. Lambert (Ed.), *Bergin & Garfield's handbook of psychotherapy and behavior change* (5th ed., pp. 493–539). New York: Wiley.

Gerhardt, S. (2004). *Why love matters: How affection shapes a baby's brain*. London/New York: Routledge.

Goldsmith, L., Lewis, S., Dunn, G., & Bentall, R. (2015). Psychological treatments for early psychosis can be beneficial or harmful, depending on the therapeutic alliance: An instrumental variable analysis. *Psychological Medicine, 45*(11), 2365–2373.

Hawkins, J. (2005). Living in pain: Mental health and the legacy of childhood abuse. In S. Joseph & R. Worsley (Eds.), *Person-centred psychopathology: A positive psychology of mental health* (pp. 226–239). Ross-on-Wye: PCCS Books.

Holdstock, T. L., & Rogers, C. R. (1977). Person-centered theory. In R. J. Corsini (Ed.), *Current personality theories* (p. 136). Itasca, IL: Peacock.

Johnstone, L. (2014). *A straight talking introduction to psychiatric diagnosis*. Monmouth: PCCS Books.

Joseph, S., & Worsley, R. (2005). *Person-centred psychopathology: A positive psychology of mental health*. Ross-on-Wye: PCCS Books.

Kirschenbaum, H., & Henderson, V. (1989). *The Carl Rogers reader*. London: Constable.

Proctor, G. (2002). *The dynamics of power in counselling and psychotherapy: Ethics, politics and practice*. Ross-on-Wye: PCCS Books.

Prouty, G. (1994). *Theoretical evolutions in person-centred/experiential therapy: Applications to schizophrenic and retarded psychosis*. New York: Praeger.

Rogers, C. R. (1957). The necessary and sufficient conditions of therapeutic personality change. *Journal of Consulting Psychology, 21*, 95–103.

Rogers, C. (1961). *On becoming a person: A therapist's view of psychotherapy*. London: Constable.

Rogers, C. R. (1967). The findings in brief. In C. R. Rogers, E. T. Gendlin, D. Kiesler, & C. B. Truax (Eds.), *The therapeutic relationship and its impact: A study of psychotherapy with schizophrenics* (pp. 73–94). Madison, WI: University of Wisconsin press.

Rogers, C. R. (1980). *A way of being*. Boston and New York: Houghton Mifflin.

Stiles, W. B., Barkham, M., Twigg, E., Mellor-Clark, J., & Cooper, M. (2006). Effectiveness of cognitive-behavioural, person-centered and psychodynamic therapies as practiced in UK National Health Service settings. *Psychological Medicine, 38*, 677–688.

Tolans, J., & Wilkins, P. (2012). *Client issues in counselling and psychotherapy*. London: Sage.

Traynor, W., Elliot, R., & Cooper, M. (2011). Helpful factors and outcomes in person-centred therapy with clients who experience psychotic processes: Therapists' perspectives. *Person-centred and Experiential Psychotherapies, 10*, 89–104.

Wampold, B. E. (2001). *The great psychotherapy debate: Model, methods, and findings*. Mahwah, NJ: Lawrence Erlbaum Associates.

Warner, M. (2005). A person-centred view of human nature, wellness, and psychopathology. In S. Joseph & R. Worsley (Eds.), *Person-centred psychopathology: A positive psychology of mental health* (pp. 91–109). Ross-on-Wye: PCCS Books.

11

THE RELATIONSHIP WITH THE THERAPIST

Client's perspective

Annie Blake[1]

Throughout this book we have so far focused on specific therapies and approaches. However, there are many 'common ingredients' that different therapies share. These common ingredients include the quality of the relationship between client and therapist, and this seems potentially important when it comes to determining the outcome of therapy. In this chapter Annie shares her account of integrative Cognitive Behavioural Therapy, but a key theme is the relationship she builds with her therapist. This is something that Amanda and I then pick up and discuss further in the second section of this chapter.

– Peter Taylor

Introduction

In the autumn of 2012, I found out that my father had been arrested for the possession of child pornography. He was also threatening to commit suicide. Up until that point, I had a good relationship with my father. I looked up to him and respected him. The trauma of discovering this revelation and the mental pressure of my mind's attempt to make sense of a senseless and incomprehensible situation triggered a manic psychotic episode. A year and a half later, I embarked on six months of Cognitive Behavioural Therapy (CBT) for psychosis. In this chapter I plan to explore how therapy aided my recovery. I will cover which topics to expect in therapy sessions, (e.g. family, relationships, attitudes and commitment to therapy), different exercises I found useful or challenging, how I see the roles within a therapeutic relationship, the context of my difficulties, and how therapy gave me practical tools to confront painful issues, be kinder to myself, and begin to let go of the past and move on. In this chapter, all real names have been replaced with pseudonyms in order to maintain confidentiality.

Accessing therapy

The practical requirements for therapy are minimal. On the face of it, all that is needed is a small and at times stuffy room, two chairs, and a strategically placed tissue box. If you are lucky there might be some artwork on the wall. Just two people in a room, talking. It is remarkable then, how through this simple set up, such transformative personal developments are possible.

My first experience of seeking out and getting therapy was out of desperation. My brother had died five years earlier and I had just come out of a five year relationship with one of his friends. I felt in utter despair, experiencing frequent suicidal thoughts. When I was referred to have six weeks of therapy sessions I had no idea what to expect. I just felt I was having an existential crisis and would try anything to take the pain away. I kept a diary and wrote down my nightmares. I also read a book about how therapy had assisted other people, called 'Love's Executioner' by Irvin D. Yalom (1991). I found this very helpful, and after six weeks, the depression I had been experiencing for the last two years lifted. So when I approached my more recent period of therapy, which will be the focus of this chapter, I already knew a few things that might help make the sessions more successful. Keeping a diary is a way of ordering your thoughts, making notes of what you would like to bring up, and reflecting on what you have covered in a session. This helped me enormously.

I think it is important to assess for yourself when the time is right for therapy, although it could be a good idea to get yourself on a waiting list for therapy even when you are not feeling like it, as you may have changed your mind by the time your name gets to the top. One gauge for how ready you are feeling might be how optimistic you are that talking therapy could complement your other coping strategies on the path to recovery. My most recent experience of therapy, with CBT, involved a commitment to keeping weekly appointments for six months. Commitment, a positive attitude, and a belief that I could make sense of psychotic and bipolar experiences through being open about my memories and feelings from these periods helped me enormously. The remainder of this chapter will focus on my experience of CBT.

Telling my story

In my experience, talking to a therapist is very different from talking to a friend. In friendships, boundaries and agendas may not be clear. While suffering with mental health problems, it can be very hard to discuss the disturbing and distressing elements of your issues like suicidal thoughts, paranoia, delusions, and feelings of being out of touch with reality, through fear of being a burden or being misunderstood. By speaking out, it can sometimes feel like risking further isolation and alienation. My role, as I saw it, was to be as open and vocal as possible about my experiences. I found the role of the therapist was often to be a sounding board which reflected my perceptions back to me but with new and consistently useful insights. It was a focused partnership. There were also clear, unspoken boundaries between us. At times I felt curious about my therapist's life. I would wonder how his week had been or imagine what his home was like or if he had a partner. Due to my respect for the boundaries I felt, which were about him being a professional who was employed to listen and help heal me, I had the feeling that it would have been inappropriate to ask him about his personal life and this prevented me from asking any questions which may have crossed this line.

The therapist who delivered my CBT was called Sone. Early on in therapy I was asked (along with the numerous questionnaires I was asked to fill out) what I wanted to get out of therapy and if I had any goals. I said I would like to try to make sense of my psychosis. The main goal I had was to come to some kind of resolution with regard to the feelings towards my father. I knew this was a big ask but I also knew that at the root of my episode were the fears, shock, and terror that had sprung from finding out that my father was not the man I thought he was.

I began by describing in great detail what had happened during my manic psychotic episode. This took up three hour-long sessions, which I think gave the rest of my sessions a very firm foundation, as I truly felt that my therapist understood what I went through. I showed my therapist a sketch book I had made just after my episode with drawings and writing about my experiences. I also surprised myself by how much I could remember, the insomnia, the automatic writing, the over spending, the Truman show complex, delusions of grandeur, paranoia, increased energy. I ticked all the manic psychosis boxes, but alone and without context, I find these labels of symptoms hollow and lacking in meaning. It is hard to generalise when everyone's experiences of these symptoms are so different. So I spoke in great detail about the nature of my psychosis, what I could remember happening and how I felt looking back.

One example of the things that we covered in the sessions was how, in a great state of agitation and having had little sleep, I went to a charity for elderly people and demanded a wheelchair for a woman I knew with a heart condition and limited mobility. Her name was Beatie and I volunteered to walk her dog for her on a regular basis. At this point I was convinced that my father was trying to kill me and that there were hitmen outside the charity shop. I also believed I was having telepathic visions of my father, as Satan, in a straightjacket. When I looked at all the pamphlets on display, I saw messages in the words just for me. Everything held a mystic significance to me. I had asked for the wheelchair for Beatie because when I was at her house, before the revelations about my dad, she had said that she wanted to go shopping and did not have the means to go out alone. The staff at the elderly people's charity could see that I was not functioning normally. On the way over to Beatie's house, I started talking in a deep voice about my dead brother and then I felt as though my brother was talking through me.

I spoke about how I believed that my brother had invented the Internet. I said that we were twins, but I had been frozen and our mother artificially inseminated five years after his birth. We got to Beatie's and I went upstairs to hide behind a cupboard because I thought someone was trying to shoot me through the window. Beatie was shocked and confused. A few weeks later I heard from the charity that Beatie's absent son had heard about what had happened and no longer wanted me to walk the dog. This is just one example of the devastating consequences of this kind of episode. I lost my home, my job, my friends, and my relationship with

Beatie and her dog, Teddy. This is just one of the anecdotes I told my therapist, Sone, in an effort to describe how these symptoms manifested for me. In telling my story there was a great sense of catharsis.

Through my sessions, space was given for new life events such as, among other things, a break up in a new relationship. These important and emotional events sometimes took the focus away from my original goal, but my therapist was extremely accommodating, and I was able to shape the direction I wanted the therapy to take. By the end of therapy, we had identified three rough segments: psychosis and my father, relationships, and more generally how to lead a 'good life'. This was the general arc of therapy for me. Along that arc, topics were revisited and there was room for change and expansion depending on what was going on in my life.

Although naturally curious at times, I never felt the impulse to ask anything about Sone's personal life even though he knew so much about mine. This may seem unbalanced or one sided, but in fact it released me from the usual complexities of social interactions. The therapist's purpose is to focus their attention, knowledge, and compassion on you. The boundaries create a safe space where you are not obliged to take on the other person's worries, concerns, and day-to-day life circumstances. Yet my therapist regularly told me that he was learning from me and so the relationship became mutually beneficial. We learnt from each other.

Exercises and interventions in therapy

In each session I would tell Sone how my week had been, how I had been feeling, and what I had been doing. We would recap on what we had spoken about in past sessions and usually a natural focus for the session would emerge as we spoke. Often we spoke about the stresses and strains I was experiencing in my family life. My relationships with my mother and brother had been put to the test by the whole situation and especially by my hospital admission. I was still harbouring some anger and resentment toward them, as well as my father. By focusing on the way in which I was thinking about these relationships and my attitudes towards them, I was able to consider with Sone a range of ways I could perceive their actions. In turn this gave me insight in to different ways that I could respond in my behaviour towards them. This helped me to repair or accept certain aspects of these complex relationships.

This process involved a lot of standing back from the situation and analysing what may have been going on. When I was in a crisis it was very hard for me to separate myself from my emotions and I felt I was in a whirlwind of pain, anxiety, and stress. Therapy gave me the chance to look back and process my reactions and emotions. This gave me the chance then to look forward and consider fully how my behaviour now could best promote my recovery. By changing the way I was thinking about my past, it directly impacted on the way I could function for the better in the present. For example, I was holding on to a lot of anger at my mother for not leaving my father. I was almost blaming her out of association with my father. I discussed with Sone how my relationship with my mother was separate and existed in its own right. Then I went on holiday with my mother for a week to an animal sanctuary. Sone stressed how important this time was for us. By thinking about my relationship with my mother in a new way, and not connecting her so much to my father, I was able to enjoy the week away.

Over the six months of therapy, I recall doing three exercises that I found very useful. The first of these was in preparation for seeing my father. After almost two years of not speaking to my father, I was able to invite him to a therapy session and talk to him directly about how his actions had impacted my life. In preparation, I was invited to imagine that he was sitting in the chair in front of me and I was given the chance to rehearse all the things I would like to say to him. As I have a vivid imagination, I found it easy to put myself in this imagined situation, and although it was hard emotionally, I found the experience invaluable when it came to the day. In another exercise, I was invited to imagine that it was my 90th birthday party and several guests (alive or dead) approached me and told me what I had brought to their life. I immediately started crying as I visualised each guest. My dead brother was there, my best friend, and my dog. It was an amazing exercise for realising your self-worth and good qualities that others see in you. The third exercise was aimed at making more balanced decisions. I was invited to sit in one chair and give an account of all the reasons why I should do something, then sit in another chair and give all the reasons why I should not. Then sit in a third chair and give a more balanced assessment based on all the pros and cons. Perhaps it was my drama training that helped, but I found this exercise easy and enlightening. It was far more revealing than simply writing a list of pros and cons.

After describing my psychotic, manic reaction to trauma, I spoke about the resentment I held towards my father. Sone said that resentment is like holding a hot coal, ready to throw at someone else, but that it is only hurting you. When it came to arranging a meeting, my father was very amenable and immediately said yes. With the above in mind, I wrote down my thoughts in preparation for the meeting, including reasons why I wanted to meet, what I would like to get out of it, how I see the relationship now, and what I need from him in the future. The way in which Sone facilitated the meeting helped me feel safe and prepared. I felt like finally I was taking some control over my life situation. Sone held the space expertly. He created a space in which I was able to tell my father exactly how his actions had negativity impacted my life. He also gave my father and mother a chance to speak, prevented anyone from talking over each other, and was there to suggest a time out if emotions ran too high.

There is no simple resolution to the struggles with my father, but to have the chance to meet on my terms and express my pain to him in a controlled and safe place proved to be very cathartic, and in some ways released me from the heavy burden I felt from keeping my feelings inside.

I came to realise that perhaps my father was incapable of really empathising with the torment I had been through, or with the horrifying consequences that those countless abused children had to face day by day. The most helpful moments were those which sprung from my and Sone's authentic mutual respect and honest connection. Rather than dictating the best way I should think or feel about a situation, Sone would gently offer his insights which might have signposted a direction of thought to me, but on which no pressure was placed to go down those trails of thought. More often than not, Sone would lead me to thinking about situations and relationships in new and different ways, and his insights would often trigger valuable realisations, leaving me feeling empowered that I could make my needs known without damaging connections. I did find the structured exercises helpful, but I think this had a lot to do with Sone's expert timing and the relevance of the exercises to the general flow of therapy. In isolation and without the sensitivity to know which exercises might be of use, I do not think they would have been as helpful. Therapy is such a personal journey and I believe everyone is ready at different times.

How therapy helped

The key way in which therapy helped me was by helping me make sense of what had been labelled psychosis and mania. While studying at University, I had some lectures on mental health. This was before my bipolar diagnosis, but as it runs in my family and I was dating someone at the time who suffered from it, my attention was grabbed. Bipolar, psychosis, schizophrenia, they were all described using a tick list of symptoms, but the labels remained just that. The lectures gave me no insight into what the symptoms might look like in reality. I think words like 'delusional' and 'paranoid' need a context in order to gain meaning. That said, after days of insomnia as I gradually slipped into mania, I held that tick list in my mind and one by one mentally crossed them off as I experienced each symptom. For a long time I felt health care professionals saw me as a tick list of symptoms and it was not until I met Sone that I truly felt someone was hearing my trauma and the potential meaning in my madness. Sone gave the space for the possibility that my episode was my mind's way of coping; a necessary escape from a reality that was too overwhelmingly harrowing to cope with in any other way; a normal reaction to an abnormal situation. This allowed me to actually value my experience, however painful it was, rather than feel ashamed and pathologised as I had done in the past. The stigma of being branded bipolar still burns bright in my psyche, and for a long time I lived in denial, but therapy helped me see that I am so much more than my condition. I have heard bipolar being compared with asthma. People with asthma are not constantly having an attack, for most of the time they are asymptomatic, as am I. I know this is not the case for all people who have bipolar, but I found it a useful comparison for me.

Therapy built my resilience, which has been tested a great deal in the year and a half since I finished therapy, including another hospital admission. I do feel therapy gave me the hope to bounce back and the grit to carry on when I felt in utter despair. We explored practical tools such as the exercises I have described, writing a journal and more willingly expressing my needs to others, along with others such as meditation, mindfulness, exercise, and limiting my alcohol intake. These are all very helpful, but ultimately it was a matter of rebuilding my self-esteem and my sense of control over my life, which has most helped in my journey of recovery and staying well.

I resented the feelings of being judged by health care professionals who neglected to take a thorough history of my past traumas or current challenges. With going to therapy though, I often felt like I was stepping in to a warm bath. I felt safe, secure, listened to, and cared for. Despite my past, I did not have a problem opening fully to the experience of therapy and to the trust I had to forge with my therapist for the relationship to be fruitful. Therapy also allowed me to listen to myself and my instincts more readily. I am aware that CBT can be challenging for many, the family sessions I had, seeing my dad again, were particularly hard, but on the whole my experience of therapy was extremely positive, and the sessions became something I looked forward to each week.

I am still striving to find balance in my life, and doing all I can to come to terms with the traumas I have experienced. Six months of therapy did not prevent a relapse in my case, but without having been to therapy and gained so much insight into my difficulties, I know I would not have been able to cope so well with a second period spent in hospital and the aftermath of that. In therapy we discussed my triggers and early warning signs. I had already drawn up a comprehensive relapse prevention plan with my social worker, but it was the holistic approach to healing which has really helped me. The mysteries of the mind are vast and deep, and bipolar is a devastating and unpredictable condition. Therapy may not have stopped me from having another episode, but it has certainly contributed to me making the most of my life when I am well, and in dealing with the consequences of a manic episode and the crushing hopelessness of depressive symptoms. It has made me realise that I can and do have an influence on my external environment, and that in every area of my life I can learn to help myself.

Conclusion

Therapy has had a lasting impact on my life. It has changed the way I relate to my experience of mental illness in such a positive way. Although I still make mistakes and have setbacks, it has allowed me to be more honest and truthful in my relationships, both platonic and romantic. I have been much more able to recognise my emotional landscape and have a greater knowledge of the path which is best for me. In my experience, a therapist may not talk about their training or the technicalities of how they deliver their treatment. Inherent in the therapeutic relationship should be that they have your best interests at heart and that you can trust them to guide the sessions in such a way that leaves room for inevitable life changes and developments, but also gives space to address goals and concerns you have at the start of your therapy. Ultimately, the healing begins when there is a genuine meeting of hearts and minds. It starts with connection, and can grow into a life changing experience which offers hope, insight, and dignity.

Practitioners' perspective

Amanda Larkin and Peter Taylor

Introduction

The preceding personal account focuses on the positive attributes and behaviours of the therapist as experienced by Annie. It highlights the importance of the relationship between client and therapist, an idea that has been supported by research into differing therapeutic modalities across different presentations. More widely, the importance of the relationship with the therapist has been a common theme across the experiences of clients captured within this book (see Chapter 12 for examples of this). A relationship between client and therapist exists in all psychological therapies, and appears to be a key component of effective therapy. For every therapy covered in this book, there is a recognition, at least to some extent, that this relationship is an important part of the therapy.

This section will aim to focus on the idea of the relationship between client and therapist, briefly reviewing how this relationship can be defined and understood. We will next review evidence that this relationship is important in influencing the outcome of therapy. Lastly, we will consider how difficulties within the relationship with a therapist could affect clients' experiences of therapy, and what clients might be able to do about such difficulties.

Defining the relationship with the therapist

The relationship between client and therapist can be broadly defined as "the feelings and attitudes that therapist and client have toward one another, and the manner in which these are expressed" (Norcross & Lambert, 2011, p. 5). From this definition we can identify various properties of this relationship.

First, it is a multifaceted thing; it has many components (e.g. Dziopa & Ahern, 2009; Kelley, Kraft-Todd, Schapira, Kossowsky, & Riess, 2014). There is an emotional aspect, the way clients and therapists feel about each other, covering both positive (e.g. concerned, supportive, appreciative) and negative (e.g. irritated, annoyed) emotions. There is a cognitive or attitudinal component, what clients and therapists think about each other. There is also a behavioural component, the way in which the client and therapist behave towards each other and the way they express their thoughts and feelings about each other. Both client and therapist may be more aware of some aspects of this relationship than others.

Second, the relationship between client and therapist is clearly reciprocal (Sandhu, Arcidiacono, Aguglia, & Priebe, 2015). There is the therapist's experience and the client's experience, and it is the ongoing interaction between these two positions that is the relationship. This means that when we think about the things that influence the client-therapist relationship, we have to consider both the therapist and the client.

Third, it becomes clear that this relationship is a dynamic thing. Feelings towards a client or a therapist can change and evolve. They may change as therapy progresses (e.g. Zilcha-Mano & Errázuriz, 2017), and moment to moment shifts in feeling and behaviour are also possible. A client may start to feel able to open up more about how they feel, or a therapist may start to feel a stronger positive regard towards a client. One individual may also start to feel irritated or disappointed in the other. This changeability is important because it suggests that a difficult relationship has the potential to improve, and that bad patches or 'ruptures' in the relationship may be overcome. When ruptures in the relationship occur and are overcome or 'repaired', this can contribute to positive outcomes for the client (Safran, Muran, & Eubanks-Carter, 2011).

The relationship is at times described as something that is distinct from the specific techniques a certain therapy makes use of, such as testing out unhelpful beliefs in Cognitive Behavioural Therapy or using mental imagery in Compassion Focused Therapy (Norcross & Lambert, 2011). This distinction can sometimes be helpful when we try to understand what the client-therapist relationship is, or how it might be measured. Within this chapter we consider the relationship between therapist and client as distinct from the techniques used in therapy. However, these two aspects of therapy are still likely linked, because the impact of effectiveness of any therapeutic technique or method is likely to depend on the underlying relationship (Norcross & Lambert, 2011).

What makes a good client-therapist relationship?

The multifaceted nature of the client-therapist relationship means that it is not something that can be easily described as simply being 'good' or 'bad'. However, it is clear that certain relationships will be less effective or helpful when it comes to therapy. A helpful or effective relationship would be one that best supports the progression of the therapy towards a positive outcome (both client and therapist will have an idea of what a positive outcome would be), whether that is the reduction of psychotic experiences or an improvement in well-being. The relationship may hinder or prevent progress in therapy for various reasons. This could happen if a client is unable to engage with or try out the techniques suggested by a therapist, perhaps because of a lack of trust or faith in the therapist and their approach. Alternatively, where a therapist finds it hard to emotionally connect with a client's experiences, they may not be able to offer the empathy a client needs to experience. For people experiencing psychosis, who may have unusual explanations for their experiences, it may be detrimental to the relationship if the therapist does not adequately convey a sense of a shared understanding of the experiences. These are just examples, and the way the relationship can facilitate or hinder success in the therapy will depend on the particular therapy being used. In the previous section, Annie writes that she felt that her role in therapy was to be as open and vocal as possible about her experiences. This might have been very difficult for her to do without trusting her therapist.

Clinicians and researchers have tried to identify perceived qualities that are associated with a more positive or helpful client-therapist relationship. It has been suggested that, at least in relation to some forms of therapy, a helpful relationship is one in which a therapist is able to foster perceptions of trust, honesty, genuineness, warmth, empathy, respect, and positive regard for the client (Roberts, Fenton & Barnard, 2015; Kazantzis, Dattilo, & Dobson, 2017; Nienhuis et al., 2016; Rogers, 1957). One study in mental health nurses (Dziopa & Ahern, 2009) suggested nine components of an effective client-therapist relationship (empathy and understanding, individualised care, providing support, being available, genuineness, equality, respect, clear boundaries, self-awareness). This study focused on the position of the nurse or clinician, and so tells us less about the client's contribution to this relationship. However, research focused on clients' perceptions of therapy suggests that experiencing moments of connection and engagement with the therapist may be an important part of this relationship (Cooper, 2013; Knox & Cooper, 2010). Where this sense of connection has been present, clients' perceptions of therapists included them being warm and empathic, sharing their perspective, reliable, and creating a safe and welcoming atmosphere (Knox & Cooper, 2010).

Winnicott, contributed to the ideas of object relations theory (mentioned above), has also influenced ideas about what might count as a 'good enough' relationship, based upon his ideas about being a good enough parent. From this perspective, a good enough relationship in therapy might be one that is initially adapted or attuned to the needs of the client, helping the client to feel protected and safe, but also which gradually supports a client to become more autonomous (Borg, 2013; Winnicott, 2002). This 'good enough' relationship is not perfect, and feelings of frustration or disappointment may not necessarily suggest problems but can be part of a therapy that is going well, where the client is able to be in touch with painful aspects of reality.

The working alliance

One influential approach to understanding the relationship between client and therapist, and what characterises a helpful relationship, has focused specifically on a component of this relationship called the 'working alliance' (Bordin, 1979). The working alliance has been defined as a combination of three factors: (a) client and therapist agreement on the goals of therapy, (b) client and therapist agreement on how to achieve these goals (task agreement), and (c) the development of a personal bond between the client and therapist. A good working alliance is viewed as a common factor that helps promote a positive outcome from therapy, regardless of the specific type of therapy being used. An advantage of this idea of a working alliance is that it is something that can be measured during the course of therapy, and so can help guide the therapist. A more positive working alliance appears to be strongly associated with clients' perceptions of therapists as more genuine and having greater empathy (Nienhuis et al., 2016), supporting the idea that the working alliance overlaps with other aspects of the relationship between therapist and client.

The relationship with the therapist and the link to the client's other relationships

A number of different theories have suggested that the relationship between therapist and client has additional importance, as it provides an impression of a client's relationships with other people in their lives, both past and present (Lemma, 2015; Ryle & Kerr, 2002). From this perspective, the relationship is like a mirror, reflecting other relationships in a client's life. For example, an individual who finds it difficult to accept care or support from their friends or family might also struggle to accept the help of the therapist. These theories suggest that a person's expectations and perceptions develop from their previous experiences of relationships. Object relations theory (Flanagan, 2016), for example, describes how we all, including therapists, internalise the interactions we have with other people, starting with our earliest caregivers. This internalised inner world of relationships is believed to then affect what we need and expect from others in our lives, and how we perceive their behaviour towards us. A person's prior experience of external interpersonal relationships may also influence their experience of particular aspects of psychosis, such as their relationship to voices that they hear (Birchwood, Gilbert, Gilbert, & Trower, 2004), which may also influence their relationship with a therapist.

In some therapies the therapeutic relationship is therefore used as a tool to help understand the client's current problems and this understanding can then help support people to change problematic patterns (Lemma, 2015; Ryle & Kerr, 2002). The therapy relationship may also be used as a vehicle for helping the client, by providing an opportunity for the client to have a different type of relationship experience to the patterns that have normally played out in their lives. Thus, for example, the client who struggles to accept care from others may use the therapy relationship as a safe space within which they can experiment with acting differently and accepting care. In Chapter 5, for example, Alex talks about how therapy was a space to experiment with being more open about the difficulties she was facing.

Within psychodynamic theory, the concepts of transference (where a client's internal world or past experiences of relationships distort or affects the relationship with their therapist) and countertransference (the emotional response a therapist has in response to a client) have been developed to help understand the feelings that emerge within the therapy relationship (Lemma, 2015). These ideas have also been adopted by other theories (Bennett, 1995). Importantly, these theories highlight how the client-therapist relationship is a two-way process, influenced by both the client and the therapists' experiences and behaviour. These theories also highlight how the way that the therapist and client might experience and influence the client-therapist relationship can be unintentional or even unconscious.

The therapist as attachment figure

Another influential theory when thinking about the relationship between client and therapist has been Attachment Theory (Bowlby, 1973, 1980, 1982, 1988). This theory developed out of object relations theory (see above). It focuses on our early relationships with caregivers, and the way we are predisposed to forming an 'attachment' with them, seeking proximity, comfort and protection, from a young age. These early interactions lay down a template for how we interact with and experience relationships with others in the future. These early interactions are also believed to affect the way we see ourselves and our ability to handle our emotions (Bartholomew & Horowitz, 1991; Cassidy, 1994). Thus early relationships that were abusive, neglectful, or not well attuned to a child's needs may leave a lasting impact on how this individual feels towards and responds to other people in their lives.

Whilst initially concerned with caregivers, this theory has been extended to think about therapists as other potential attachment figures (Mikulincer, Shaver, & Berant, 2013; Obegi, 2008). From this perspective, a helpful relationship with a therapist is one where a therapist can come to be seen as a 'secure base', from which the client feels able to explore difficult experiences or feelings, knowing that the therapist is available and able to contain or manage the distress they might experience. Also, attachment theory would suggest that therapist behaviours that promote a good attachment are likely to be similar to the behaviours that would allow a caregiver to create a good attachment. Therefore, a therapist who is more attuned or in touch with what a client is experiencing, and is responsive to this, will potentially build a stronger attachment with the client (Mikulincer et al., 2013).

Another implication of attachment theory is that clients who have not experienced an optimal relationship with their caregivers and have formed a less 'secure' pattern of attachment (where seeking support or comfort from others becomes more difficult to do) may find it harder to form a helpful relationship with their therapist. There is evidence that less secure (or insecure) attachment patterns are associated with a poorer working alliance, but this association is statistically strongest when we focus on the attachment clients have with their therapists (Mallinckrodt & Jeong, 2015; Mikulincer et al., 2013; Taylor, Rietzschel, Danquah, & Berry, 2015a). These results suggest that the attachment a client forms with their therapist may be an important determinant of the quality of the working alliance they form.

Notably, though, it is not just a client's pattern of attachment that seems to matter, but also the therapist's own attachment pattern. A more secure therapist attachment pattern is also typically associated with a better working alliance, for example (Mikulincer et al., 2013). There is also evidence that attachment patterns can change during therapy, so that helpful therapy might be able to lead towards a more secure and adaptive attachment pattern for the client (Taylor, Rietzschel, Danquah, & Berry, 2015b).

The client-therapist relationship in psychosis

For people who experience psychosis, there may be additional considerations when thinking about the client-therapist relationship. People who experience psychosis, or receive a diagnosis of schizophrenia, report a high level of stigma and discrimination (Rose et al., 2011; Lasalvia, Penta, Sartorius, & Henderson, 2015). A good relationship may therefore be even more important for people experiencing psychosis (Kvrgic, Cavelti, Beck, Rusch, & Vauth, 2013), because it is even harder to talk about stigmatising experiences, and because a sense of being valued is even more important. Annie describes feeling that she and her therapist were learning from each other, indicating that she had felt respected and valued through the therapeutic process. Particular experiences of psychosis may also affect the relationship. For example, some clients might experience paranoia or other distressing thoughts about their therapists, and this can create a barrier to forming a more helpful relationship (Lawlor, Hall, & Ellett, 2015). Some voices may forbid a person from talking about certain experiences, and this again could create a barrier in therapy. As mentioned above, these experiences can also mirror prior interpersonal experiences which may act as a barrier to forming a relationship with a therapist. People experiencing psychosis may have faced difficult reactions from others when discussing their experiences, and this may influence how open they feel they can be with their therapist. Receiving an empathetic and normalising response from mental health professionals has been noted by clients to be a positive experience (Byrne & Morrison, 2010). It appears that such challenges do not necessarily mark the end of therapy and can often be overcome, for example, through the collaborative discussion of these difficult thoughts (Lawlor et al., 2015).

What is the evidence that the client-therapist relationship affects therapy outcomes?

Numerous reviews of the existing research, considering a range of different therapies, have suggested that aspects of the client-therapist relationship, including a stronger working alliance, greater empathy, and genuineness, have all been associated with better outcomes from therapy (Ardito & Rabellino, 2011; Elliott,

Bohart, Watson, & Greenberg, 2011; Kolden, Klein, Wang, & Austin, 2011). If we look at research specifically concerning people with experiences of psychosis, then reviews suggest again that the client-therapist relationship matters, with a better relationship (or a better working alliance) being associated with more positive outcomes (Priebe, Richardson, Conney, Adedeji, & McCabe, 2011; Shattock, Berry, Degnan, & Edge, 2018). This included outcomes like a reduction in the severity of psychotic experiences, but there was also some evidence that outcomes to do with self-esteem or returning to hospital are affected by the client-therapist relationship. Interviews about the therapeutic experience of people with psychosis have shown that clients value the relationship between themselves and the therapist (Kilbride et al., 2013), as well as viewing it as important for undertaking the sometimes difficult work involved in therapy.

There is also evidence that the effect of the client-therapist relationship on therapy outcomes is reciprocal; a better relationship is associated with improved outcomes, but this in turn is associated with further improvements in the relationship (perhaps because clients' trust and belief in the therapist and their methods are strengthened; Xu & Tracey, 2015).

A limitation with the research described above is that it does not rule out the possibility that other factors might explain the association seen between the client-therapist relationship and therapy outcomes. This means it is still difficult to say whether a better relationship with therapists *causes* a better therapy outcome. A consequence of this is that we cannot say for sure if the effect we see on therapy outcomes is caused by the quality of the relationship or some other overlapping factor (e.g. perhaps clients with better client-therapist relationships may also tend to have difficulties that recover more readily). A recent study has applied more advanced statistical methods to increase our confidence that the relationship actually *causes* a better outcome from therapy for psychosis (Goldsmith, Lewis, Dunn, & Bentall, 2015). This study found that a better therapeutic alliance early on led to greater improvements from therapy. It also found that where a good alliance did not develop early on, clients actually tended to experience a worsening outcome from therapy. This is only a single study, but provides us with further evidence that the client-therapist relationship is important in determining the outcome of therapy for psychosis.

Promoting a good enough client-therapist relationship

Difficulties within the relationship are not uncommon in therapy (Safran et al., 2011). A client may feel a loss of trust in their therapist, doubt their genuineness, or their ability to help. Problems in the relationship experienced by clients or therapists could be due to the actual behaviour of one of these individuals during therapy, or the perceptions or expectations that the therapist or client have brought to the therapy. Within this book, there are some examples of difficult moments and experiences with therapists. For example, in Chapter 8, Mystic Leaf notes how an earlier therapist's approach felt 'cold, factual, and objective', and ultimately this therapy did not appear helpful. In contrast, in Chapter 10, Jules Haley describes how a possible rupture (anger at her therapist around a cancelled appointment) was overcome. Importantly, therefore, whilst ruptures in the relationship are not uncommon, and whilst some may lead to the end of the therapy, this does not have to be the case. There is evidence that ruptures can be overcome or resolved through discussion in the therapy itself (e.g. Bennett, Parry, & Ryle, 2006).

There are various things that may help to foster a more helpful relationship. For therapists, supervision has been recommended as an important process for helping them to think about how they can improve their relationship with clients (Safran, Muran, Stevens, & Rothman, 2007). Where problems occur in the relationship, it may be that therapists need to adjust or alter their approach or style (e.g. perhaps being less directive or more empathic), and supervision may be helpful in reflecting on the need for such changes. It has also been suggested that therapists receiving therapy themselves may be helpful (Orlinksy, Schofield, Schroder, & Kazantzis, 2011). This might particularly be the case where the expectations or perceptions of clients that therapists bring with them to their sessions are getting in the way of a better relationship forming (e.g. perhaps because of the therapists own history or experiences, as outlined above). Different therapy approaches also offer different ways of thinking about ruptures or problems in the relationship with clients, and working to resolve these.

For clients, where a choice of therapist is available, it may be helpful to choose a therapist who inspires a feeling of hope that therapy with them will be beneficial. However, there is often limited choice regarding the type of therapy offered and the therapist who is available (though this will vary across locations). In such cases, there may still sometimes be a value in asking about alternative therapists when a good relationship is not forming. However, it is also important to note that for some therapies, a key part of the therapeutic work is about noticing and responding to difficulties in the relationship (e.g. this may be the case for CAT and psychodynamic approaches), and as such, ending relationships too soon could miss an opportunity for change and improvement in difficulties. From our perspective, where difficulties in the relationship are apparent for a client, an important first step is often to raise this in the therapy itself where possible.

Raising these concerns gives the opportunity to discuss and potentially work through these difficulties, and to see how a therapist responds to such concerns. Attending to and working on these concerns can enhance the therapeutic relationship, and potentially the client's experience and outcome of the therapy (Stiles et al., 2004).

For those who have previously experienced a particular kind of therapy where it has not been helpful, we believe it is common to draw the conclusion that this particular therapy is not for them (e.g. "I've had CBT, it did not work, so it's not for me"). Anecdotally, we know this can be frustrating when an individual has few other therapy approaches available to them. In these situations, given that the relationship with the therapist is important to how beneficial the therapy ultimately is, it may be that the same therapeutic approach, but with a different therapist (one a client is better able to form an effective relationship with) could still be beneficial.

Conclusion

There is no clear single idea of what a good relationship is, though various attempts to define the beneficial elements of the client-therapist relationship exist, such as thinking about working alliance, or what a 'good enough' relationship might be. The relationship between client and therapist plays an important part in therapy, irrespective of the therapy approach taken. This relationship is related to the outcome of therapy, including therapy for problems related to psychosis. Given its potential importance it is likely beneficial that both therapists and clients are mindful of this relationship.

Note

1 The author has preferred to remain anonymous and use a pseudonym.

References

Ardito, R. B., & Rabellino, D. (2011). Therapeutic alliance and outcome of psychotherapy: Historical excursus, measurements, and prospects for research. *Frontiers in Psychology, 2*, 270. doi:10.3389/fpsyg.2011.00270

Bartholomew, K., & Horowitz, L. (1991). Attachment styles among young adults: A test of four-category model. *Journal of Personality and Social Psychology, 61*, 226–244. doi:10.1037/ 0022–3514.61.2.226

Bennett, D. (1995). The use of transference in CAT: Refinement of a proposed model. *Reformulation, Spring*. Retrieved from www.acat.me.uk/reformulation.php?issue_id=27&article_id=326

Bennett, D., Parry, G., & Ryle, A. (2006). Resolving threats to the therapeutic alliance in cognitive analytic therapy of borderline personality disorder: A task analysis. *Psychology and Psychotherapy: Theory, Research and Practice, 79*, 395–418. doi:10.1348/147608305X58355

Birchwood, M., Gilbert, P., Gilbert, J., Trower, P., Meaden, A., Hay, J., . . . Miles, J. N. (2004). Interpersonal and role-related schema influence the relationship with the dominant 'voice' in schizophrenia: A comparison of three models. *Psychological Medicine, 34*, 1571–1580. doi:https://doi.org/10.1017/S0033291704002636

Bordin, E. S. (1979). The generalizability of the psychoanalytic concept of the working alliance. *Psychotherapy: Theory, Research & Practice, 16*, 252–260. doi:10.1037/h0085885

Borg, L. K. (2013). *Holding, attaching and relating: A theoretical perspective on good enough therapy through analysis of Winnicott's good enough mother, using Bowlby's attachment theory and relational theory*. Unpublished doctoral dissertation, Smith College School for Social Work, Northampton, MA.

Bowlby, J. (1973). *Attachment and loss: Vol. 2. Separation: Anxiety and anger*. New York: Basic Books.

Bowlby, J. (1980). *Attachment and loss: Vol. 3. Sadness and depression.* New York: Basic Books.

Bowlby, J. (1982). *Attachment and loss: Vol. 1. Attachment* (2nd ed.). New York: Basic Books. (Original work published 1969)

Bowlby, J. (1988). *A secure base: Clinical applications of attachment theory.* London: Routledge.

Byrne, R., & Morrison, A. P. (2010). Young people at risk of psychosis: A user-led exploration of interpersonal relationships and communication of psychological difficulties. *Early Intervention in Psychiatry, 4,* 162–168. doi:10.1111/j.1751–7893.2010.00171.x

Cassidy, J. (1994). Emotion regulation influences of attachment relationships. *Monographs of the Society for Research in Child Development, 59,* 228–249. doi:10.1111/j.1540-5834.1994.tb01287.x

Cooper, M. (2013). Experiencing relational depth in therapy: What we know so far. In R. Knox, D. Murphy, S. Wiggins, & M. Cooper (Eds.), *Relational depth: New perspectives and developments.* Basingstoke: Palgrave McMillan.

Dziopa, F., & Ahern, K. (2009). What makes a quality therapeutic relationship in psychiatric/mental health nursing: A review of the research literature. *The Internet Journal of Advanced Nursing Practice, 10,* 1–9. Retrieved from https://espace.library.uq.edu.au/view/UQ:177415

Elliott, R., Bohart, A. C., Watson, J. C., & Greenberg, L. S. (2011). Empathy. *Psychotherapy, 48,* 43. doi:10.1037/a0022187

Flanagan, L. M. (2016). Object relations theory. In J. Berzoff, L. M. Flanagan, & P. Hertz (Eds.), *Inside out and outside in: Psychodynamic clinical theory and psychopathology in contemporary multicultural contexts* (4th ed.). London: Rowman & Littlefield.

Goldsmith, L. P., Lewis, S. W., Dunn, G., & Bentall, R. P. (2015). Psychological treatments for early psychosis can be beneficial or harmful, depending on the therapeutic alliance: An instrumental variable analysis. *Psychological Medicine, 45,* 2365–2373. doi:10.1017/S003329171500032X

Kazantzia, N., Dattilio, F. M., & Dobson, K. S. (2017). *The therapeutic relationship in cognitive-behavioural therapy: A clinician's guide.* New York: The Guilford Press.

Kelley, J. M., Kraft-Todd, G., Schapira, L., Kossowsky, J., & Riess, H. (2014). The influence of the patient-clinician relationship on healthcare outcomes: A systematic review and meta-analysis of randomized controlled trials. *Plos One, 9,* e94207. doi:10.1371/journal.pone.0094207

Kilbride, M., Byrne, R., Price, J., Wood, L., Barratt, S., Welford, M., & Morrison, A. P. (2013). Exploring service users' perceptions of cognitive behavioural therapy for psychosis: A user led study. *Behavioural and Cognitive Psychotherapy, 41,* 89–102. doi:10.1017/s1352465812000495

Kolden, G. G., Klein, M. H., Wang, C. C., & Austin, S. B. (2011). Congruence/genuineness. *Psychotherapy, 48,* 65–71. doi:10.1037/a0022064

Knox, R., & Cooper, M. (2010). Relationship qualities that are associated with moments of relational depth: The client's perspective. *Person-Centered & Experiential Psychotherapies, 9,* 236–256. doi:10.1080/14779757.2010.9689069

Kvrgic, S., Cavelti, M., Beck, E. M., Rusch, N., & Vauth, R. (2013). Therapeutic alliance in schizophrenia: The role of recovery orientation, self-stigma, and insight. *Psychiatry Research, 209,* 15–20. doi:10.1016/j.psychres.2012.10.009

Lasalvia, A., Penta, E., Sartorius, N., & Henderson, S. (2015). Should the label "schizophrenia" be abandoned? *Schizophrenia Research, 162,* 276–284. doi:10.1016/j.schres.2015.01.031

Lawlor, C., Hall, K., & Ellett, L. (2015). Paranoia in the therapeutic relationship in cognitive behavioural therapy for psychosis. *Behavioural and Cognitive Psychotherapy, 43,* 490–501. doi:10.1017/s1352465814000071

Lemma, A. (2015). *Introduction to the practice of psychoanalytic psychotherapy* (2nd ed.). Chichester: Wiley Blackwell.

Mallinckrodt, B., & Jeong, J. (2015). Meta-analysis of client attachment to therapist: Associations with working alliance and client pre-therapy attachment. *Psychotherapy, 52,* 134–139. doi:10.1037/a0036890

Mikulincer, M., Shaver, P. R., & Berant, E. (2013). An attachment perspective on therapeutic processes and outcomes. *Journal of Personality, 81,* 606–616. doi:10.1111/j.1467-6494.2012.00806.x

Nienhuis, J. B., Owen, J., Valentine, J. C., Winkeljohn Black, S., Halford, T. C., Parazak, S. E., . . . Hilsenroth, M. (2016). Therapeutic alliance, empathy, and genuineness in individual adult psychotherapy: A meta-analytic review. *Psychotherapy Research,* 1–13. doi:10.1080/10503307.2016.1204023

Norcross, J. C., & Lambert, M. J. (2011). Psychotherapy relationships that work II. *Psychotherapy, 48,* 4–8. doi:10.1037/a0022180

Obegi, J. H. (2008). The development of the client-therapist bond through the lens of attachment theory. *Psychotherapy Theory Research & Practice, 45,* 431–446. doi:10.1037/a0014330

Orlinsky, D. E., Schofield, M. J., Schroder, T., & Kazantzis, N. (2011). Utilization of personal therapy by psychotherapists: A practice-friendly review and a new study. *Journal of Clinical Psychology, 67,* 828–842. doi:10.1002/jclp.20821

Priebe, S., Richardson, M., Cooney, M., Adedeji, O., & McCabe, R. (2011). Does the therapeutic relationship predict outcomes of psychiatric treatment in patients with psychosis? A systematic review. *Psychotherapy & Psychosomatics, 80,* 70–77. doi:10.1159/000320976

Roberts, J., Fenton, G., & Barnard, M. (2015). Developing effective therapeutic relationships with children, young people and their families. *Nursing Children & Young People, 27,* 30–35. doi:10.7748/ncyp.27.4.30.e566

Rogers, C. R. (1957). The necessary and sufficient conditions of therapeutic personality change. *Journal of Consulting Psychology, 21,* 95–103.

Rose, D., Willis, R., Brohan, E., Sartorius, N., Villares, C., Wahlbeck, K., & Thornicroft, G. (2011). Reported stigma and discrimination by people with a diagnosis of schizophrenia. *Epidemiology and Psychiatric Science, 20,* 193–204. doi:10.1017/S2045796011000254

Ryle, A., & Kerr, I. B. (2002). *Introducing cognitive analytic therapy: Principles and practice.* Oxford: Wiley Blackwell.

Safran, J. D., Muran, J. C., & Eubanks-Carter, C. (2011). Repairing alliance ruptures. *Psychotherapy, 48,* 80–87. doi:10.1037/a0022140

Safran, J. D., Muran, J. C., Stevens, C., & Rothman, M. (2007). A relational approach to supervision: Addressing ruptures in the alliance. In J. D. Safran & E. P. Shafranske (Eds.), *Casebook for clinical supervision: A competency-based approach* (pp. 137–157). Washington, DC: American Psychological Association.

Sandhu, S., Arcidiacono, E., Aguglia, E., & Priebe, S. (2015). Reciprocity in therapeutic relationships: A conceptual review. *International Journal of Mental Health Nursing, 24*, 460–470. doi:10.1111/inm.12160

Shattock, L., Berry, K., Degnan, A., & Edge, D. (2018). Therapeutic alliance in psychological therapy for people with schizophrenia and related psychoses: A systematic review. *Clinical Psychology & Psychotherapy, 25*, e60–e85. doi:10.1002/cpp.2135

Stiles, W. B., Glick, M. J., Osatuke, K., Hardy, G. E., Shapiro, D. A., Agnew-Davies, R., . . . Barkham, M. (2004). Patterns of alliance development and the rupture-repair hypothesis: Are productive relationships U-shaped or V-shaped? *Journal of Counselling Psychology, 51*, 81–92. doi:10.1037/0022–0167.51.1.81

Taylor, P. J., Rietzschel, J., Danquah, A., & Berry, K. (2015a). The role of attachment style, attachment to therapist, and working alliance in response to psychological therapy. *Psychology & Psychotherapy, 88*, 240–253. doi:10.1111/papt.12045

Taylor, P. J., Rietzschel, J., Danquah, A., & Berry, K. (2015b). Changes in attachment representations during psychological therapy. *Psychotherapy Research, 25*, 222–238. doi:10.1080/10503307.2014.886791

Winnicott, D. W. (2002). *Winnicott on the child*. Cambridge, MA: Perseus Books Group.

Xu, H., & Tracey, T. J. (2015). Reciprocal influence model of working alliance and therapeutic outcome over individual therapy course. *Journal of Counselling Psychology, 62*, 351–359. doi:10.1037/cou0000089

Yalom, I. D. (1991). *Love's executioner*. London: Penguin.Zilcha-Mano, S., & Errazuriz, P. (2017). Early development of mechanisms of change as a predictor of subsequent change and treatment outcome: The case of working alliance. *Journal of Consulting & Clinical Psychology, 85*, 508–520. doi:10.1037/ccp0000192

12

CONCLUSION

Peter Taylor and Naomi Fisher

Introduction

In this book we have brought together first-hand examples of people's experiences of having therapy following their experiences of psychosis, alongside therapists' account of delivering these forms of therapy. We have presented a range of different therapeutic approaches, though there remain many approaches we do not cover in this book (e.g. group therapies or arts-based therapies). Our goal in doing this has been to help raise awareness of some of the psychological therapies that are available, build understanding of what those different therapies may involve, and illustrate what it can be like as a client undertaking them. The accounts given by therapists in this book share a lot of important and useful information about the therapies covered. What we feel is particularly novel is the sharing of the client voice and being able to have both the therapist and client account to provide a context to each other. As the client's voice is less represented in descriptions of therapies or information available to people deciding if a therapy may support them we would like to focus this concluding chapter largely on the clients' experiences.

Every client's experience of therapy is unique, and depends, not just on the type of therapy but also the therapist themselves, the client and their history and experiences. However, when reading about clients' experiences within the chapters of this book we were struck by the commonalities that emerge across different contributors' accounts. These commonalities are important, because they can tell us something about the common elements of the therapy experience. They can be helpful in thinking not only about what someone about to start therapy might expect it to be like, but also in thinking about how therapy itself operates. With this in mind, this final chapter is an opportunity to reflect back over the clients' experiences captured in the various chapters in this book, and draw out some of the common themes and ideas that were most apparent to us. This is by no means an exhaustive list. It reflects our perspectives, as individuals who had psychological therapy to help with experiences of psychosis and as researchers interested in understanding what can help individuals struggling with psychosis.

Figure 12.1 'Moving on', a short comic on experiences of therapy by Annie Blake

The insights that only personal accounts can provide

It is a privilege to read these first-hand accounts of therapy and experiences of psychosis. Reading these very honest personal accounts confirms the value of sharing both the client and therapist perspectives on therapy. Each account contains observations that will be of interest to people considering therapy and those who recommend or provide it. Many of the contributors describe their experiences of psychosis, how real delusional thoughts feel and how immersive they can be, as in what Annie describes as being in a 'Truman show' (Chapter 11). Alex (Chapter 5) also describes the sense of meaningful and tangible connection, which is lost when no longer experiencing psychosis. Reading these accounts helps highlight how those of us who experience psychosis may not talk about it for fear of upsetting those who have been scared by our actions. This can lead to important and often relationship altering experiences being 'off limits' which we feel can perpetuate a sense of isolation or shame. Our hope is that these chapters provide an insight into psychosis and therapy as a shared human experience that can be talked about.

There is humour and piercing insight into the role that the therapist and client are expected to assume in therapy such as Yarburgh's (Chapter 2) concerns of being ushered out when the time is up, based on movie portrayals of therapists. This may be hard for therapists to read but is important to understand how therapy is experienced. For example, for Zara (Chapter 3), although she appreciated the understanding conveyed by her therapists through a compassionate nodding, this was not the same as being heard by someone who had experienced psychosis and has felt its impact on friends and family. The accounts illustrate how the change that can come through therapy can take a long time rather than being what Nick would describe as an instant fix (Chapter 9) Yarburgh (Chapter 2) talks of how the therapy he received was like trying to re-programme the way he thought and acted in different situations and was not something that could happen overnight. It is also worth noting that for many contributors this was not the first time they had assumed the role of the client. Such as Annie (Chapter 11) who arrived in the "small stuffy room with a strategically placed box of tissues" with ideas already about the value of committing to this work.

Therapy is hard work but can also be helpful

We thought long and hard about a subheading for this section that accurately communicates the challenges without suggesting that the hard parts of therapy are always helpful. For some, previous experiences of therapy were not right, or with the right therapist or at the right time. However, many of the experiences of therapy in this book were described as being "hard but . . ." For example, Jules (Chapter 10) describes the importance of having someone willing to "witness, touch and hold the pain of others'" rather than viewing experiences through a "lens of mental illness" that isolates and reduces people to a tick box of criteria for diagnosis. The bravery required to open up what has often been hidden and overcome considerable difficulties through what Alex (Chapter 5) describes as skilful coping strategies should not be underestimated. Paul-Newell (Chapter 7) suggests that the disclosing and sharing of painful psychological 'wounds' was for him part of the process of the therapy. Many describe real anxiety at the outset, and fear of being judged (Chapters 3, 6 and 10) and for Mystic Leaf (Chapter 8) not just as a client but also as a woman who had not yet reached what society perceived as important milestones. Mystic Leaf (Chapter 8) illustrates the value of a therapeutic approach that tenderly worked with the experience of compassionate Angels. The Angels were not dismissed as delusions without use, but were used within therapy to see what she needed now and in the time that led up to the psychotic experiences. This tenderness is reflected in how clients felt when they did share what was deep inside them and the safe place that a therapeutic space can become (see Chapters 3, 6, 10 and 11).

The work of therapy does not happen in isolation and there are illustrations of how transformative therapy has been not just for the person who took on the role of client but also their family and friends. Junaid (Chapter 4) describes how he really benefited from his family having the chance to talk to his care-coordinator as this meant they could ask questions and reduce their anxiety. The ripples of change can continue to be seen beyond therapy, for example in Zara's family in a greater ability to be talk honestly as a family about the normal difficulties of life and not just about psychosis (Chapter 3). It was inspiring to hear that tools, exercises and the pacing of therapy were felt to be guided by what was going on whilst people had therapy (see Chapter 6). It was also important to hear how therapy for Zara and Rebecca continued during or was interrupted by episodes of psychosis (Chapters 3 and 6). Doing the homework and practising a different way of relating to your self is hard and often hindered by a doubt in one's own capacity to be different. For Alex, not doing the homework for fear of failing and then avoiding her therapist allowed her to see a pattern that had led to isolation in her life (Chapter 5). For Mystic Leaf the practice of compassion and belief that she could 'ask for something good' only came through 'laboriously' repeating the exercises developed through therapy (Chapter 8).

The qualities of a good therapist

One of the common themes across the chapters concerns reflections on what makes a good therapist. In particular, many clients refer to the interpersonal qualities of their therapists, what are they were like as a person or the way they come across, as being important. For example, Mystic Leaf (Chapter 8) notes how her therapist "seemed gentler, and her voice was softer and more soothing" and for Jules her therapist's understanding and flexibility in using email contact allowed therapy to continue when words would not come in face to face sessions. Nick (Chapter 9) describes how the members of the Open Dialogue team that helped him provided a "supportive and sympathetic audience" to his account of his difficulties. He further emphasises how the team's capacity to accept, acknowledge and validate his experiences was a key part of how they helped him. Annie (Chapter 11), similarly, talks about her therapist's willingness to listen and hear out her experiences as an important quality. Junaid (Chapter 4) describes how his care co-ordinator "had such a personality that she would liven up the house when she came to see me".

In some cases this interpersonal style or manner of the therapist seems inextricably linked to the therapy itself. For example Jules (Chapter 10) describes how she valued her therapist's 'empathic understanding' and acceptance, which are seen as essential therapist qualities in Person-Centred Therapy. Similarly, within Cognitive Analytic Therapy, Alex highlights how the collaborative style of the therapy, which sees the therapist and the client as equal partners, ultimately felt like the right approach (Chapter 5). For others, there were important turning points in developing a strong relationship with their therapist. Paul-Newell (Chapter 7) describes a time when he left mid-session, after feeling "extremely worked-up". Returning to the session and his therapist's response was seen as a key turning point in the relationship. Similarly, Rebecca (Chapter 6) describes how disclosing some of her most difficult experiences helped strengthen the relationship she had with her therapist.

Summarising across the chapters, the ability to listen in an accepting, empathic and non-judgemental way appears to be key. This is captured by Mystic Leaf (Chapter 8) when she states "I think for clinical psychologists and other psychological therapists, the importance of being non-judgemental and really listening to a client talk about their 'psychotic symptoms' is a powerful, healing thing to do". However, the sense that one's therapist is competent and knows what they are doing also seems important. Zara (Chapter 3) mentions that whilst at times in therapy she could feel patronised by the therapist's tone she also got the feeling of being in 'safe hands' with her therapists from the start.

The interpersonal qualities of therapists also appear to be important for some clients in distinguishing experiences of therapy that were not helpful from those that were. Mystic Leaf (Chapter 8) mentions how she did not find CBT helpful as the approach came across as 'cold, factual, and objective', but she also notes the qualities of the therapist themselves were important here, stating that the CBT therapist was not connecting with her 'inner world', and so seemed to struggle to take on board and make sense of her psychotic experiences. Mystic Leaf formed a better connection with her therapist when receiving Compassion Focused Therapy (CFT), and emphasises how it was important that she saw her therapist as being in a similar situation to herself ("I saw a woman in a parallel world; single, just like me, and dreaming of getting married one day and 'having it all'; but it had not happened for her yet either").

For both Mystic Leaf and Jules (Chapters 8 and 10), the valued qualities of their therapists became therapeutic goals for themselves. Mystic Leaf notes "that is when I realised I really wanted an internal climate like the psychologist's: one that automatically cushions you when you are low; one that helps you to keep perspective when things are sad and serious". Jules talks about taking her therapist's "willingness to share her humanity" and "way of being" into her own life and "making it my own".

The qualities that make a good therapist are likely closely tied to what helps to build a strong therapeutic relationship as described in Chapter 11. In this chapter it is highlighted how the relationship that is formed with a therapist appears to be a powerful factor in determining what the outcome of the therapy is, whether it helps or not. It can be seen across the chapter how the qualities of the therapist could help build this relationship. Nick (Chapter 9) comments on how he has "grown to know and to trust the Open Dialogue team and they have come to know my story". This relationship appears essential to being able to share experiences and feel supported and understood by the team.

The tools of therapy

The observation that the interpersonal qualities of therapists and the relationship that is formed with them are important for the outcome of therapy leads to an important question. Is it just the relationship with the therapist, not their specific therapeutic approach (e.g. Cognitive Analytic Therapy, Cognitive Behavioural Therapy, Compassion Focused Therapy, etc.) or is it the particular techniques they use, that make the difference when it comes to therapy? Some of the therapists writing in this book suggest there may be something in this idea, referring to the 'Dodo Bird Verdict' (Luborsky et al., 2002) that different types of therapy tend to be about as effective as one another (the name is a reference to the book *Alice's Adventures in Wonderland*, and the line "everybody has won, so all shall have prizes"; Carroll, 1869, p. 34). There is a great deal of debate amongst researchers about this, and it is not something we have space to explore in any great depth here (e.g. Beutler, 2002; Luborsky et al., 2002; Marcus, O'Connell, Norris, & Sawaqdeh, 2014). However, looking back further at the chapters there is an indication that there is something more than the personal qualities of therapists and the relationship one has with them that matters when it comes to therapy.

Whilst many clients mention their relationship with their therapist as being important, they also often name the specific tools and techniques that belong to a certain therapy as being helpful. Rebecca describes how re-imaging a nightmare so that it had a different, more positive ending (a technique called imagery re-scripting; Chapter 6) helped with this problem. She also highlights the value of other imagery-based techniques like imagining a safe place. In Alex's chapter on Cognitive Analytic Therapy (Chapter 5), she notes how the reformulation letter (a written summary of the shared understanding of a client's problems and strengths that is put together with the therapist) was a powerful tool, helping her to feel confident in the therapy. Similarly, Yarburgh (Chapter 2) talks about how the new understanding of his difficulties that he gained from Cognitive Behavioural Therapy gradually started to help him when he was facing challenging situations. Junaid (Chapter 4) talks about how the use of the SMART goals technique helped him achieve the targets that mattered to him. Some clients note that, following the end of therapy, they have not needed to use the techniques they learnt (Rebecca, Chapter 12), whereas others still found specific techniques, such as mindfulness meditation, helpful (Chapter 8).

Whether or not a particular tool or technique is helpful may still depend a lot on the individual. Both Alex and Annie (Chapters 5 and 11) talk about using a diary to record their thoughts and feelings during therapy. In both cases, this was something they had done prior to therapy and so the idea of keeping a diary fitted well for them. Yarburgh (Chapter 2) had mixed feelings about the use of *attentional training*, a technique that was introduced to him as part of his Cognitive Behavioural Therapy, noting that the idea did not make sense to him at the time.

Overall, we get the impression that for many people it is the qualities of their therapist as a person that makes the initial big impression, and allows a positive relationship to form (or not in some cases), but this relationship in turn allows individuals to make best use of the particular tools, methods or techniques involved in that therapy and so benefit further from the work involved. It is also important to add that the distinction between what is the therapeutic relationship and what are the tools, methods or techniques of the therapy is hard to make, as actively working with the therapeutic relationship and using this as a means to help the individual, is a part of many of therapies covered here.

Final thoughts

To conclude we would like to return to the comments that are made in the introductory chapter: research and clinical practice relating to psychosis is complex and constantly developing. The way we understand and think about psychosis is evolving, and may look very different in five or ten years to the way we think about it now. For example see the recently published Power Threat Meaning Framework, which suggests a different way of thinking about psychiatric difficulties in general (Johnstone & Boyle, 2018). Similarly, as research takes place new therapies are likely to be developed and evaluated.

Within this book we see some common themes, that therapy can often be challenging and difficult but also worthwhile and beneficial, and that there are many different aspects of a therapy that may contribute to whether it is a 'good' or helpful experience (the therapist, the techniques, the approach itself). Ultimately, we believe this book highlights the value of listening to the voices of those who have undertaken therapy, and incorporating these into the wider conversation about the therapies that are offered for those who struggle with experiences like psychosis.

References

Beutler, L. E. (2002). The dodo bird is extinct. *Clinical Psychology: Science & Practice*, 9, 30–34. doi:10.1093/clipsy.9.1.30

Carroll, L. (1869). *Alice's Adventures in Wonderland*. Boston: Lee & Shepard.

Johnstone, L., & Boyle, M., with Cromby, J., Dillon, J., Harper, D., Kinderman, P., Longden, E., Pilgrim, D., & Read, J. (2018). *The power threat meaning framework: Towards the identification of patterns in emotional distress, unusual experiences and troubled or troubling behaviour, as an alternative to functional psychiatric diagnosis.* Leicester: British Psychological Society. Retrieved from https://www1.bps.org.uk/system/files/user-files/Division%20of%20Clinical%20Psychology/public/INF299%20PTM%20Main%20web.pdf

Luborsky, L., Rosenthal, R., Diguer, L., Andrusyna, T. P., Berman, J. S., Levitt, J. T., . . . Krause, E. D. (2002). The dodo bird verdict is alive and well – mostly. *Clinical Psychology: Science & Practice, 9*, 2–12. doi:10.1093/clipsy/9.1.2

Marcus, D. K., O'Connell, D., Norris, A. L., & Sawaqdeh, A. (2014). Is the dodo bird endangered in the 21st century? A meta-analysis of treatment comparison studies. *Clinical Psychology Review, 34*, 519–530. doi:10.1016/j.cpr.2014.08.001

INDEX

Indexer: Dr Laurence Errington.

acceptance in compassion-focused therapy 121, 128, 129
actualising tendency 157, 158, 159, 164
adaptive information processing model (AIP) 88
adaptive ways of coping 713
adolescents, family therapy 35; *see also* teenagers
agenda-setting in CBT 20
Aino (fictional client) 143–144
Alex (client) 61–67, 176, 187, 188, 189; biography x, 173, 175, 178, 187, 189, 191
angels (human), Mystic Leaf's 116–117, 118–119, 122, 188
anger: person-centred therapy 153; psychodynamic therapy 99; therapeutic relationship 169–170; trauma-focused therapy 82
antidepressants 49, 51, 144
antipsychotics *see* medication
anxieties and worries, hearing voices 23
assessment: in care co-ordination 55; in psychodynamic therapy 107; of risk 56; in trauma-focused therapy 79, 90
attachment figure, therapist as 177–178
attention: attentional training 13–14, 191; on present moment 14, 120, 127
attention deficit hyperactivity disorder (ADHD) 30, 50
attunement (therapist) 161, 175, 177
Austin Riggs Centre 97

Becky *see* Rebecca
beginning of therapy *see* start
behaviour, changes in *see* changes

beliefs: in CBT (and challenging them) 13, 19, 23–24; Mystic Leaf's 116–117, 118, 119
bipolar disorder 68; clients' experiences 133, 135, 136, 167, 171, 172
Blake, Annie (client) 166–172, 178, 187, 189, 191; biography x; comic strip 9, 44, 186
Borchers, Pekka (practitioner) 34–42; biography x
boundaries 167, 169; in person-centred therapy 151–152, 160; in psychodynamic therapy, interpersonal 99, 100
brain, evolving 123–124
Buddhism and compassion-focused therapy 126
bullying 30, 70, 71, 74, 144

care co-ordination 43–59; challenges 57; client's perspective 43–50; day-to-day practice 53–57; evidence for 58; history 51–52; practitioner's perspective 51–59; role of care co-ordinator 52–53
caregiver relationships (early life) 177
care programme approach (CPA) 52
carer support 56–57
chairwork 128, 129
changes (in life or behaviour or personality): cognitive analytic therapy and 61–75; cognitive behavioural therapy and 15–16; person-centred therapy and 158–159; psychodynamic therapy and 106–107
Chatalos, Peter Andrew (practitioner) 156–165; biography x–xi

193

INDEX

childhood (early life): caregiver relationships 177; school life 30, 143–144, 145; sexual abuse 86, 89; *see also* adolescents, family therapy; past life events; teenagers

choice/selection: of therapies 3–4, 111, 180; of therapist 180

cognitive analytic therapy (CAT) 61–75; client's perspective 61–68; ending 67–68, 74; evidence 74; history/development 71; practitioner's perspective 69–76; structure/process/practical aspects 72–74; theory and language 69–71

cognitive behavioural therapy 8–26; in action 20–24; clients' perspective 8–16, 117, 120, 168, 169, 189; evidence 24–25; practitioner's perspective 17–26; trauma-focused (TF-CBT) 90, 91, 92, 93

cognitive model 17–18

cognitive model, psychosis and 18–19

cognitive processing during trauma 80

collaborative empiricism in CBT 21

community psychiatric nurses (CPNs) 27, 29, 62, 149

compassion-focused therapy 115–132; client's perspective 115–122; evidence 128–129; key concepts 123–125; practice 126–127; practitioner's perspective 123–132; theory 126

conditions of worth 158, 159, 163

congruence (or genuineness) 159

consent, informed 21

contentment system and compassion-focused therapy 12, 115–116, 119, 121, 124–125, 126, 127, 128

coping: cognitive analytic therapy and 71; psychodynamic therapy and 99; trauma-focused therapy 81

countertransference 73, 75, 108, 177

couples therapy 39

crisis teams 78, 134, 135, 139

Crossley, Jon (practitioner) 123–132; biography xi

Danish study of psychodynamic therapy 110

depression: clients' experiences 134, 136, 137, 148, 167; compassion-focused therapy and 129; drugs for (antidepressants) 49, 51, 144

diagnoses and person-centred therapy 163–164

dialogism 140, 141, 142, 145

diary *see* journal or diary-keeping

difficult processing 161

disclosure of feelings and experiences in open dialogue 135–136

disintegration 158

distance therapy 101

dose-related response to trauma 86

dreaming (and trauma-focused therapy) 87; nightmares 78, 79, 82, 85, 90, 91

drive system and compassion-focused therapy 115, 121, 124–125

drug abuse 10

drug therapy *see* medication

dynamic therapeutic relationship 174

Early Intervention (for Psychosis) Service/EI(P)S 51, 52, 53, 58; Junaid Sarwar 43, 45, 46, 47, 48, 49, 50; Mystic Leaf 117, 122; Niklas Granö 143; Rebecca 78; Zara Zaks 28

early life *see* childhood

education and training: care co-ordination practitioners 75; client's needs 57; *see also* psychoeducation

emailing therapist 150

EMDR (eye movement desensitisation and reprocessing) 22–23, 88, 90–91, 92, 93

emotions (and feelings): compassion-focused therapy and 115, 123–126; emotional needs 46–47, 69; open dialogue and 135–136, 137; psychodynamic therapy and 99–103, 104, 105, 106, 107, 108; three system model 115, 121, 124–125, 126, 127; trauma-focused therapy and 81, 82, 83, 87, 93; *see also* anger; jealousy; shame and compassion focused therapy

empathy 174, 175, 176, 178, 189; person-centred therapy 151, 153, 159, 160–161, 162; psychodynamic therapy 108

employment (job/work/occupation) 57; client experiences (having/not having) 85, 116, 118, 119, 120, 121, 134, 139

ending/terminating therapy: cognitive analytic therapy 67–68, 74;

INDEX

psychodynamic therapy 102, 107; trauma-focused therapy 84
evidence (from research of outcomes/benefits): care co-ordination 58; cognitive analytic therapy evidence 74; cognitive behavioural therapy evidence 24–25; compassion-focused therapy 128–129; open dialogue 145–146; person-centred therapy 162–163; psychodynamic therapy 110–111; systemic family therapy evidence 38–39; therapeutic relationship 178–179; trauma-focused therapy 92
evolving brain 123–124
exercises (in therapy) 169–171
experiences: in open dialogue, disclosure 135–136; of past life events (*see* past life events); in psychodynamic therapy 108
experiments (real-life) in cognitive analytic therapy 66–67
eye movement desensitisation and reprocessing (EMDR) 22–23, 88, 90–91, 92, 93

facilitative conditions for change 158–159, 160, 161
family: care co-ordination and 47; open dialogue and 137, 138, 140, 141, 142, 145; *see also* parents; partner; siblings
family therapy/work: care co-ordination and 56–57; evolution/developments 35–38; people's perceptions of 28–29; systemic (*see* systemic family therapy)
father *see* parents
feelings *see* emotions
Finnish national schizophrenia project 140
Finnish need adapted approach 34, 38, 39
Fisher, Naomi (practitioner) 185–192; biography xi; chapter comments 8, 96, 133
flagellatory self-judgement 99, 100
flexibility (of support team in open dialogue) 141, 142, 145
Fluoxetine 134
formulation: care co-ordination 54–55; CBT 12–13; compassion-focused therapy 127; trauma-focused therapy 79, 90; *see also* reformulation, cognitive analytic therapy
free-association 96, 97, 98, 109

genuineness (or congruence) 158
Gianfrancesco, Olympia (client and researcher) 1–7; biography xi; chapter comments 27, 61, 148
goals: care co-ordination 48; CBT 20, 31–32; *see also* SMART goals technique
'goodbye letter' 68
Granö, Niklas (practitioner) 140–147; biography xi–xii
Haley, Jules (client) 148–155, 187, 188, 189, 189–190; biography xii
Hayes, Nick (client) 133–139, 187, 188–189, 190; biography xii
hearing voices 22, 125, 126, 128; Aino (fictional client) and open dialogue and 143, 144; Paul-Newell Reaves and psychodynamic therapy 97; Rebecca and trauma-focused therapy and 77, 78, 79, 81, 84, 85; Sue (fictional client) and CBT 22–24; Yarburgh and CBT 10, 13–14, 22
holistic approaches 46, 172
homework 188; CBT 14–15, 20; *see also* journal or diary-keeping; worksheets, cognitive analytic therapy
hospital admission/inpatient stay: Alex 61, 62; Annie Blake 169, 171; Julia Hayley 149; Nick Hayes 133, 134, 139, 141; Paul-Newell Reaves 97; Rebecca 77, 78, 79, 81; Zara Zaks 28, 29
human angels, Mystic Leaf's 116–117, 118–119, 122, 188
humanistic psychology 157
human nature, positive regard *see* positive regard
Hutton, Jane (practitioner) 17–26; biography xii
hybrid therapy 112–113

ideas, challenging, in CBT 13
imagery: compassionate imagery 118, 121, 127–128; image rehearsal therapy (IRT) 90, 91
immediate help provision (in open dialogue) 141, 142, 145
incongruence 158
individual-centred therapy *see* person-centred therapy
information processing system (IPS) 88–89

195

INDEX

informed consent 21
inner voice 71, 74
inpatient *see* hospital admission/inpatient stay
insights (incl. making sense of situations) 187; Annie Blake 171, 172; Junaid Sarwar 49; Mystic Leaf 117; Nick Hayes 139; Sue (fictional client) 23; Yarburgh 13–14; Zara Zacs 32, 33
interpersonal boundaries and psychodynamic therapy 99, 100
interpersonal qualities of therapists 189
interventions (in therapy): care co-ordinators and 56, 58; client's experiences 169–171; trauma-focused, evidence base 92
intrusive thoughts: care co-ordination 48; CBT 13–14, 15

jealousy 102
job *see* employment
journal or diary-keeping 167, 191; cognitive analytic therapy 66, 68
judgement: flagellatory self-judgement 99, 100; non-judgemental therapists 107, 108, 118, 154, 162, 189

Keane, David (practitioner) 86–95; biography xii
Kelly, James (practitioner) 51–60; biography xii–xiii
Koch, Siobhain (practitioner) 51–60; biography xii–xiii

labelling 103, 163–164, 171
Lancashire Traumatic Stress Service (LTSS) 89, 90, 93
'language': cognitive analytic therapy 69–71; of mental conditions 102–103
Larkin, Amanda (practitioner) 173–184; biography xiii
letters (writing): compassionate 119, 120, 121, 128; 'goodbye' 68; reformulation letter 64–65, 72, 73
life, changes in *see* changes
life events: new, space given for 169; past (*see* past life events)
lithium 133, 134
long distance therapy 101

Mad Pride 102
mania, client's experiences 134, 135, 171

mapping in cognitive analytic therapy 64, 65, 66–67, 68
medication (pharmacological agents incl. antipsychotics): in care co-ordination 52, 54, 55; CBT combined with 24; clients' perspectives 10, 28, 45, 46, 49, 61, 133, 134, 135, 138, 142, 144, 149; in trauma-focused therapy 90; *see also specific drugs*
memory of trauma, nature 80
Milan systemic family therapy 36
mind, psychodynamic ideas 104
mindfulness 14, 120, 121, 122, 127, 128, 129
mirroring 151
mix of therapies 112–113
mobility (of support in open dialogue) 141, 142, 145
moment-to-moment experience in psychodynamic therapy 108
mother *see* parents
Mystic Leaf (client) 115–122, 188, 189–190; biography xiii–ix

narrative therapies 37
National Institute for Health and Clinical Excellence *see* NICE
negative thoughts/thinking 45, 47, 48, 49, 81, 91, 120, 121
NICE (National Institute for Health and Clinical Excellence) recommendations/guidelines: person-centred therapy 112; psychodynamic therapy 112; trauma-focused therapy 92
nightmares and trauma-focused therapy 78, 79, 82, 85, 90, 91
non-directive attitude in person-centred therapy 149, 150, 156, 159–160
non-judgemental therapists 107, 108, 118, 154, 162, 189
normalisation 38, 146, 178; in care co-ordination 55, 57; in CBT 21

object relations theory 70, 104, 175, 176, 177
occupation *see* employment
olanzapine 134, 138
open dialogue 133–147; client's perspective 133–139; literature and clinical implications 145–146; meaning/concepts/principles 140–143; practical example 143–144; practitioner's perspective 140–147
outcomes *see* evidence; recovery

paranoia 1; Mystic Leaf and compassion-focused therapy 117, 118, 126, 128, 129; Zara and systemic family therapy 27, 33

parents (father and/or mother): care co-ordination and 46, 47, 48, 49; open dialogue and 137–138, 143–144; systemic family therapy and 31; therapeutic relationship and 166, 168, 169–170, 171; *see also* family

partner: Mystic Leaf's need for 115, 116, 118, 119, 120, 121; Nick Hayes' help from 134–135, 136, 137, 138; *see also* family

past life events/experiences (of significance incl. adversity and trauma) 21, 55, 77–95, 105–106; cognitive model 18, 19; dose-related response 86; in eye movement desensitisation and reprocessing, processing of trauma 82–83; getting stuck 83, 88; memory of, nature 80; modular approach to treatment 89–91, 93–94; person-centred therapy and 154; psychodynamic therapy and 100, 107, 176; relationship with therapist and 169–170, 172; reliving/re-experiencing 82, 83, 87, 88, 89, 91; systemic family therapy and 29; *see also* childhood

peer mentors and support 112, 135, 137, 139

perfectionism 67

personality change *see* changes

person-centred therapy 148–165; client expectations 160–164; client perspectives 148–155; concepts and theories 156–160; evidence 162–163; practitioner's perspective 156–165

pharmacological agents *see* medication

physical activity (incl. sport) 47

physical health in care co-ordination 55–56

'poisoned parrot' technique (Rebecca's) 81, 85

positive regard (for human nature) 157; unconditional 157, 159, 163

post-Milan approaches in systemic family therapy 36

post-traumatic stress disorder (PTSD) 10, 92, 93

power threat meaning framework 191

practitioner *see* therapist

present moment: attention to 14, 120, 127; listening to what clients actually say in 37

problem in CBT: prioritised problem 22–23; problem list 20, 31–32

processing, difficult 161

psychodynamic therapy 96–114; aims 106; classical approach 109; client's perspective 96–103; current guidelines 112; definition 104; evidence 110–111; factors affecting outcome 112; how it works 106–107; modified approach/supporting techniques 109; practitioner's perspective 104–114; practitioner's role 108; what happens in 107–108

psychoeducation 38, 55, 127–128

psychological contact and continuity: in open dialogue 141–142, 145; in person-centred therapy 149–150, 152, 158, 161–163

psychological distress: CBT and 20; person-centred therapy and 157–158

psychology, humanistic 157

psychosis: cognitive model and 18–19; contested notions 125–126; evidence for therapies (*see* evidence); meaning 1–2; psychodynamic ideas and therapy in 105–106, 110–111; therapeutic relationship in 178

psychotherapy *see* therapy

quetiapine 49

Reaves, Paul-Newell (client) 96–103, 113, 188, 189; biography xiv

Rebecca/Becky (client) 77–85, 93, 94, 188, 189, 190, 191; biography xiv

reciprocal role procedures (RRPs) 70, 71, 72, 73, 74

reciprocity in therapeutic relationship 174, 179

recognition phase of cognitive analytic therapy 73–74

recovery (getting better): care co-ordination and 45, 47, 54, 56, 58; psychodynamic therapy and 102–103; trauma-focused therapy and working on 84

reflecting teams (in systemic family therapy) 29, 31, 36

reflections (client's): in compassion-focused therapy 121; in open dialogue 136

INDEX

reflections (therapist's personal) 188; trauma-focused therapy 92–94
reformulation, cognitive analytic therapy (CAT) 64, 64–65, 72–73
relapse prevention 57, 91, 172
relational approach of person-centred therapy 158–159
relationship: with others, link to therapeutic relationship 176–177; with therapist (see therapeutic relationship)
religious and spiritual needs 46–47
reliving/re-experiencing trauma 82, 83, 87, 88, 89, 91
research evidence see evidence
responsibility (of support team in open dialogue) 141, 142, 145
revision in cognitive analytic therapy 74; client experiences 66–67
risk assessment and management 56
Rogers, Carl 152, 156–157, 158, 159, 162, 163

Sarwar, Junaid (client) 43–50, 188, 189, 190–191; biography xiv
Scandinavia, open dialogue 140
schizophrenia 37; Finnish national schizophrenia project 140; meaning 1
school life 30, 143–144, 145
Seddon, Claire (practitioner) 69–76; biography xiv–xv
Seikkula, Jaakko (Professor) 140, 143
selection see choice
self, losing sense of 136
self-care 103
self-concept 158
self-direction in person-centred therapy 149, 150, 152–153, 156
self-judgement, flagellatory 99, 100
self-stigma 102
sense: losing 136; making (see insight); of self 105, 136, 162
sequential diagrammatic reformulation (SDR) 72
sertraline 49
setting: compassion focused therapy 117; person-centred therapy 160; psychodynamic therapy 107
sexual abuse (childhood) 86, 89
shame and compassion focused therapy 123, 126, 127, 128, 130
Shapiro F. and trauma 88–89

shared understanding of client's experiences 64–65, 175, 190; care co-ordination and 54–55
siblings (brothers/sisters): Annie Blake's 168, 169; Milan systemic family therapy and 36; Mystic Leaf's 116; Zara Zak's 29, 30, 31, 32
silence in therapy 32, 37, 109, 150, 151, 160
sleep and trauma-focused therapy 81–82, 90; see also dreaming
SMART goals technique 48, 190–191
social constructivism 36
social network (and open dialogue) 141, 142, 145
solution-focused therapy 35
specialist therapy skills in care co-ordination 56
spiritual and religious needs 46–47
sport 47
start/beginning (of course of therapy): care-cordination 46; CBT 20; cognitive analytic therapy 61–62; systemic family therapy 40; trauma-focused therapy 78–79
stigma 156, 163–164, 171, 178; self-stigma 102
strategic therapy 35
structural family therapy 35–36
substance (drug) abuse 10
Sue (fictional client) 21–24
suffering, turning towards 126, 129
suicidal feelings and thoughts 10, 66, 68, 78, 81, 154, 167
Summers, Alison (practitioner) 104–114; biography xv
systemic family therapy 27–42; client's perspective 27–33; evolution 35–38; meaning 34–35; practitioner's perspective 34–42; research evidence 38–39

talking therapy see therapy
Taylor, Peter (practitioner) 1–16, 185–192; biography xv; comments on chapters 77, 115, 166; on therapeutic relationship 173–184
teenagers: open dialogue example 143–144; problems of teenage life 30, 43; see also adolescents, family therapy
terminating therapy see ending

198

INDEX

therapeutic relationship/alliance 166–183; in care co-ordination 53–54; client's perspective 166–172; in cognitive analytic therapy, ruptures 73; defining 173–174; evidence for outcome effect 178–179; factors contributing to good relationship 174–175; in person-centred therapy 150, 153–154, 159, 160, 161, 163; promoting a good relationship 179–181; in psychodynamic therapy, client's view 96, 97–102; in psychodynamic therapy, practitioner's view 106, 108, 112; in psychosis 178; in trauma-focused therapy 84; trust 43, 102, 152, 153–154, 159, 161

therapist (practitioner): as attachment figure 177–178; attunement 161, 175, 177; choice 180; client reaction to (transference) 73, 75, 109, 175–176; client relationship with (*see* therapeutic relationship); emotional response to (countertransference) 73, 75, 108, 177; good, qualities 16, 188–190; in psychodynamic therapy, role 108; reflections (*see* reflection (therapist's personal))

therapy (psychological/talking therapy): access to 155–157; beginning and ending (*see* ending; start); choice 3–4, 111, 180; hard work 79, 82, 187, 187–188; helpfulness 187–188; meaning 2; mix of 112–113; in psychosis 3; tools and techniques 190–191

thoughts and thinking: challenging, in CBT 13; intrusive (*see* intrusive thoughts); negative 45, 47, 48, 49, 81, 91, 120, 121; of past adversity and trauma 87–88

threat (and threat system) and compassion-focused therapy 115, 121, 123–128; *see also* power threat meaning framework

training *see* education and training
transference 73, 75, 109, 176–177
transformative therapy 188
trauma-focused therapy 77–95; client's perspective 77–85; evidence 92; practitioner's perspective 86–95; *see also* Lancashire Traumatic Stress Service; past life events; post-traumatic stress disorder
trust (in therapeutic relationship) 43, 102, 152, 153–154, 159, 161
turning towards suffering 126, 129

uncertainty in open dialogue, tolerance of 142, 145
unconditional positive regard 157, 159, 163
unconscious and psychodynamic ideas 104, 105, 108

voices: hearing (*see* hearing voices); inner 71, 74
vulnerability 35, 125, 158; psychodynamic therapy and 101–102
Vygotsky, L.S. 71

Ward-Brown, Joanna (practitioner) 94; biography xv
Winnicott, D.W. 175
work *see* employment
working alliance 175–176, 177, 178, 179, 181
worksheets, cognitive analytic therapy 66
worries and anxieties, hearing voices 23
worth, conditions of 158, 159, 163
writing *see* journal or diary-keeping; letters

Yarburgh (client) 8–16, 187, 190, 191; biography xv

Zaks, Zara (client) 27–33, 37–38, 187, 188, 189; biography xvi

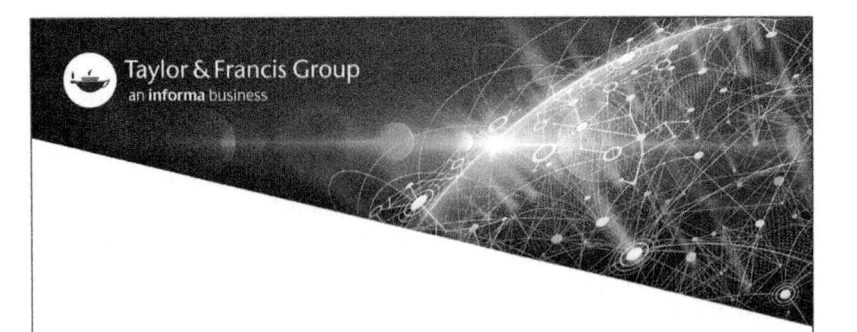